Platonic

Platonic

How the Science of
Attachment Can Help You
Make—and Keep—Friends

Marisa G. Franco, PhD

G. P. PUTNAM'S SONS
New York

PUTNAM
— EST. 1838 —

G. P. Putnam's Sons
Publishers Since 1838
An imprint of Penguin Random House LLC
penguinrandomhouse.com

Library of Congress Cataloging-in-Publication Data

Names: Franco, Marisa G., author.
Title: Platonic: how the science of attachment can help you make—
and keep—friends / Marisa G. Franco, PhD.
Description: New York: G. P. Putnam's Sons, [2022] |
Includes bibliographical references and index.
Identifiers: LCCN 2022019244 (print) | LCCN 2022019245 (ebook) |
ISBN 9780593331897 (hardcover) | ISBN 9780593331903 (ebook)
Subjects: LCSH: Friendship. | Attachment behavior.
Classification: LCC HM1161 .F728 2022 (print) | LCC HM1161 (ebook) |
DDC 302.34—dc23/eng/20220426
LC record available at https://lccn.loc.gov/2022019244
LC ebook record available at https://lccn.loc.gov/2022019245

International edition: 9780593543009

Printed in the United States of America
4th Printing

For my friends: my lifelines, my soul mates, my healers, and my everyday joys

Contents

Contents

Platonic

Author's Note

The stories of friendship you'll read in *Platonic* are all based on true stories. I'm indebted to the people who shared their stories with me to help me bring the research to life. Out of respect for them, I've changed many of their names and identifying characteristics. At times, I've combined stories from multiple people to further anonymize.

The advice I share in *Platonic* comes from hundreds of scientific studies and my consultations with dozens of experts. I believe in this research, but I also must acknowledge its limitations. Much of the research on friendship is older, is conducted in the US, and uses small samples of predominately White, heterosexual college students. Some people might not see their life experience in this research, and they are right to critique my work. To give you research-based advice that I can feel confident in, I've read widely and shared advice that's based on multiple studies, rather than on any single one. Still, we need much more research on friendship to make stronger, more nuanced claims that best reflect the diversity of our lived experiences.

I'm thrilled for you to read *Platonic*. I hope it gives you as much value as I have received through writing it. I must admit I have an agenda in writing this book: to help create a world that is kinder, friendlier, more loving. And I'm so proud of you, reader, for embarking on this journey.

Introduction

The Secret to Making Friends as an Adult

In 2015, I grieved brutally. A burst of promising romance ended in disaster. I thought about it when I rocked on the elliptical machine every morning, when I teared up walking between classes, and basically whenever my mind had nothing else to cling to as a distraction. Coming out of the grief required a series of revelations. First, I had to understand why I had taken this loss so hard, why it had caused me so much suffering. I had to articulate the ways I held romantic relationships in such high regard so that they controlled my happiness: as if there was no love in my life at all without this kind of love.

Why did I place so much importance on romantic love when up until that point, it had not been particularly fulfilling? I had been breathing in some deeply held cultural convictions. *Finding romantic love is my purpose. The moment that I find romantic love is the moment at which life will truly begin. Failing to find romantic love means being fundamentally flawed in the way of being human. And without romantic love, there is no love at all.*

To recover from my grief, I gathered a few of my very best friends to start a wellness group. Every week, we met up and one of us chose a self-care activity we could engage in together and hosted us all with snacks included. There was yoga, cooking, reading, meditating. But most curative of all, there was community. Being around people who loved me and whom I loved healed me. Although I had, until then, devalued the significance of friendship in favor of romance, after the wellness group, I could no longer diminish the colossal importance of friends.

In 2017, I suitcased my life and moved out of my six-year home in Washington DC, over to Atlanta, Georgia. I didn't know many people in Atlanta, but some of my very best friends in DC made it their goal to ensure I wouldn't be lonely when I reached Atlanta. Packed away in my suitcase was a jar full of fortune cookie–like scrolls on which my friends had listed their favorite memory of us together. I also had a two-by-three framed collage with pictures of me and my friends beaming, parading, and embracing. The year before had been one of the golden ages of my life, and this was undoubtedly because I had amassed people who knew and loved me.

I threw a combined going-away/birthday party in May 2017, when I knew I was leaving DC. We had all gone to a funky art show concert together and then returned to crowd into my small apartment for cake and champagne. I made a toast to the seven or so of us left in a circle in the living room. The champagne was setting in, giving me its permission to give a toast of the vulnerable kind: "I want you all to know that I was in a rough place this time last year. And each and every one of you in this room's friendship has been part of the force that has lifted me out of it."

That birthday, along with my wellness group, was part of my metamorphosis. I started turning toward, recognizing, and actively valuing friends. In the years before, when I figured only romantic relationships were meaningful, whenever my hopeful romantic trysts were combusting, I despaired. My sadness was nourished by gaps in my thinking. I was zooming in only to what was wrong in my life (romance) and disregarding all that was right (friendship). This sort of tunnel vision left me using these failed romances as evidence that made me question whether I could form meaningful relationships at all, whether I was worthy of love. I was unlearning this process of absorbing myself so much in one type of love that I discounted all the love that was around me, that had always been around me. I had so much love. And just because it came from friends, why should it matter less?

Platonic love lies at the lowest rung of the hierarchy our culture places on love. But I've learned it's a devastating loss to us all if we dispose of it there. I wrote this book because I'd like for our culture to level this hierarchy. But because we don't always value friendship, we lack knowledge on how to cultivate it. If we're going to realize friendship's full potential in our lives, we need to know how to make and keep friends.

When we've asked how to make friends, people have likely told us to join a meetup group or find a hobby. But somehow, the advice slips away from us. Because when we're told this, the part about facing our social anxiety, enduring fears of rejection, tolerating intimacy, and risking the further shredding of our self-worth is silent. To make friends, we need deeper work—to fundamentally reconcile with who we are and how we love. That's the journey we're on in *Platonic*. Friendship is worth it.

When I was a graduate student getting my PhD in counseling psychology, I was tasked with co-leading therapy groups in a college counseling center. We would convene in a large room with high ceilings, more space to contain all the secrets that would be shared. My co-therapist and I would sit on opposite ends of the room so we could each catch different facial expressions and be attuned to opposing aspects of the group dynamic. Students would silently march into the room and take a seat—either on the comfy couch, close to others, or in a chair, claiming their separate space. The students were almost always nervous, and my co-therapist and I had to build our tolerance for sitting through long stretches of silence. The quiet would eventually be broken by a student whose anxiety about sharing became surpassed by their anxiety about silence.

It usually took us a while to recruit enough students to run a group, since students were often reluctant to take part in group therapy. I didn't blame them. *I have to discuss my childhood trauma, in front of strangers? What could be more awful?* They typically opted to see a counselor, someone who could give them individual attention about their issues and who was trained to be nonjudgmental (unlike the question marks in the therapy group). It wasn't intuitive to these students that group therapy would be helpful. The attention they would have gotten from a one-on-one session with a psychologist was sliced among seven different people.

Although at first, we trainees felt less enthused about group work, as we gained experience running groups, my co-therapist and I began to love them, and wish we too could join one, because something curious always happened in that high-ceilinged room. Students manifested the issues they had in the outside world within the group. One student, Marquee, was working through a breakup with a chaotic and self-destructive man with whom he had stayed for so long because he thought he could rescue him from himself. We'd go on to see this very same savior complex on display from Marquee in the group. As others shared their issues, he would give them all advice on how they could fix their lives. He liked the saving process. He needed to feel needed, which was what seemed to attract him to these self-destructive relationships, but those same caretaking behaviors also exasperated the other group members.

There was another student, Melvin, whose mother was addicted to drugs. Melvin adjusted to this trauma by pretending everything was fine, just fine, never better. Every week when we checked in with one another, Melvin insisted everything was good. He adjusted to his trauma by being the person who was always okay, never suffering, always rolling with the punches, even when the punches were catastrophes that needed to be addressed. Every time he'd share something tragic in the group, he'd smile and give us an OK sign, as if to say, "Don't worry about me, I'm fine. There's nothing wrong here." He thought he was being self-sufficient, but how were other members supposed to help him if he didn't even acknowledge his need for support?

And then there was Lauren, a student with debilitatingly low self-esteem. She came because she was being ignored and discarded by her friends. They'd go on trips without her, and the last straw that brought her to the group was when they decided to all room together the following year and left her out. She was the ghost hovering over her friendship clique. In our therapy group, she played a similarly anonymous role; in fact, she was so reserved that it was a struggle to get her to say anything at all, and sometimes we'd almost forget, just like her friends, that she was a part of our group.

As these students re-created the problems they had in the outside world within the group, they revealed how our mental health issues are fueled by kinks in how we relate to others.

- Marquee faced the pain of tumultuous breakups because he was looking to fulfill the role of "savior" in his relationships, which attracted him to relationship partners who were unstable and unsupportive, and he made group members (and, surely, others in his life) feel patronized and resentful toward him.

- Melvin—who was always okay, always fine—was in truth depressed, in part because he kept others at a distance and could never share the vulnerable side of himself. The group didn't feel close to a smiling emoji, and the smiling emoji didn't feel close to anyone either.

- And Lauren, who was experiencing a lack of self-esteem, would make herself so minuscule around the group that it was easy to forget she was there, thus further diminishing her self-worth.

As the weeks passed, in the safe space of our therapy group, I saw each of them try new ways of relating to others. I was so proud when I saw Lauren, despite her low self-esteem, disagree with someone else in the group, challenging other group members to share more and taking more ownership of the group space. I cheered internally when Melvin recounted a recent breakup and appeared visually distraught; other group members remarked that this was different for him, that he was revealing more of himself, and they felt closer to him. And when a group member shared that they were getting into fights with their parents over money, and Marquee was able to ask about their pain (rather than offer his litany of fix-it solutions), I cheered internally.

Lauren, Melvin, and Marquee each took major steps forward because they were in a space where they felt connected to others, which ultimately allowed them to grow. The group was safe not only because it was a place where they could share their shame and still be loved, but also because it was a place where people could gently and honestly give them feedback to help them evolve. And the strong relationships they developed with the other group members helped them appreciate and accept this feedback, not as putdowns but as acts of love.

Connection Fundamentally Shapes Who We Are

The group was a microcosm that revealed how connection changes us. We've all heard the saying "Love yourself before someone can love you." But what does that mean, exactly? And how does that self-regard happen? Do people grow to love themselves through some magical process, holing up in a cave somewhere with a flashlight and a mirror while staring at their dimly lit reflection and repeating to themselves, "I am important. I am worthy. I am loved," until their psyche is ripped?

It's a little more complicated than that.

What the group revealed about the impact of connection is the basis of this book: connection affects who we are, and who we are affects how we connect. When we have felt connected, we've grown. We've become more open, more empathic, bolder. When we have felt disconnected, we've withered. We've become closed off, judgmental, or distant in acts of self-protection. Our personalities, alongside the way we show up as friends, then, are shaped by our past—we feel lovable because someone loved us well. We are prickly because someone hasn't loved us enough. That's the theme we'll explore in Part I of this book, and it'll help us figure out where some of our strengths and weaknesses come from in making friends. Like Lauren, Melvin, and Marquee, our disconnection wounds may be causing problems in our ability to connect, and we may be pushing people away without even knowing it. So, we'll journey through how connection—or a lack thereof—affects who we are, because the first step to developing rich, thriving friendships is understanding what might be getting in the way. As writer James Baldwin puts it, "Nothing can be changed until it is faced."

The other thing the group revealed was that when we feel accepted and loved, it helps us develop certain qualities that lead us to continue to connect better (the rich get richer, as they say). In group therapy, my clients cultivated these qualities. When Marquee experienced true and safe connection, he became more empathetic. Melvin became more self-expressive and vulnerable. Lauren began to take more initiative in her relationships. When students were able to face some of the wounds that led them to fear others, to shrink up in order to protect themselves, what was left was love for themselves and others, the thing that friendship is made of.

We've all heard the line that humans are social creatures. It's true. Our mirror neurons are entire clumps of our brains that lead us to experience others' lives as if they were our own. Babies cry when they hear other babies cry. We are loving and caring, and we lose sight of this when our past injuries entreat us to protect ourselves first and foremost. To me, this means we have a natural knack for making friends.

Who We Are Affects How We Connect

In Part II, we'll look at all the practices we can engage in to build better relationships. Because the friendships we've built aren't random; they reflect our internal hardware, our ability to develop certain characteristics that nurture friendship. These are a set of mindsets and behaviors that we'd naturally gravitate toward if we weren't so wounded by past experiences of disconnection, so afraid of rejection, so fearful or mistrusting of others, and, consequently, so out of touch with our inner core of love. They include initiative, vulnerability, authenticity, productive anger, generosity, and affection. These traits protect friendship through its life cycle. Initiative ignites friendship, while authenticity, productive anger, and vulnerability all sustain it by permitting us to show up as our full selves.

Generosity and affection deepen friendships by verifying to friends just how much we love them. These practices strike a balance by allowing us to express our inner truth, while we create space to welcome our friend's.

When we lean into these traits, we become something like how David Brooks describes good people in his *New York Times* article "The Moral Bucket List": "They listen well. They make you feel funny and valued. You often catch them looking after other people and as they do so their laugh is musical and their manner is infused with gratitude. . . . Those are the people we want to be." He goes on to describe these good people as having what are called eulogy virtues: "The eulogy virtues are the ones that are talked about at your funeral—whether you were kind, brave, honest or faithful. Were you capable of deep love?" These traits allow us to live in harmony with and in celebration of others.

This is how we make friends as an adult. We grow—we become braver, more empathic, kinder, more honest, more expressive. Like Marquee, Melvin, and Lauren, we grapple with the ways that we push others away, or maintain unhealthy relationships, and cause ourselves and others pain. This book is about becoming a better friend. It's also about becoming a better human.

Take Action for Friendship

Throughout this book, I weave in stories of people who—just like you and me and everybody—are trying to figure out the slick terrain of connection. Many of them preferred to remain anonymous, so I've altered names and details and have sometimes knitted together stories from different people to respect their privacy. I quote many experts, whose quotations have been abridged for clarity.

A few months after I started writing this book, I was in a Tibetan bookstore in New York, and I picked up a book on Buddhism and flipped to a random page. There are, the author stated, two types of learning: the learning that comes through instruction and that which comes through *experiencing.* Throughout this book, you'll learn a lot about friendship, but knowing alone cannot change your life; this book will also provide practical takeaways for how to improve your friendships. It'll guide you to not just understand friendship differently, but also to do something different in your life to experience—and enact—it.

You can treat this book as a compass to help you chart the waters of friendship. I welcome you to not just soak in all the information but also to use it to show up differently in your friendships. Because it won't matter if you learn that initiating is essential to developing friendships if you're not willing to muscle through your fear of rejection to say hello. How can knowing that self-disclosure is the life-force of friendship serve you if you don't channel this knowledge toward welcoming vulnerability? And if you know that showing love and care joins people closer, but you're stuck doing never-ending work, then your life will only change if you're willing to shift.

I've chosen to present this book in a way that entwines knowing and experiencing to highlight the importance of letting the research settle into our bones. Our quest here is not just to obtain knowledge of friendship but to use that knowledge to evolve.

PART I

Looking Back

How We've Become
the Friends We Are

CHAPTER 1

How Friendship Transforms Our Lives

Connecting with Others Makes Us Ourselves

"Some of the widowed sit at home and watch television for the rest of their lives. They may be alive, but they're not *really* living," seventy-three-year-old Harriet remarks, referencing the members of the grief group she attended after her husband's death. Harriet could have easily faced this same fate if it wasn't for one thing: friendship.

Harriet didn't always value friendship. In fact, up until she married Federico at the age of fifty, it wasn't a priority. She was ambitious, working twelve-hour days and traveling enough to eventually meet her goal of visiting every country in the world. To ascend in her career, she moved across the US, chasing jobs—from the Northeast to the Midwest to the West and back to the Northeast again—disposing of friendships along the way.

But her ambitions never impeded her search for a spouse. "That was the training of my culture—to live your life to find a husband," she says. She had a string of boyfriends throughout her life, and when those relationships clipped, she would hunt for someone new. She remembered visiting her co-worker Denise's home and envying how she had it all: an impressive job, a husband, beautiful twins. Single at forty, she struggled to accept the reality that she might never have the husband and children she dreamed of. But, without the towering domestic obligations that arose from family life, she filled her hours with work.

Harriet admits friendship wasn't all that fulfilling in her younger years because of how she approached it. She was ashamed of her childhood, as she grew up on a farm, dirt poor. During the summers, she worked on neighbors' farms to pay for school. As she rose in her career, and her network increasingly churned with wealthy elites, she never felt like she belonged. Friendship was a place for her to live a double life, to perform the culture of affluence she never felt fully accustomed to: attending estate sales, dropping Benjamins on dinners, arguing over mundanities like the color of neighbors' lawns. She never let herself get too comfortable around friends, lest they figure out where she really came from, who she really was.

Then, two things happened that resuscitated her view on friendship. First, when she married Federico, a social butterfly, she acquiesced to hosting friends in their home for regular gatherings. "People wanted to be around us because of how happy we were," she says. From him, she learned that being around others could be a joy rather than a toll.

But it wasn't until Federico died that she truly understood the value of friends. To heal her grief, she attended counseling for the first time, where she learned how to be vulnerable. She transferred the skill of vulnerability to her friendships. When she did, she experienced old friendships in new ways, as her bonds ceased to be places of pretend. While some friendships buckled under the honesty of her grief, others deepened, and she realized that being vulnerable, asking for support, could be a portal to deep intimacy.

In her old age, Harriet values friends more than ever. One friendship, she realized, has been her longest love story. She met Shirleen in college, when she was studying abroad in Marseilles. Shirleen was the least judgmental person she ever met, one of the only people Harriet could open up to. Although they lost touch after college, fourteen years later, Shirleen tracked her down and called her. Shirleen lived in London but made the effort to visit Harriet in Washington DC five times over the course of a couple of years. As much as Harriet loved Federico, he wasn't one to talk about feelings, so throughout her life, Shirleen was her only true confidante. "For our life to feel significant, we crave someone to witness it, to verify its importance. Shirleen was my witness," Harriet says. They still talk weekly, despite their five-hour time difference, and Shirleen has brought up moving to DC to be closer to Harriet.

Now, for Harriet, having friends is more important than having a spouse. She has a male friend with whom she goes for walks, and she's unsure whether the relationship will remain platonic or become romantic. But she's at peace either way: "I take measure of the value of the relationship in terms of whether we enjoy each other's company, do things together, and share things with each other. The answer to all those questions is yes." She's in no rush to determine the fate of the relationship because "friendship is good too, and it's not a second resort."

At seventy-three, Harriet describes the way she's come to value friendship as a sign that "I've finally grown up." Every evening, she meets a friend for tea, dinner, or a walk. In this way, friends help her slow down and be present for life. "I don't know about you, but when I'm alone, I eat standing up," she says. "When I'm with friends, I eat paying attention." In her old age, Harriet can't travel as extensively as she used to, but instead she gets her thrills through the adventure of interacting with her different friends.

Harriet doesn't have many regrets in her life—certainly not marrying Federico, even though he was nineteen years her senior and she spent a few years being his caretaker after he slipped into dementia. But she does wish she could have recognized the power of friendship sooner. Still, she's thankful she came to value it before it was too late: "As you approach the end of your life, you realize each day is a gift, and you want to spend it in ways that are truly important. And for me, that means spending it with friends."

Harriet's trajectory reveals what we sacrifice when we diminish the importance of friends and what we gain when we value it. In Harriet's time, and still today, friendship is cast as a lesser relationship, a buffer to soften the purgatory between leaving our family and finding a new one. But friendship doesn't have to be so second-rate. As Harriet learned, it can be powerful, deep, and loving. And just like what happened with Harriet, friendship can save and transform us. In fact, it likely already has.

Why Friendship Matters

Friendship's impact is as profound as it is underestimated. Ancient Greeks philosophized that it is a key to eudaimonia, or flourishing. Aristotle, for example, argued in *Nicomachean Ethics* that without friendship, "No one would choose to live." Priests in the Middle Ages distrusted friendship, fearing its love could eclipse our love for God. Then, in the seventeenth century, it enchanted priests, who saw it as a channel to demonstrate our love for God.

These days, we typically see platonic love as somehow lacking—like romantic love with the screws of sex and passion missing. But this interpretation strays from the term's original meaning. When Italian scholar Marsilio Ficino coined the term "platonic love" in the fifteenth century, the word reflected Plato's vision of a love so powerful it transcended the physical. Platonic love was not romantic love undergoing subtraction. It was a purer form of love, one for someone's soul, as Ficino writes, "For it does not desire this or that body, but desires the splendor of the divine light shining through bodies." Platonic love was viewed as superior to romance.

The power of friendship isn't just a relic of ancient thinking. It's demonstrated by science. Psychologists theorize that our relationships, like oxygen, food, and water, are necessary for us to function. When stripped of them, we cannot thrive, which explains why friendship powerfully influences mental and physical health. Scientists have found that of 106 factors that influence depression, having someone to confide in is the strongest preventor. The impact of loneliness on our mortality is akin to smoking fifteen cigarettes a day. One study found the most pronounced difference between happy and unhappy people was not how attractive or religious they were or how many good things happened to them. It was their level of social connection.

Friendship files down the barbs of life's threats. When men were alone, a study found, they rated an alleged terrorist as more imposing than when they were with friends. Another study found that people judged a hill as less steep when they were with friends. I remember a time when I was arguing with a boss who refused to dole out my final paycheck. The conflict gave me a constant edge of anxiety until I told my friend Harbani how I was feeling over chai at a teahouse. As the story poured out, and the chai poured in, I felt better. It was the first peace I had had in weeks.

The healing force of friendship extends past our mental health and into our physical. In Marta Zaraska's book *Growing Young: How Friendship, Optimism, and Kindness Can Help You Live to 100,* she assesses the usual suspects that contribute to our longevity, such as diet and exercise, but she concludes that *connection* is the most powerful contributor. Meta-analyses have found, for example, that exercise decreases our risk of death by 23 to 30 percent, diet by up to 24 percent, and a large social network by 45 percent. When I shared this research with a colleague, she said, "Now I can feel better about being a social couch potato." We all can.

While we can experience many of these benefits through other close relationships, like those with family and spouses, friendships have unique advantages. Friends, distinct from parents, do not expect us to live out their hopes and wants for us. With friends, distinct from spouses, we are not shackled with the insurmountable expectation of being someone's everything, their puzzle piece to completeness. And distinct from our children, we aren't the sole propagator of our friends' survival. Our ancestors lived in tribes, where responsibility for one another was diffused among many. Friendship, then, is a rediscovery of an ancient truth we've long buried: it takes an entire community for us to feel whole.

Friendship, in releasing the relationship pressure valve, infuses us with joy like no other relationship. Without needing to plan for retirement, fulfill each other's sexual needs, and work out who should be scrubbing the shower grime, we are free to make friendships territories of pleasure. One study, for example, found that hanging out with friends was linked to greater happiness than hanging out with a romantic partner or children. This was because, when around friends, people had fun—doing things like going bowling, or to the pumpkin patch, or to the dog park to steal some OPP (other people's puppies)—whereas around spouses or children, they did the mundane, like washing dishes, paying bills, and reminding one another to floss.

Of course, friends too can sink into what friendship-memoirists Ann Friedman and Aminatou Sow call "the intimately mundane." Friendship can be a relationship of grocery shopping, chores, and shared retirements. As people unbundle sex, romance, and life companionship, they see that friends can make marvelous significant others. An *Atlantic* article called "The Rise of the 3-Parent Family" profiled David Jay, founder of the Asexual Visibility and Education Network, who discussed spending his life with a friend he had "really intense energy with." That didn't work out, but he eventually settled into co-parenting with another couple. Friendship is flexible, depending on our needs. It can bring us a once-a-month lunch friend or a soul mate.

A key source of joy in friendship is in how unlimited it is: you can have many friends, whereas other core relationships are finite—a couple of caregivers, one spouse (for the monogamous among us), 2.5 children. Buddhism identifies *mudita,* or sympathetic joy, as vicariously experiencing others' joy. In the Bible, Paul alludes to *mudita* when he writes of all of Jesus's followers, "If one part is honored, every part rejoices with it." Our spouse, our children, our parents, they'll all ping us with *mudita,* but with many friends to celebrate, joy becomes infinite.

I experienced the power of friendship for repeatedly invoking joy when I sold this book. My romantic partner at the time was excited for me, bringing me champagne and a strawberry shortcake with the word "BOOKED" written across it. We had a lovely night in. When I called my friends with the announcement, I got to reexperience this joy again and again, as they told me how excited they were, how they wanted to take me out to celebrate, and how much they hoped I would be interviewed by Oprah so they could come to the taping.

We choose our friends, which allows us to surround ourselves with people who root for us, get us, and delight in our joy. There's no looming vow, formal ritual, or genetic similarity to retain us in friendship's open palms. Through friendship, we can self-select into some of the most affirming, safe, and sacred relationships of our lives, not because of pressures from society to do so, but because we elect to do so. Cleo, who works for the government, told me that after her mother died, she felt alone and uncomfortable at the funeral. Her strained relationships with her family made her scared to break down. But when her friend Stephanie showed up, surprising her by flying in from Michigan, Cleo let herself weep.

The electiveness of friendship, coupled with its usual absence of romantic love, means that in friendship, we are free to choose relationships based on pure compatibility. British author C. S. Lewis once said, "Eros [romantic passion] will have naked bodies; Friendship naked personalities." The consuming feelings of romantic love can sometimes drive us into mismatched relationships, as we erroneously use these consuming feelings as a litmus test for compatibility. But, as psychologist Harriet Lerner states, "Intense feelings, no matter how consuming, are hardly a measure of true and enduring closeness. . . . Intensity and intimacy are not the same." When choosing friends, we are freer to prioritize the truest markers of intimacy, such as shared values, trust, admiration of each other's character, or feelings of ease around each other. We don't always do this, of course, which I'll explore later in a chapter on navigating anger and conflict.

Friends don't just support us personally; they benefit us collectively. When we zoom out to evaluate the merits of friendship on a macro level, we see how these relationships better society. As societies aim to increase justice and decrease prejudice, friendship provides a means. Research finds that having one friend in an outgroup (i.e., a group you're not a part of) alters people's response to that entire outgroup and even increases people's support of policies benefitting the outgroup, suggesting that friendship may be necessary (but likely not sufficient) to trigger systemic change. Another study finds our hostility toward outgroups decreases when our friend is friends with someone in that group, signaling that friendship across groups can have ripple effects throughout entire networks. Prejudice thrives in the abstract, but once we become friends, others become complex beings who hurt and love just like we do, and no matter how different we think they are, we see ourselves in them.

A 2013 meta-analysis found friendship networks had been shrinking for the preceding thirty-five years, and the impact of this trend on society is grave. Friends, research finds, increase our trust in others, and trust is necessary for society to operate. A study with participants from Germany, Czech Republic, and Cameroon found that across all three cultures, people who felt disconnected experienced something called social cynicism, "a negative view of human nature, a biased view against some groups of people, a mistrust of social institutions, and a disregard of ethical means for achieving an end." Robert D. Putnam, author of *Bowling Alone,* emphasized how when we share a social network with someone, we develop "thin trust"—we trust people we don't know well—but, he argues, "as the social fabric of a community becomes more threadbare, its power to undergird norms of honesty, generalized reciprocity, and thin trust is enfeebled." For banks to run, we trust that our bankers won't pocket our retirement and vacation in Katmandu. For grocery stores to run, we trust that our kumquats aren't laced with arsenic. For schools to run, we trust that the teacher won't force our children to spend the day clipping coupons for (arsenic-free) kumquats. And yet, this trust trembles when we're disconnected.

Friendship Is the Underdog of Relationships

By now, it may sound like I'm saying that to keep society from crumbling, we need to file for divorce, disown our families, twist up our tubes, and seek friends. That's not it. What I am trying to convey is that, counter to how our culture treats friendship, it is as meaningful as the other relationship Goliaths. And yet, if you deeply value friendship, you've likely experienced your platonic love being relegated to second-class.

"What's going on between you two?" people remark of close friends, their assumption being that platonic love alone cannot explain a tight bond. If two people aren't romantically involved, then they're not friends—they're *just* friends. If they want to become romantic, they'll say, "Let's be *more* than friends." People with friendship at the center of their relationships are unfairly cast as lonely, unappealing, or unfulfilled, spinsters with a choir of cats, or bachelors who never quite matured. This happens when, all the while, research finds that *friendship is what gives romantic love its strength and endurance,* rather than the other way around.

We don't just assume that friendship is a second-tier relationship; we act to make it so. Compared to our families and romantic partners, with friends, we invest less time, are less vulnerable, and share less adoration. We see romantic relationships as the appropriate relationship to hitch a flight to see each other, toil through tension, or nurse each other back to health. We see family as appropriate relationships to move across the country for or to stay committed to despite problematic Uncle Russ getting drunk and testy every holiday.

Queer and asexual people, who developed terms like "queerplatonic" (friendships that go beyond social norms for platonic relationships) and "zucchini" (your queerplatonic partner), show us that, while typically our friends are not as close to us as our spouse or sibling, they *can* be. The only reason they aren't is because the rest of us unnecessarily compartmentalize friendship into happy hours and occasional lunch dates. The same factors make *all* relationships succeed—familial, romantic, and platonic. We scalpel the tissue of deep intimacy out of friendship, all the while assuming our friendships are shallower than other relationships because of friendships' inferior DNA. Because our culture trivializes friendship, we don't realize how we act to deplete our friendships of intimacy. We see it as the natural way of things.

It wasn't always this way.

When Abe moved to Springfield, Illinois, he was as broke as a mirror flung down a spiral staircase. With his last few dollars, he hoped to purchase a new bed. He went to the store, plopped his bag on the counter, and asked the store's owner, Josh, how much a bed cost. When Josh told Abe the price, Abe admitted he couldn't afford it. Josh, sensing Abe's despair, offered an alternative. He lived above the store, in a bed that was big enough for two. Would Abe like to move in and share his bed? Abe, thrilled, dropped off his bags and declared himself moved.

Abe and Josh were opposites in many ways. Abe was tall enough to make average-size Josh look pint-size. He was slightly hunched, with ungainly limbs and deep-set green eyes. Josh looked like a handsome poet, his eyes a whirlpool of blue, his head adorned with curls. Abe wasn't educated and grew up poor. Josh grew up wealthy and had gone to a prestigious college until he dropped out. But the two soon came to find that they were more similar than they thought.

They spent every waking moment together outside of work, and sometimes Josh would even accompany Abe on his work trips. They woke up in their bed, had bitter coffee and a light breakfast together, and, in the evenings, went to a nearby friend's house for dinner. They'd return to hang out in Josh's store, where other guys would gather to hear Abe tell stories and crack jokes.

But the friendship had its challenges. Abe was often sad, and not just any sad—the hard-to-get-out-of-bed, keep-sharp-objects-away kind of sad. Medicine didn't help. It only aggravated his mood. Abe had endured many tragedies, the most acute occurring when he was nine, when his beloved mother suddenly died from food poisoning. "All that I am or ever hope to be I owe to her," Abe once said. His father was moody, and his cousins were erratic. One was even institutionalized. Abe feared he was doomed to the same fate.

Another major trigger for Abe's depression was his botched relationships. During their friendship, Abe and Josh each got into romantic entanglements that soon unraveled as they pushed away women who loved them so much. Once, Abe got engaged to a woman named Mary, but he broke it off, as the relationship surged fears of intimacy that likely originated from his mother's death. He felt so guilty that he spiraled into psychosis—depressed, hallucinating, suicidal, and babbling incoherently. Josh was the only one Abe allowed by his side. Josh chatted with him every day and kept him safe by hiding his razors.

While Abe was recovering, Josh moved to Kentucky to reunite with his family. There, he got engaged to a woman named Fanny. The looming marriage struck Josh with the same distress that had besieged Abe. The two friends wrote letters to each other, and Abe coached Josh through his intimacy fears.

Yet the letters were not just about Josh's distress. They also expressed the intimacy they felt with each other. Abe wrote, for example, that he felt Josh's distress as piercingly as he did his own, that his desire to be Josh's friend was everlasting and would never cease, and signed his letters "yours forever." Abe anxiously requested that Josh reply to his letters immediately upon receipt.

Sleeping in the same bed, nurturing each other through ailments, writing loving letters: Abe and Josh's relationship was so intimate that many have suspected it sexual, but the two lived during a time when their sort of deep friendship was much more accepted than it is now. The fateful day where the two met at Joshua Speed's store was April 15, 1837. Abe is a man we know quite well. His full name was Abraham Lincoln.

In his book *Your Friend Forever, A. Lincoln: The Enduring Friendship of Abraham Lincoln and Joshua Speed,* author Charles Strozier writes, "It takes a leap of imagination to enter into a time in American history when, on one hand, sex between men was regarded as loathsome and if known was severely punished and the basis for social ostracism while, on the other, intimacy—including sleeping together—and closeness, mutuality, and expressions of love were strongly encouraged and even regarded as desirable."

Once Lincoln shared a hotel room with Judge David Davis. When Lincoln's friend and advisor Leonard Swett came in, he found the two huffing from a pillow fight, Lincoln was scantily clad in a long yellow tunic that was held together by a single button at the throat. Swett stated that he shuddered when he thought of "what might happen should that button by any mischance lose its hold."

In Lincoln's era, homosexuality was so squarely forbidden that intimacy between friends didn't raise concerns of its presence. This freed people to be as close to friends as they wished, with the only boundary being genitals. Daniel Webster, a congressman and former secretary of state, greeted his friend James Hervey Bingham in letters with "Lovely Boy" and "Dearly Beloved." In one of those letters, he wrote, "You are the only friend of my heart, the partner of my joys, griefs, and affections, the only participator of my most secret thoughts." If marriage didn't work out for them, Webster shared his hope that "we will put on a dress of old bachelors, a mourning suit, and having sown all our wild oats, with a round hat and a hickory staff, we will march on to the end of life, whistling as merry as robins."

I'm not endorsing a return to this era, a time when sexual intimacy among people of the same sex was even more deeply stigmatized. Joshua Speed enslaved people, further highlighting the obvious—this was not a golden era for relating to our fellow humans. But exploring this time reveals the depths of what friendship could truly be.

When we diminish friendship, we stifle the potential of a relationship that can become every bit as deep as Josh and Abe's. In fact, no matter our age, we've likely experienced a time when a friend was who we felt closest to in the world. But as we age, we embrace a collective amnesia that disregards the ways our friends have impacted us. We pretend growing up means shedding friendship, like molting dead skin, to focus on relationships that matter, which flouts research that verifies Harriet's conclusions, finding that as we get older, friends matter even *more* for our health and well-being. In fact, our friendships have likely already transformed us, molding us into who we are and foretelling who we will become.

Friendship Makes Us Whole

On an Uber ride back to their shared apartment, Selina and her best friend Jesse texted about the anime show *Higurashi no Naku Koro ni* (or *When They Cry* in English) and what it illuminated about their friendship. "I'll always be fighting beside you," Jesse texted, referencing a theme from the show. It was the affirmation Selina needed to hear in order to confess something she'd hidden from everyone. "Can I tell you a secret? I can't tell anyone else," Selina texted Jesse.

When Selina arrived home to meet Jesse, her breath grew shallow, and she averted her eyes. If she hadn't already texted Jesse she was ready to confess, she'd likely have aborted the mission. She imagined Jesse's response to what she was about to share. "That makes no sense. Why would you lie like that?"

Selina's secret? She didn't have celiac disease, despite telling people for a decade she did. While this may seem trivial, for Selina, this lie was tumbled up in shame. Before she was born, in her father's previous marriage, his first son was stillborn. Throughout Selina's life, he feared she'd die, just like his son had. So, he searched and searched for something wrong with Selina. Then, he could find the cure and feel like he had regained control of Selina's mortality. Selina was ushered to the doctor weekly, and when one doctor said nothing was wrong, she was herded to the next.

Finally, her father arrived at the possibility that Selina had celiac. Selina, so exhausted by the doctors, the tests, and even the minor surgeries her father goaded her into, surrendered. "Yes. That must be it, Dad. I have celiac," she said, knowing she was lying. And that was the beginning of a decade of lying: to her friends, and to family, and to anyone who knew her. While the lies saved her from being further caught up in her father's hysteria, she sacrificed her self-esteem in the process: "I felt fucked up and guilty and was questioning my character. I remember my cousin Katie, who had celiac, and she'd have seizures if she ate gluten. Thinking of her, I felt terrible faking that. It felt like I was faking cancer."

Harry Stack Sullivan, a prominent psychiatrist, has a word for what Selina felt in her shame over her lie—"unhuman." Our shame, he argues, is excruciating because it cleaves us from humanity. When we get fired, we don't feel bad because we screwed up. We feel bad because, in screwing up, we alienated ourselves from everyone who hasn't. When we divorce, our grief is compounded because the breakup estranges us from those living "normal lives" in happy marriages (even though divorce is normal). When we feel shame over our bodies, it's because we sense our skin hangs saggy, flabby, or jiggly beyond comparison (also normal). Our shame, according to Sullivan, comes less from the inherent agony of our experiences and more from the agony of these experiences severing us from humankind.

How do we feel human again? Through friendship, according to Sullivan. When we confide our shame, and friends accept us or even identify with us, we learn our disappointments don't make us unhuman. They make us deeply human. Our friends permit us to accept our flaws, to allow them to be a piece of who we are rather than our scarlet letters.

Selina's experience illustrates Sullivan's points. Before she disclosed the truth to Jesse, she was confronted with her lie every day. Friends would cook gluten-free or choose gluten-free restaurants on her behalf. Occasionally, Selina would squirrel away a bagel or muffin. All the lying made Selina feel quite literally unhuman: "When I ate gluten, I literally had this image of a bridge troll crawling out from the shades and grabbing something from the trash."

But when she shared her secret, Jesse didn't question her character as she feared. They empathized and even celebrated Selina: "I was met with immediate grace and support. There wasn't even a hitch. They said, 'I'm excited to eat these foods with you. We're going to reclaim this, make it fucking great. We'll go to brunch and drink mimosas and eat a ton of gluten.'" A week later, Jesse and Selina went to brunch and ate waffles and French toast, or, as Selina put it, "gluten with extra gluten." That night, the two got some (gluten-filled) cookie dough ice cream with brownie bits and ate it together. As Selina cried, Jesse said, "Cry, Selina. Let it out. I'm so happy you could tell me this."

Jesse's acceptance gave Selina the confidence to reveal her secret to everyone in her life. "I don't think they'll judge. They might just think it's fun to eat donuts with us," Jesse said reassuringly. Selina told her brother first, and then other friends, while Jesse advocated for her. "This is exciting, and we're all going out for lunch," Jesse would chime in after Selina's disclosure, steering the conversation away from any probing questions about Selina. Eventually, Selina even told her father, whom she feared telling the most.

Because we avoid what we feel shame over, we miss out on the opportunities to explore those pieces of our identity. For Selina, revealing her shame allowed her to understand the slice of her suppressed by the shame. She "underwent a transformation in what food meant to me," realizing she loved cooking—barley, farro, and all types of gluten. Before she shared her secret, the acts of restricting and hiding food to maintain her pretense of celiac would trigger food binges for Selina, since "even though they're not the same, the situation and motivation put me in a similar mental space as when I had bulimia, where I was like, I'm this monster who hoards food." After her disclosure, her bulimia symptoms lessened.

When we feel shame, we feel fragmented, like Selina. Shame prompts us to ignore, bury, or distance a piece of ourselves. But in our obsession with hiding that flaw, it absorbs us, and ironically, as we try to detach from it, it becomes engulfing. One of my neighbors who is gay disclosed that he started feeling like his true self only when he came out, because hiding his sexuality exhausted all his energy, consuming his whole personhood. What we try to suppress defines us (more on this in the vulnerability chapter), or, in the words of one of my psychology supervisors, "Anything unspeakable to you is affecting you." That's why we don't heal shame by hiding it. When we share it, and our friends love and accept us, we are released from the labor of guarding our shame. Whatever alleged flaw triggered our shame becomes a part of who we are, not the entirety of who we are. This is how the empathy we receive from friends makes us whole.

Selina did indeed feel whole again after she shared her shame with Jesse. "I look up and there's no troll bridge, no garbage," she said. "It was like looking down at my ugly, gnarly troll hands and realizing that they're regular hands, like everyone else's. I'm normal. I looked in the mirror after that night, and thought, 'Why do I feel so beautiful?' Because if somebody like Jesse loved someone like me, then I'm someone worth loving. I was human again and deserving of love."

Friendship Makes Us Empathic

Of course, anyone can offer us this empathy—our family, our spouse, our boss, our Instagram followers, a Zumba instructor, a candlestick maker, a reluctant Uber driver. But friends are there when we need this empathy the most. Research finds that shame is highest when we're teenagers, decreasing steadily throughout our lives and then increasing again to similarly high rates only in old age. Research finds that at this awkward time, we don't turn to family or the boyfriend we invented when we were younger to seem interesting. We turn to friends. Friends have such a lasting impact on our identities because they are there during this critical and tumultuous time when we are figuring out who we are.

Friends are good candidates for providing us with empathy because friendship provokes empathy. In fact, friendship, according to Sullivan, is *how* we become empathic. In his theory of chumships, he argues that around the ages of eight to ten, friendship radically alters how we relate to others. It's the first relationship where we value another's welfare as much as our own. As kids, when it comes to parents, we take. When it comes to teachers, we obey. But when it comes to friends, we feel for and with.

Sullivan explains that a child "begins to develop a real sensitivity to what matters to another person. And this is not in the sense of 'what should I do to get what I want,' but instead 'what should I do to contribute to the happiness or to support the prestige and feeling of worth-whileness of my chum.' . . . It is a matter of *we*." When I shared this theory with my friend, she nodded and said, "I could easily confuse my kids for tiny tyrants if I never saw them with their friends."

This isn't all just theory. Dozens of studies highlight friendship's unique role in promoting empathy. For adolescents, friendship is a distinct space to practice empathy, as research finds that during adolescence, kindness toward friends increases while kindness toward family is stagnant or decreases. Friendship isn't just a space to practice empathy; it's a space to develop it. A meta-analysis found that having high-quality friendship is correlated with greater empathy. In another study on kids with languages issues, kids with better friends developed more empathy, and those with more empathy developed better friendships. There's also research that looks at empathy and friendship unfolding in the brain. It finds that seeing friends excluded activates the same part of our brains triggered when we are excluded. This is not true for strangers. Empathy, then, is part of friendship. And friendship does not only make us empathic toward our friends. It makes us empathic generally.

Empathy is a major achievement of friendship. It's enough to make the relationship vital. But friendship's positive impact extends beyond nurturing empathy, toward bettering our characters more generally. One study, for example, tested whether having friends during formative years affects who we become as adults. It compared fifth graders who did have friends with fifth graders who did not on several outcomes in adulthood. The fifth graders with friends were less depressed, more moral, and had higher self-worth as adults.

If we were asked, *How did you become empathic? More moral? Develop high self-esteem?*, for most of us, our answer wouldn't be friends. Education, self-reflection, therapy, or genes, we might say. We're not always conscious of the way friendship transforms us, but it still does. And it doesn't just make us into better versions of ourselves. It helps us figure out who we are.

Friendship Helps Us Figure Out Who We Are

It was the summer of 2016, a muggy day in the French district of Hanoi, Vietnam, when Callee opened the windows of her apartment and yelled, "SHUT UP!" at the racket below. She knew it was futile. Her voice would be drowned out by the bustle, but she had to try. She slumped back in bed and began to sob. Callee is American, and her move to Vietnam was supposed to be her great escape, a grand adventure. But several months in, she felt herself more exasperated than recharged. Sure, she enjoyed teaching English, but life outside her tiny apartment was overwhelming, and she was lonely.

"You should come out with me and my friends," her co-worker Gilda told her when she noticed Callee looking glum. Gilda introduced Callee to her friends, a well-meaning but dour group at a local bar. They didn't say much to Callee as she scooted into the booth, nor for the rest of the night. While Callee appreciated Gilda's invitation, she left feeling a different type of lonely, the type you feel when you're around people but uncomfortable being yourself. Callee has bouncy curly hair, and she is normally as bubbly as a fizzy beverage, laughing easily and greeting people with hellos that echo through the room. But around Gilda and her subdued friends, Callee felt pressure to turn down the dial on her personality.

Callee didn't see those friends again, but she continued to spend time with Gilda. Soon after, they joined a kung fu class with other expats, and Gilda gave her a rundown of the other students that included a word of advice: "The girl, Lee, she's a loud and obnoxious Australian girl. I'd stay away from her." The comment confirmed something Callee suspected about her friendship with Gilda: it could survive only if she shrunk herself. She said, "Because if Gilda *really* knew me, then she'd probably be telling some other person 'That's Callee. She's a loud and obnoxious American. Stay away.'" Ironically, Gilda's comment put Lee on Callee's radar as someone to get to know.

Luckily, Lee wasn't shy and introduced herself to Callee. The two took to each other quickly, giggling in the back of class and getting in trouble. Lee invited Callee to lunch after class and their friendship was cemented. Lee struck Callee as someone good and kind. They also shared an easy comfort from the start, something Callee was missing with Gilda. She adored Lee for her positivity, the way her smiles looked like crescent moons, and her cheeks dimpled when she laughed. Around Lee, Callee exhaled into her full laughing, vibrant self. The demure girl with Gilda at the bar wasn't Callee.

Lee was as full of joy as she was guts. She drove a moped around

Vietnam. When she didn't know how to get somewhere, she jumped on the bike and hailed passersby for directions. She went up to strangers, said hello, and asked them to lunch, as Callee witnessed. She was brave, and Callee wasn't.

One weekend, Callee visited Lee in a house she had just moved into. Lee's boyfriend, a Brazilian soccer player, was there, kind, cute, and attentive. Her tidy home was hugging the beach. Callee sighed and thought of her life. She was tired of living in the city, tired of the rumbling moped engines, yells, and stumbling drunk people outside her apartment. And somehow, that frustration started coming out in her interactions with Lee.

That weekend, when Lee hailed a stranger for directions, Callee snapped, "How do you not know where to go? You live here!" When Lee made a wrong turn, Callee chided, "You're going the wrong way." When Lee fumbled over her Vietnamese while ordering food, Callee interjected, "That's not how you say it!" and then when Lee would gesticulate wildly while telling a story, Callee would mimic her mockingly. Finally, a deflated Lee said, "C! Why are you being so mean to me?"

Why *was* she being so mean? Callee had to face the facts. "I was envious because of how further ahead in life she was. She's fearless, going anywhere the wind takes her, and she's not afraid to make changes. I was really inspired by her, but I wasn't cognizant of that, so it started to feel oppressive to be around her, because she had her shit together," she admitted. Here was someone she was curious about, even envious of, and she expressed her intrigue with jabs. Lee was a threat because she reminded Callee of the ways her life was empty.

After this revelation, Callee started to embrace her envy, as a clue for how she wanted to change her life. "I needed to remember her journey was different from mine," she said, "and the reason we are friends is because we could ignite one another and help each other grow." And so, Callee let Lee ignite her. She drove a moped around town. She invited strangers out for pho. One day, while Lee and Callee were at the gym, Lee suggested that they choreograph a dance together. They did, and Callee never stopped dancing. She began to choreograph dances when alone in her room, and she eventually became a Zumba instructor. Callee became all the things Lee showed her she could be.

There's a famous psychology study called the Bobo doll experiment. The experiment involves kids watching an adult either beat up a huge inflatable doll called Bobo or else ignore it and play with toys. When the kids were exposed to Bobo, after seeing the adult pummel him, they hammered him upside his big old head and left-hooked him in his dumb grinning face. When the kids saw the adults ignore Bobo for the other toys, they left Bobo alone. The study was revolutionary because it illustrated that learning doesn't just happen when a teacher lectures at the front of a classroom. We take on what we experience. Our classroom is what we witness firsthand.

Lee was Callee's Bobo doll experiment. As much as Gilda told Callee to enjoy and live life in Vietnam, what convinced her to do it was seeing Lee live hers. Their friendship demonstrates how friends change us. Our friends advertise the kaleidoscope of ways we can live. They expose us to new ways of being in the world, showing us another life is possible. As Anaïs Nin, the French Cuban writer, puts it, "Each friend represents a world in us, a world possibly not born until they arrive, and it is only by this meeting that a new world is born."

In psychology-speak, Callee and Lee's friendship illustrates the tenets of self-expansion theory. The theory emphasizes that our identity needs to constantly expand for us to be fulfilled, and relationships are our primary means for expansion. That's because when we get close to someone, we include them in our sense of ourselves, a phenomenon aptly termed "inclusion of others in the self." When our friends hike Kilimanjaro, it feels almost as if we did, and then we feel more ready to make the climb. When our friend gives up their accounting job to pursue watercolor, we're curious about leaving ours to make jewelry. When they've developed a frozen yogurt obsession, we find ourselves peering into the Pinkberry window. Inclusion of others in the self is actually part of why we're empathic toward friends; it feels like being empathic to ourselves.

Arthur Aron, a renowned professor at Stony Brook University, developed the concept of inclusion of others in the self. Aron told me about interesting tests he's done that suggest that we include others in our selves. He found that people who were given money were likely to divvy it up fairly between themselves and a best friend but were more selfish when sharing it with a stranger. In another of his studies, people were asked to attribute traits to themselves or another person and then to recall which traits they ascribed to whom. They were more likely to mistake traits they had attributed to themselves to a close other (friend or romantic partner) than to a media personality. Another study found that people took longer to recognize their face as theirs when it was presented alongside their friend's face compared to when it was presented alongside a celebrity's. When trying to assess differences between ourselves and close others, we get confused because they feel like part of us.

While inclusion of others in self can make us feel exhilarated, intimate, and evolved, it also has drawbacks. A small slice of people report being enmeshed with others and losing their identity, Aron told me. It also provides a window for us to take on another's unsavory traits—their chortle, love of bologna, or morning whiskey-swigging routine.

Inclusion of others in self explains why we're extra susceptible to peer pressure coming from friends. Parents worry when their kids get involved with the wrong crowd, and, based on Aron's research, they should. But Aron has faith that the positives outweigh the negatives. "We choose people for relationships because we want to become like them, after all," he shared. "It's a way for us to enrich who we are."

Aron maintains that friendship is a powerful trigger for self-expansion. A diehard researcher, he's gotten so close to his research collaborators that he sometimes forgets whose expertise is whose. I'd add that friendship has unique advantages for self-expansion. Even in my greatest romantic relationships, when I haven't seen friends enough, I've felt my personality accordion inward. One person, no matter how great, could surface only one side of me. Hanging out with different friends dilated my personality like a peacock fanning its tail.

Lincoln and Speed's friendship reveals the consequences of including others in our self. It's not just that we share joy and sorrow. We also become more similar, less distinguishable. As Aron puts it, "If I am close to you, who I am is deeply and centrally different because of you; and this difference is that who I am deeply and centrally is you." Aron goes so far as to argue that the self is simply a reflection of what we've gleaned from our relationships across our lives.

Most of us look forward to the day when our identity hardens, like a cast protecting against life's dings. When we're younger, we yearn for the moment when we'll be fully formed and have life figured out. Maybe it's when we find love, or have kids, or write that book, or retire. And then we get older and realize that moment never happens. You're never done figuring it out, but hopefully you're better equipped to tolerate not knowing. This uncertainty is also an offering—an opportunity not only to expand, evolve, and grow, but also to deepen our friendships by letting others be agents of our transformation.

Friendship Makes Us Friendlier

Friendship affects who we are—our behaviors, traits, and identity. For some additional evidence of its importance, let's zero in on its effects on our biology.

Imagine if you showed up to a research experiment, and the experimenter asked you to inhale a nasal spray. After waiting for the spritz to set in, the researcher told you he'll give you ten dollars and that you'll have to divide the sum with a stranger. How much you share is up to you. Are you generous?

Or imagine another scenario. This time, after the nasal spray spritz, the researcher gave you some money and told you that you could give some or all of it to a trustee. The researcher will top off any money you give, so the trustee can pay you back and then some and still keep a hefty amount for themselves. But they could also keep it and leave you with nothing. Do you trust them?

Your answer here, according to two studies, will depend on what was in that nasal spray. Some people got a saltwater placebo, while others were spritzed with a magical hormone that makes us more generous, giving, and all-around friendly. It's called oxytocin. People who got oxytocin were more trusting. According to other studies, the hormone triggers empathy for and attention to others.

But oxytocin doesn't just bring us connection. Connection brings us oxytocin. When we feel connected, our oxytocin rises. One study found that male chimpanzees hanging out with friends experience an uptick in oxytocin. Another study found that female monkeys who had better friendships released more oxytocin later in life. The same was true for male monkeys, in relation to a different social hormone, vasopressin. Kids with moms who had higher levels of oxytocin exhibited higher levels of oxytocin and better friendships.

Throughout this chapter, I've tried to convince you that

friendship transforms us, and oxytocin shows us how. While the evidence is still growing, studies suggest that having quality friendships in our past triggers our oxytocin and makes us more empathic, moral, and attentive and, in doing so, positions us as better friends. Our past friendships, the evidence suggests, prepare us for connection throughout our lives. According to Sullivan, the psychiatrist who created the theory of chumships, "Carrying on the businesses of life with members of one's own sex requires relations with a chum in preadolesc[ence]." Friendship begets friendship. But for those who haven't yet experienced the virtuous cycle of friendship, don't worry. The information you will learn in *Platonic* will bring you onboard.

But oxytocin, like an undergrad with student loans, takes on multiple jobs. It isn't just the key to connection; it's also the key to health—so much so that scientists have touted it as the "elixir of youth." Although much of the research on oxytocin's health-boosting effects has been conducted in animals, results are promising. Studies find that it calms stress responses and reduces inflammation. In rat studies, it has been found to decrease cortisol levels and blood pressure. In our quest to figure out why having friends makes us better connectors, and why friendship benefits our mental and physical health, we find the same source: oxytocin. In the words of Esther Perel, a famous couples' therapist, "the quality of our relationships determines the quality of our lives." Oxytocin is the common denominator.*

---

* Even when it comes to oxytocin, you can have too much of a good thing. In attaching us to people, it comes with some liabilities. There's evidence, at least in women, that it increases anxiety about losing people (whereas for men it's linked to lower anxiety).

Friendship Makes Our Souls Grow

"Friendship is unnecessary like philosophy, like art, like the universe itself," C. S. Lewis wrote with irony, implying the very opposite. At one point in our lives, friendship was at the center of all our universes, like it is for Selina. And in that time—if it was healthy—it elevated our character, making us more moral, empathic, and whole. Callee's story demonstrates that, through self-expansion, friendship helps us figure out who we are. We don't know ourselves fully until we experience ourselves in another person and recognize that force within us. Or, as the Zulu saying goes, "a person is a person through other persons."

Friendships are tiny interventions of love and empathy and oxytocin that calm our bodies, keep us healthy, and ready us for connection. In the words of Lydia Denworth, author of *Friendship: The Evolution, Biology, and Extraordinary Power of Life's Fundamental Bond,* "People think all the time about competition and survival of the fittest, but really it's survival of the friendliest. Friendship is the key to us living long and happy lives."

Friendship is a medium through which we find the truest, kindest, and richest selves. It is the in vivo class on relationships that teaches us what it means to connect with others. Friendship, in enhancing us in so many ways, prepares us for, well, friendship. Our friends mold us into people who are better prepared to form healthier, richer, longer-lasting connections. French philosopher Michel de Montaigne, in his essay "On Friendship," calls it "spiritual," a relationship that allows the "soul to grow more refined by practice." May we cherish our friends and watch our souls grow.

CHAPTER 2

How Our Past Relationships Affect Our Present

The Power of Attachment Theory in Friendship

Imagine you're back in your middle school cafeteria. The lunch servers offer today's mystery meat on one side of the room, and the kids gather at their rectangular tables on the other. Everyone's so loud that their voices twine into a tumble of white noise, like mixing all colors until they turn black. Your table is called to stand in line for lunch. As tempted as you are to skip today's muck and head to the vending machines for Cool Ranch Doritos and cheddar popcorn, you know that'll leave your stomach rumbling by seventh period, so you get in line.

As the line moves, you look back at the table where you plopped your bookbag. It's where you and your best friend, Eric, sit every day. You don't see Eric's bag or jacket anywhere by yours, and you wonder where he is. You saw him in algebra earlier, so you know he's at school. Usually, you'd wait in line together, catching each other up on your mornings. You start to feel kind of lonely, as you watch the other kids in line chat with their friends, asking, "Did you see the latest episode of *The Simpsons*?"

The line progresses until you're at the front. You consider your meal options. There's a large brick of pizza with a sheet of white cheese, or a platter of sandwiches—bologna, ham and cheese, peanut butter and jelly, roast beef, pumpkin-orange American cheese. You choose the pizza and grab a side of carrots. Sometimes there's juice too, which you were hoping for, but today there's only milk. You take a red milk carton and head to your seat.

As you get to your seat, you're relieved to see that your friend Amanda is sitting at your table. Amanda sometimes sits with you and Eric and sometimes with her friends from the school play. Today, her choice saved you from having to sit alone, hoping Eric might show.

"Have you seen Eric?" you ask her.

"Yeah. We were just in earth science together. He stopped to talk to the teacher after class. Not sure how long that'll take."

You move your backpack, peek at the clock, and settle into your seat. It's fifteen minutes into lunch. You look over your shoulder at the lunch line to see if you spot Eric. He's not there either. You turn back to Amanda and start chatting about your grade on the latest math test.

While Amanda is congratulating you on your grade, she peers behind you. Suddenly, her eyes go wide. As you turn your head, you feel liquid spilling down your shoulder, its smell consuming your nostrils. It's milk. It trickles down your chest, into your lap, before the carton bounces onto the floor. A couple of kids nearby start laughing like *Lion King* hyenas. You look behind you to figure out what's going on, and you see Eric. His face is blank. His tray is almost full—a brick of pizza, a baggie of carrots, but the square where his drink is supposed to be is empty. His milk is gone.

It's up to you to make sense of what happened. Was Eric so eager to drink his milk that he sipped it during the walk from the lunch servers back to your table? Did he then trip as he came close, perhaps rushing because he was eager to see you? Did his open carton of milk flip off his tray and onto you? Or was Eric perfectly balanced? Did he decide, sinisterly, to pry open the carton and release its

31

contents all over you in a waterfall of dairy? Was he looking to humiliate you, or is he just a well-meaning klutz?

Why might people interpret the same events in friendship so differently? In this chapter we'll explore attachment theory, a groundbreaking framework that answers this question, and along the way, we'll solve other questions about friendship, like who are we as friends and how did we become this way? How do our perceptions and behaviors impact our friendships? What type of people are most likely to make and keep friends? In our quest for friendship, answering these questions is vital and will guide us through the rest of this book.

We'll find that hundreds of studies reveal that the way we view others, interpret events, and behave have predictable impacts on whether we make and keep friends. It's not all luck, these studies scream; whether we make and keep friends depends on us. There are tiny choices we make—ones that we often don't realize—that determine the fate of our friendships. But what the heck are they?

The Power of Attachment Style

As a kid living in Israel, Omri Gillath struggled to make friends, and he wondered why others didn't. He wondered again when he moved to the US for his postdoctoral studies in psychology, separated from all the friends he knew. It was a struggle to reinvent his friendships in the US, where, he realized, people viewed friendships as disposable. They'd move and forget their friends, Omri observed. Now an immigrant in the US, moving around a lot himself, he worried there wasn't much hope.

What Omri had going for him, though, was curiosity. Now at fifty, he's bald and bearded like Sigmund Freud, but even in college, his friends nicknamed him Freud because of his voracious interest in why people do what they do. As a graduate student, he bounced between advisors and studied suicide and the meaning of life, until he finally ended up satisfying his curiosity about people through studying attachment styles.

Attachment theory helped him identify people who were experts at making and keeping friends. According to research, these "super friends" are not only better at initiating new friendships, but their friendships are also closer and more enduring. They are good at making what he described as "shovel friends"—friends who, "if you show up at two a.m. to their house and told them you need help burying the body, they'd ask you, 'Where's the shovel?'"

These super friends weren't just flourishing in their relationships. They were flourishing in all aspects of life, revealing that our ability to relate to others determines not just our friendships; it holds gravity over everything we do. Studies find that these super friends have better mental health and are more likely to feel like they matter. They are more open to new ideas and harbor less prejudice. They are more satisfied at work and are viewed more positively by co-workers. They feel less regret and are better able to roll with the punches of life. In typically stressful events, like math tests or public speaking, they keep calm. They are less likely to have physical ailments like heart attacks, headaches, stomach troubles, and inflammation. When I talked to Omri, now Dr. Gillath, a professor at the University of Kansas, we were in the middle of the COVID-19 pandemic. He speculated that super friends were adapting better to the chaos.

The super friends responded distinctly in the milk fiasco described at the start of this chapter. In several studies, kids were asked how they'd interpret their friend's actions in a similar scenario (albeit less dramatic; poetic license, people). Some judged Eric to have sinister motives, going out of his way to humiliate them, and subsequently felt angrier over spilled milk. Some wanted to seek revenge—slosh milk on Eric right back. The super friends, however, saw the saga as an accident. They were forgiving and gave Eric the benefit of the doubt, reassuring Eric that everything was okay.

What is the distinguishing quality of the super friends? It's security. According to attachment theory—the theory that changed Gillath's life and career forever—secure attachment is one of three major attachment styles, outlined as follows:

1. **Secure attachment.** Secure people assume they are worthy of love, and others can be trusted to give it to them. This belief becomes an unconscious template that trickles into all their relationships, leading them to give others the benefit of the doubt, open up, ask for what they need, support others, assume others like them, and achieve intimacy.

2. **Anxious attachment.** People who are anxiously attached assume others will abandon them. To keep themselves from being abandoned, they act clingily, are overly self-sacrificing to accommodate others, or plunge into intimacy too rapidly.

3. **Avoidant attachment.** Avoidantly attached people are similarly afraid others will abandon them. But instead of clinging to avoid this outcome, they keep others at a distance. Intimacy signals, to them, that they could be hurt, so they push others away, eschew vulnerability, and leave relationships prematurely.

We develop our attachment styles based on our early relationships with our caregivers (though Gillath's research has also found our genes play a role). If our caregivers were warm and validating, we become secure. If they were, instead, unresponsive, cold, rejecting, or intrusive—if they bark at us to stop crying when we're sad, neglect us when we want to play, or hit us when we accidentally drop our Cheerios, then we develop insecure attachment, wherein we see the world as treacherous, believing others are bound to abandon or mistreat us. To protect against the mistreatment we reason we'll endure, we act either anxiously or avoidantly. There's also disorganized attachment, which describes people who flip between these two styles in more extreme ways.

But attachment isn't all our parents' fault. One study finds that 72 percent of people maintained the same attachment style from infancy to adulthood. Another study, however, finds this rate is as low as 26 percent. Both of these studies were small, and more research is needed. Everett Waters, a professor at Stony Brook University who conducted one of the studies, told me that while early attachment experiences with caretakers do establish expectations about our relationships with people in general, these expectations likely evolve in other relationships, with our parental relationship serving only as a jumping-off point. "Once you have some experience in the peer group, initial expectations are going to give way to expectations based on actual experience with peers," he said. In other words, each new relationship can change your attachment style.

Even as attachment evolves based on our ongoing relationships, attachment theory still illustrates that how we view our relationships is not objective; it's influenced by our past and by how our parents, and then others in our lives, responded to us. But most of us don't recognize this. We see our perceptions—refracted through our attachment style—as reality.

I've had friends suspect a mutual friend doesn't like them, while in truth that friend has praised them in my company. I've gotten messages from people, hungry for friendship advice, who have let promising relationships wither because "if they aren't initiating conversation, they don't want to hear from me." Where do these assumptions come from? Not from how others view us, because we don't know others' perceptions and motives for certain. Rather, we're just unconsciously rummaging through our past to make sense of the world.

- When we assume, without clear evidence, that the only reason someone's reaching out to us is that they're bored and lonely, attachment is at play.
- When we wait for the "shoe to drop" in an otherwise happy friendship, attachment is at play.
- When we feel an overwhelming but mysterious urge to withdraw, attachment is at play.
- When we assume others will disappoint us, judge us when we're vulnerable, or turn us down when we need support, attachment is at play.
- When we assume friends don't really like us to begin with, attachment is at play.
- When we allow people to see only our strong side, our "jolly" side, or our sarcastic side, attachment is at play.
- When we maintain relationships with people who mistreat us, attachment is at play.

Attachment is what we project onto ambiguity in relationships, and our relationships are rife with ambiguity. It's the "gut feeling" we use to deduce what's really going on. And this gut feeling is driven not by a cool assessment of events but by the collapsing of time, the superimposition of the past onto the present.

Understanding our attachment is illuminating, not so we can mentally flog ourselves for our biased interpretations, but so we can understand ourselves better and grow in our friendships. If you've ever wondered, "I don't know what I'm doing wrong—why can't I make or keep friends?" identifying how your attachment shapes how you relate to others can bring fresh hope and lay the bricks of the path forward.

Determining Your Attachment Style

The following is a table that describes patterns of behavior in friendship based on attachment style.* Go through the list, and place X's throughout the chart to mark which behaviors you demonstrate. Then, sum up all your X's in each column. Your highest score represents your primary attachment in friendship.

BEHAVIORS IN FRIENDSHIP BASED ON ATTACHMENT

Secure	Anxious	Avoidant
Comfortable initiating new friendships **X**	Fear of rejection impedes initiation of new friendships ____	Uninterested in new friendships ____
Develops intimate friendships **X**	Develops intimate friendships ____	Develops shallow friendships ____
When friends are out of sight, assumes contact will eventually recommence **X**	When friends are out of sight, worries friends don't like them anymore; resentful ____	When friends are out of sight, they are forgotten ____
Generous, with appropriate boundaries **X**	Overly generous to the point of self-depletion ____	Not generous ____
Brings up issues level-headedly **X**	Ignores issues, and then blows up over issues ____	Ignores issues; minimizes or deflects when others bring up issues ____

* Though fearful attachment is important to explore, there is unfortunately not much research on it, so I focus on anxious, avoidant, and secure attachment throughout this book.

BEHAVIORS IN FRIENDSHIP BASED ON ATTACHMENT

Secure	Anxious	Avoidant
Comfortable being vulnerable ——	Overshares ——	Feels "weak" whenever vulnerable; avoids vulnerability ✗
Friends know all sides of them ✗	Friends know all sides of them ——	Friends know only their positive or strong side ——
Comfortable asking for support ——	Fears asking for support will make them a burden ✗	Fears asking for support will make them look weak ——
Comfortable providing support ✗	Comfortable providing support but may get overly involved in friend's problems: pushing advice or breaking down ——	Feels burdened when others need support ——
Prioritizes both own needs and others' needs ✗	When triggered, prioritizes own needs over those of others. Otherwise, prioritizes others' needs over own needs ——	Prioritizes own needs over needs of others ——
Comfortable admitting fault and taking responsibility ——	When admits fault, overly self-critical; otherwise denies fault or responsibility; sees the other party as at fault ✗	Denies fault or responsibility; sees the other party as at fault ——
Authentic and genuine ✗	Inauthentic to get others to like them ——	Inauthentic to avoid uncomfortable feelings; often sarcastic or humorous when serious topics arise ——
Happy for friends' success ✗	Jealous of friends' success; interprets it as an affront to personal success ——	Jealous of friends' success; feels they are more deserving ——

BEHAVIORS IN FRIENDSHIP BASED ON ATTACHMENT		
Secure	Anxious	Avoidant
Seeks relationships of mutual agency ✗	Lets others dominate them ⎯	Seeks to dominate others ⎯
Direct communication ✗	Passive-aggressive or hostile communication ⎯	Lack of communication; ghosts or withdraws ⎯
Trusts that others love and care for them ✗	Assumes others don't really like or care for them ⎯	Assumes if others show they like or care for them, they have ulterior motives; mistrusting ⎯

If you score highest on one attachment type, you may demonstrate that attachment most often, but there will be people or events that trigger you to demonstrate others. Though we have a primary attachment, attachment is a spectrum rather than a category. It's common for people to exhibit more insecure attachment patterns when stressed. For example, I scored highest on secure, but higher on avoidance than I typically do. I've been so busy (working a full-time job and writing this book), which limits my resources to provide emotional support for others. After working so much, I just want to barricade the door, splay on the couch, and watch trashy and dramatic television.

Now that you have a better understanding of your attachment, let's delve deeper into how your attachment affects how you navigate friendship.

Secure Attachment

Everybody's doing the best they can, and it's going to be all right in the end.

The psychologist Fred H. Goldner coined the term "pronoia" to describe the positive counterpart of paranoia. People with pronoia possess the delusion that, despite any evidence to the contrary, the universe is scheming for their success and that others like, trust, and want the best for them. What do you call a non-delusional pronoid? A secure person. Unless there's evidence otherwise, their default assumption is that others are trustworthy, like them, and want the best for them. They aren't Pollyannas—they adjust this optimism based on additional data. But this initial optimism, the belief that everything is going to be all right in the end, is why "life is just easier" for the secure, explains Gillath. "Being secure in our relationships prepares us to be secure in all aspects of our lives."

It's tempting to assume secure people are setting themselves up for disappointment. By thinking others are trustworthy, won't they get hurt? And won't they overlook people out to harm them? But actually, assuming the best sets secure people up to receive the best. One study involved a finance game, where students were told to invest money with a "trustee" and were instructed to then threaten, or else disregard, a financial penalty exacted if they didn't return on the investment. The trustee provided the highest returns when the penalty was disregarded and the lowest returns when it was threatened. "If you trust people, you make them more trustworthy," said Ernst Fehr, a professor at the University of Zurich and one of the authors of the study. The study lends credence to a psychological theory called reciprocity theory, which emphasizes that people treat us like we treat them. If we are kind, open, and trusting, people are more likely to respond in kind. Secure people, then, don't just assume others are trustworthy; they make others trustworthy through their good faith.

And when untrustworthy people weasel through the cracks and cause harm, secure people are less, rather than more, impacted than the insecure. Studies find that security is a strong predictor of resilience and stress regulation. One study found that when people were primed with security, their heart rate variability (changes in the time between heartbeats) didn't fluctuate as significantly when they were socially excluded. But when people weren't primed with security, it did. Heart rate variability fluctuates when our heart is responding to stress, leading the study's authors to conclude, "Attachment may provide an important mechanism to increase adaptive responding to the distressing experience of social exclusion." Whereas insecure people expect others' mistreatment, carrying the lead backpack of suspicion all the time, even when unnecessary, secure people endure only when others disappoint. Their faith in others also reassures them that they'll have support when disappointed.

Accompanied by this resilience and good faith, secure people are freed up to take risks in friendship. "What would you do if you could not fail?" a card at Whole Foods once asked me, dragging me into an existential crisis when I was just hoping to buy some egg white cheese curls. The secure live the answer to this question. As mentioned, they're more likely to initiate new friendships, as well as productively address conflict and share intimate things about themselves. As we'll find out later in this book, these risky behaviors are vital for friendship's success (but they have their limits, as we'll find when we explore anxious attachment). When Nick, a secure doctor, moved to St. Louis, he met Lawrence through a mutual friend, and the two instantly bonded. Though Lawrence was slated to move to New York in a few months, "I said even though you're leaving, let's still hang out. I voiced a commitment to be friends, which is something I do often. The worst that can happen is nothing comes of it." When Nick met Lawrence's friends and liked them too, he told Lawrence, "I like your friends, but you're leaving and you were our connector. Maybe we can start a group chat?"

Nick became tight with Lawrence's friends, but he later heard from Lawrence that they talked about him behind his back: his wife had filed for divorce and broke his heart, and according to their shared friends, he was a broken record in talking about it. But instead of being angry, Nick was understanding: "I related to them. Sometimes one friend will go through something and you're like, 'He keeps talking about this. That is so annoying.' You vent to another friend, but it doesn't take away from the love that you have for that person and the support that you will continue to show them. I'm accepting of that, and it's part of the dynamics of friendships."

A solid sense of self, unrattled by the skirmishes that inevitably arise in close relationships, gives secure people the composure to grant others grace, which explains why, research finds, they are better at maintaining friendships and less likely to get into conflict. And when conflict does arise, secure people are less likely to use harmful strategies like withdrawing or over-complying. Whereas insecure people think solely about whether others meet their needs, secure people climb the emotional observation deck and consider their needs alongside others'. As Nick revealed, even when critiqued, the secure don't go into a self-defensive mode where they protect themselves, disregard others, and unwittingly damage their relationships. They freely express their needs, not looking to blame or accuse, but to understand and be understood (more on this in the anger chapter).

Tons of other positive qualities arise when we're not feeling threatened. Secure people are more giving, forgiving, and authentic. They are comfortable with intimacy and with engaging in behaviors that promote it, such as giving and receiving support and being vulnerable. Terry Real, a therapist and author, was right when he wrote in his book *How to Get Through to You,* "Sustaining relationships with others requires a good relationship to ourselves. Healthy self-esteem is an internal sense of worth that pulls one neither into 'better than' grandiosity nor 'less than' shame."

In being open to other's needs, seeing them not as an assault to one's ego but as an opportunity to treat others better, secure people continuously grow into better friends. This lack of defensiveness helps them better attend to others and, research finds, increases their security over time. Jack, a copy editor who lives in Washington DC, remembers a time when his friend was GChatting him about difficult things she was going through. He kept giving her advice, and she responded, "What I need from you is to say 'I'm sorry,' or 'that sucks.'" "Our communication got so much better after that," he said. "She would get things off her chest, I would empathize, we could move on and talk about other things, whereas using 'my model' of offering advice, we'd be dwelling on the subject with a back and forth that she wasn't interested in and didn't ask for." Now Jack is better at validating friends' feelings.

Secure friends make you feel safe. You're scared to tell someone you experience bouts of depression, or broke ties with your great-aunt, or put ketchup on your eggs, and your secure friends make you feel loved regardless. Researchers found that secure people report being more accepting of others and better listeners. In chapter 1, we discussed how friends can make us feel human again when we experience shame. Secure friends do this better than anyone else. They provide us with friendships that heal.

The "hedgehog's dilemma" is an apt metaphor that can shed light on attachment. Created by the German philosopher Arthur Schopenhauer, the dilemma describes a group of hedgehogs shivering in the cold. They huddle together for warmth, but their quills prick one another, so they retreat: avoidant hedgehogs. But when they're cold again, they huddle too close: anxious hedgehogs. It's Schopenhauer's metaphor for the perils of intimacy—we're out in the cold without it but injured with it. But intimacy isn't so perilous for every hedgehog. The secure have learned to strike the right balance of safety and warmth.

Avoidant Attachment

I don't need anyone. All I need is myself.

In our individualistic American society, defined by the Protestant work ethic, we are goaded to pull ourselves up by our bootstraps, prized for our ability to endure life's obstacles alone, and heralded for our strength when we are unmoved by life's tragedies. "Don't cry" we are told, instead of "Cry; it's healthy to feel." Our notion of cool is marked by unnatural nonchalance: holy is the one who just doesn't care. Some scientists attributed the word "cool" to skin conductance—unflappable people release less sweat when under duress, making their skin literally cooler and "thicker." The thick-skinned, the unfeeling, are our heroes, which makes it hard for us to admit that when people display these behaviors, something is wrong. They're avoidantly attached.

Jared, a fifty-nine-year-old former military officer, was born to a fifteen-year-old mother. His earliest memory was of her packing her bags to leave him. He remembers being jealous of his mother's boyfriends—that they might get closer to her than he was. His grandparents, who raised him, instilled in him extreme indepen-dence. Don't depend on others, and don't let others depend on you. It was a cardinal sin, his grandmother said, to go to someone's home and accept the tea they offered.

Jared, like most avoidants, learned from his family that if you get too close to people, or depend on them, they'll let you down. So he didn't. He had a best friend but otherwise kept most people at a distance. From his family, he "always got the sense that friends were an annoyance, not something that made your life better." Once, his grandfather complained about a neighbor asking to borrow his sledgehammer, a tool he hadn't touched in a decade.

Avoidants, like Jared, push others away, perceiving relationships not for the joy and fulfillment they bring but for their pressures and responsibilities. When people try to connect with them, avoidants are closed off and distrusting, assuming others have ulterior motives. Their friends often describe them as a "mystery" or an "enigma" since they avoid sharing much about themselves.

To keep others at bay, avoidants bury their heads in work, further satisfying our American ideals. Compared to other attachment styles, avoidants, research finds, are more likely to claim their work affects their happiness more than their relationships. An avoidant patient in couples' therapy with one psychologist commented on his relationship partner: "She can't work when she's upset. I must work when I'm upset." Philippe Lewis, a long-haired, middle-aged, formerly avoidant love and relationships coach, used to prefer friends who were also business partners—justifying their worthwhileness by providing him with something other than pure connection.

But work isn't the only way avoidants maintain their distance. They also erect rigid boundaries around friendships. They tend to be uninterested in mixing friends from different circles or migrating friends from one context to another, like inviting a work friend to their home for a potluck. As Gillath put it in one of his articles, "By allowing each friend to fulfill only one or a smaller number of functions than nonavoidant individuals, avoidant individuals reduce their dependence on each specific friend. This potentially reduces their concerns regarding trust and reliance."

One way avoidants push others away has to do with a psychological concept called object permanence. Without object permanence, things no longer exist when they aren't directly in front of us—able to be seen and felt. If an infant is absorbed by a rattle, and you hide it under the place mat in front of them, the infant will look around, confused over where it went. Infants grow out of this stage at seven months, but avoidants never quite do, psychologically speaking. Friends move or change jobs, and when out of sight, they drop out of mind. Lewis said, "When friends were no longer around, I didn't miss them. I didn't call or write, and they would get upset, but I didn't feel the need to."

Avoidants also distance themselves by simply ending friendships, even ones with friends they've known awhile. Discomfort with emotions makes it tough for avoidants to work through conflict successfully. Research finds avoidants are more likely to end friendships. And because breakups can surface powerful emotions, avoidants, according to research, prefer to eject using indirect routes, like ghosting. When Jared noticed his college roommate, Leroy, retelling other people's stories and splicing himself into them as the protagonist, he realized Leroy was untrustworthy. "I just stopped answering his phone calls," Jared recalls. He withdrew from another friend he met while deployed by ignoring him in their shared group chat.

It may seem like avoidants are strong. They possess incredible self-sufficiency and don't *seem* to need anyone. But we are social creatures, remember? We are hardwired to need people, and when we claim we don't, something is amiss. Studies find that even though avoidants appear cool and collected during times of strife, inside their bodies are freaked, their nervous systems frenzied and their blood pressure spiking. The pain they repress doesn't disappear. It ravages them inside (something we'll learn more about in the vulnerability chapter).

It'd be more accurate to say, like all of us, avoidants do need people, but they're just afraid of depending on them. Their distancing behaviors overcompensate for their fears—that if they let people close, they'll be rejected and disappointed. Charlie, a formerly avoidant entrepreneur living in Denver, told me he used to see his friendships as being about power: the person who cares the least wins (an avoidant mantra). When friends asked him to come over, he'd say no, because rejecting them made him feel powerful and in control. As an adult, Charlie realized that he was concealing his insecurities. "I was very, very afraid of being rejected," he said. "I would manifest that fear by pretending like I didn't care, or downplaying friendship opportunities so that if something went wrong, I could say it didn't really mean that much to me."

This fear and distrust of others make avoidants struggle to both ask for and receive support. So, instead of turning toward others in times of need, they shut down and withdraw. In chapter 1, we learned the importance of voicing our pain to feel fully human and counteract shame, which means, without relying on others, avoidants are shame-prone. Others typically help us release and process our emotions, but for avoidants, their emotions get clogged in their bodies. Studies have found, for example, that avoidant attachment is related to poorer immune functioning, severe headaches, and chronic pain. Despite all this injury, avoidants' shame justifies their continued withdrawal, in a self-reinforcing cycle, since they are convinced no one truly cares if they're gone. In Jared's words, "My mother was fourteen and pregnant. My father never acknowledged me. My grandfather was an alcoholic. My mother used to give me the ten dollars she'd get in food stamps each month, but I'd never use them because I had a lot of shame."

Avoidants' go-to strategy for coping with emotions is repressing feelings. When uncomfortable feelings arise, they withdraw or stonewall. Often others perceive their disengagement as callous, but when avoidants withdraw, they are actually emotionally overwhelmed. Lewis, the love and relationships coach, said he felt "sensations and not feelings" before becoming secure. He described tolerating emotion as a "muscle" avoidants haven't built up. When he feels avoidant, "Other people's emotions are really loud, and I can't hear anything else," so he inevitably withdraws.

The withdrawal frustrates those close to avoidants, who look for an explanation for their behavior. Others pry, coming up with complex and often unflattering hypotheses for avoidant behavior like "He's a sociopath!" For Lewis, because he didn't understand himself, he felt defenseless in rebutting these harsh accusations. Without feelings as a guide, avoidants often don't know what is going on with them or why they act the way they do. When Lewis is in distress, it's like he's "trying to scream without a mouth." Another avoidant described the urge to cry as "turning on the faucet, but no water is coming out." The grave cost of appearing cool all the time, it seems, is feeling estranged from yourself.

Although Lewis worried about being perceived as a villain, the truth is that many avoidant behaviors hurt others. Their compulsive need to be strong and avoid feelings is a rule they not only hold themselves to, but one they hold others to as well. One avoidant, Leanne, a project manager, told me about how she thought it was "weak" and "pathetic" that someone was upset and asked for support on Facebook. But "everything that irritates us about others can lead us to an understanding of ourselves," according to Swiss psychiatrist Carl Jung. When others are distressed and need reassurance, avoidants struggle to provide this, telling friends they're too sensitive or need to get over their problems, and in doing so, they transmit their avoidance to others. This pattern is apparent, though less sophisticated, in avoidant kids, who are more likely to bully other kids. "Whenever I see a teacher who looks as if she wants to pick a kid up by the shoulders and stuff him in the trash," Alan Sroufe, an attachment researcher and professor at the University of

Minnesota, said, "I know that kid had an avoidant attachment history."

As we'll see later in this book, vulnerability, asking for support, working through conflict, accepting others—the gamut of behaviors that avoidants shun—are the lifeblood of friendship. This explains why avoidants have less warm, supportive, and close friendships. Avoidants engage in various behaviors that explain why their friendships are weak. Studies find they are less invested, committed, and ultimately satisfied in their friendships. Another study finds that avoidants are less likely to initiate new friendships and maintain existing ones.

The avoidants would drop Eric over spilled milk, never truly trusting him in the first place. They might sit alone at lunch for the rest of the year, or tack on to a friendship group they didn't much care for to keep up appearances. They might feel safer from others when at a distance, but they'd be giving up the joy and purpose of life itself. Avoidants may argue they are fine alone, but in shunning connection, research finds, they experience less enjoyment and intimacy. By keeping others at a distance, avoidants opt out of the responsibilities of connection, but they also opt out of its balm—its ability to make us feel whole, seen, supported. They surrender the ways that connection imbues us with a zest for life, enlivens us, and brings our lives meaning.

Anxious Attachment

I'm afraid everyone will leave me.

After Carolina's divorce, she joined a belly dancing class that met for four hours every Sunday. The dance crew would socialize in someone's home afterward, which is how Carolina became close to Zoe, the dance instructor, who was known for having a strong personality. But Carolina was drawn to Zoe because she was sometimes sweet, remarking at their yearly Friendsgiving that she "waited 364 days to spend this time with [Carolina]." Carolina also appreciated how quickly she became Zoe's confidante, as Zoe disentangled from her own divorce. Zoe reached out to Carolina for support often, which made Carolina feel special. "My default was feeling unwanted. I wake up in the morning and feel alone until someone reaches out," she said.

But Zoe could also be abrasive. Zoe had a photo shoot at the dance studio and started kicking people's belongings and pelting their coats aside. "What's wrong?" Carolina asked. "Nothing," Zoe responded. A half hour later, Zoe unleashed: "I went through a divorce and no one cares about me. You only asked if I was okay once. I'm leaving!" Zoe also snapped at Carolina when they were out at dinner and Zoe unloaded about her ex-husband. "He sounds truly awful," Carolina responded. To Carolina's surprise, Zoe, hurt that Carolina had spoken negatively of her ex, despite her calling him trash throughout the conversation, yelled, "That's bogus," and left their dinner.

How did Carolina respond to all this volatility? She clung to Zoe harder. "I would apologize for being condescended to, ask her, please don't leave me. I was forty years old. I had a master's degree. I had a number of houses. But I still felt like a little girl."

People with anxious attachment try to merge with people they're close to, building relationships of such closeness that their sense of self dissolves. Such intimacy soothes their fears of abandonment while making them vulnerable to an unhealthy friendship dynamic like Carolina and Zoe's. Anxious people demonstrate qualities that prime them to get into crooked relationships where they give more than they receive, also known as co-dependent, or, more recently, evoked in the term "trauma bonding." They desire to build intimacy rapidly, to mitigate fears of rejection, diving into relationships where trust isn't yet built. You'll meet them at a party and ask how they're doing, and they'll tell you about their childhood trauma, their surgery, their suicidal urges, hoping the vulnerability will entreat you. Secure people, in contrast, let relationships unfold over time, and critically, while they are trusting, they adjust their initial optimism based on feedback they receive from others in real time. Research finds, for example, that secure people modulate their disclosures depending on whether the other person reciprocates, whereas anxious people disclose, no matter the response of the other party.

Another reason anxious people might end up in lopsided friendships is that anxious people martyr themselves in relationships, silencing their needs and prioritizing those of others, convinced that voicing their needs will drive others away. But because their giving can be more of a means to gain love than to express love, they'll give to people who mistreat them and in ways that compromise personal boundaries (more on this in the generosity chapter), like Carolina did when she apologized after Zoe scolded her.

Anxious people's suppressed needs don't disappear. Anxious people stew, building resentment for their unmet needs, endorsing statements like "I boil inside but I don't show it." They leak their feelings passive-aggressively, other studies show. When Carolina's childhood friend Clara returned to their hometown and didn't update her on local happenings, Carolina felt hurt. When Carolina visited their town and Clara reached out to get the details of her trip, Carolina said, "I didn't respond much because I was angry she didn't include me. It's a young response, but I decided to withhold and reject her."

Eventually, the pressure of muffled feelings becomes too much, and anxious people erupt. Lexi Darcel, a YouTube influencer with anxious attachment, described these episodes as "temper tantrums" and referenced that anxious attachment tantrums can come off to others like they are being handed a child to raise.

Borey, an anxious person working in IT, described these eruptions as an out-of-body experience, as "going bananas." He recalled an instance when he erupted on a friend. Once, Borey sent his coworker Sherry a kind email identifying all the things he appreciated about her and wishing her the best as she transitioned to a new job. She responded with brevity: "It was a pleasure to work with you. Wishing you all the best." The message replayed in his head, making him angrier at each encore. He sent her a heartfelt message, and that was all she had to say? Had he done something wrong? Did she not like him? He obsessed. It distracted him from work, woke him up at 3:00 a.m., and made it hard for him to eat. Studies find that anxious people tend to wallow, obsess over issues, and blame themselves. As Lexi explains, "Dealing with anxious thoughts—it's incessant. It's nonstop, and it's very draining. It is truly taxing mentally and physically."

For many, Borey's and Lexi's responses seem intense. But for the anxious, an instance of rejection feels like an assault on their bodies and minds. Consider how your response would differ if someone stole your lunch and you had a refrigerator stocked with food at home versus if that was all the food you had; or if someone took your clothes and you could easily slip back into another outfit from your wardrobe versus if now you had to go naked. Secure people, because of their history of available and abundant love, internalize the sense that they are connected to others—a sense that stays with them, even when rejected. Anxious people have no such resources. When others reject or leave them, the loneliness feels omnipresent and unbearable. They might feel, as Carolina described, "like a piece of paper burned down to its ash."

Neuropsychology sheds light on why the anxious are more sensitive to rejection. One study found that when rejection was simulated in the laboratory, the more anxious someone was, the more the regions of the brain associated with distress lit up. Similarly, another study found that when anxious people viewed a threatening face, their amygdala—the part of their brain associated with negative emotions and stress—was triggered more intensely. When others are confused as to why anxious people freak out over trivial issues, they assume anxious people have the same neural wiring they do. But anxious people's brain response illustrates that they experience the same events fundamentally differently and more painfully.

If you felt as alone as anxious people tend to, you'd probably do anything you could to feel better, and for anxious people, this looks like rage. "When you feel like the other person is about to leave you, there's this overwhelming amount of emotion that makes you want to charge at that person to get them to make you feel better. I feel like I'm just out of control of my emotions and I need someone to soothe me because I can't soothe myself," Lexi stated. When Borey got to his breaking point, he lashed out at Sherry: "Your response to my heartfelt message was cold and impersonal. Clearly, you're not the person I thought you were. I would never respond to a message like you did. You're a terrible friend."

Borey's actions display something called vulnerable narcissism. Vulnerable narcissists reveal the self-centeredness of pain, how we prioritize our needs and shun those of others when we're hurting. They agree with statements like "I need compliments from others in order to be sure of myself" and "When others get a glimpse of my needs, I feel anxious and ashamed." They feel low self-worth and are reactive and hostile. Vulnerable narcissists don't mean to cause harm. They focus on getting their needs met, and dismiss those of others', because as research finds, they assume (often incorrectly) that they're the ones being slighted. For vulnerable narcissists, or to some extent for anxious people (and avoidants too, for that matter), there's so much attention given to how others are slighting them that this concern eclipses their evaluation of how they treat people. Mario Mikulincer, an attachment expert and professor at Bar-Ilan

University, wrote that "whereas avoidant attachment is associated with overt narcissism or grandiosity, which includes both self-praise and denial of weaknesses, attachment anxiety is associated with covert narcissism, characterized by self-focused attention, hypersensitivity to other people's evaluations, and an exaggerated sense of entitlement."

This dynamic of being hurt and so absorbed by your own reality that you don't consider others' played out between Borey and Sherry. When Sherry received Borey's text, she was surprised. Her message had been short because she was in the middle of completing an international move for her new job in Singapore. She was also closing out her old job, returning her laptop and keys, and delegating tasks to new employees. Then, the day her job ended, she felt a lump in her breast, and she was nervous it could be cancer. The brevity of her response, she explained, had nothing to do with Borey.

Borey and Sherry's story also reveals how anxious people often misfire, projecting rejection in benign circumstances. For example, anxious people were quicker at recognizing jumbled letters as representing words that conveyed rejection, such as "abandoned," or "ridiculed," even if these jumbled words were preceded by a signal of approval, like a smile. Anxious people are so vigilant for rejection that they register cues of it while ignoring signals of their acceptance.

But what does this all mean for anxious people's friendships? Because they're comfortable with intimacy, they're able to grow close bonds just as easily as the secure, but research finds their relationships are more emotionally intense and volatile. In not registering red flags in others, like Carolina with Zoe, and in projecting anger and assuming rejection, like Borey, their friendships are addled by fragility. Because they take relationship issues personally, they perceive transgressions as more serious and forgive others less, studies find. They have trouble considering others' motives, understanding how others' behaviors are explained by factors that aren't personal to them. They assume Eric spilled his milk because he hates them, and assuming negative intent in others frays their bonds and their peace.

A Self-Fulfilling Prophecy

Insecure attachment is a way for us to protect ourselves from the milk spills of connection, but it's a system gone haywire. We keep others at a distance to protect ourselves, but this also harms us. We reject before potentially being rejected to protect ourselves, but this also harms us. We cling to protect ourselves, but this also harms us. At some point, all the self-protection becomes self-harm. Robert Karen, in his book *Becoming Attached: Unfolding the Mystery of the Infant-Mother Bond and Its Impact on Later Life,* wrote, "The behavior of the insecurely attached child—whether aggressive or cloying, all puffed up or easily deflated—often tries the patience of peers and adults alike. It elicits reactions that repeatedly reconfirm the child's distorted view of the world. People will never love me, they treat me like an irritation, they don't trust me, and so on." Alan Sroufe at the University of Minnesota similarly said, "The disorder leads to conditions that foster the disorder." We act in ways that invite the prophecy of our greatest fears.

I'm not *haywire,* I thought to myself before I started interviews for this chapter or dug deep into the research. I've been anxious sometimes in romantic relationships but have experienced friendship as a sanctuary in which I'm secure. Without the throes of romance and the ambiguities of the dating process, the best side of me arose around friends. Or so I thought.

As I heard stories from people with insecure attachment, I was surprised at how I related to them. Attachment in friendship, I realized, can manifest with subtlety. I remember turning down invitiations from high school friends to hang out and being confused about my behavior. They'd ask me to go to the mall and I'd just say no. "She doesn't want to hang out with us," they said to one another. I did, though. It just felt vulnerable to admit it. It was my avoidance speaking.

As I listened to the anxious, I had an epiphany. My tendency to entertain only a tight circle, rather than a sprawling network, my cliquishness in friendship, masks my feelings of unsafety and fears of rejection around more casual connections. When I meet a new group of people, my inclination is to find the few I can be comfortable with and forget the rest. The friends I do maintain are wholesome, reliable, emotionally intelligent, and "person-centered"—they don't just talk about themselves but are curious about others. They make me feel safe. These are qualities that anyone appreciates in a friend, but people with insecurities might place these traits at a greater premium.

My compulsion for safety is especially triggered in group settings. When I was a resident assistant (RA) in college, I felt left out by the other RAs. I didn't relate to their cheery, outgoing, bulletin-board-constructing energy, so I skipped our social gatherings. In my mid-year review, my boss told me he wished I collaborated more with the other RAs. I rationalized my behavior by assuming "we just don't vibe," but the truth is, I felt threatened by all the new people, worried they wouldn't like me, so I didn't give us a chance to connect. I told another RA, Ife, that I felt left out. I remember sitting in the mailroom, sorting packages, talking to Ife, when other RAs came and, ignoring me, asked Ife to lunch. He turned to me and asked if I wanted to join. I told him I didn't, and he cocked his head, baffled. I declined because I imagined I'd feel uncomfortable if I joined them for lunch, but the deeper feeling I feared was unsafety. Ife never invited me out again.

I recognize how my fears of rejection led me to reject others. But when I was fearful or nervous, I didn't think about how I was treating others. The stress narrows your focus; that's the self-centeredness of pain, the obliviousness to how we perpetrate harm when hurt. When others experience us as closed off, like I was to the RAs, they typically assume it's because we don't like them or we're mean. But often we're closed off because we're scared. We're not trying to reject others; we're trying to protect ourselves. We need most of all for someone to show love and acceptance of us, and yet by shutting them out, we invite the opposite.

There are also many ways I'm secure in friendship. When I meet someone I like, I'm not shy about asking them to hang out and even following up to check in if I haven't heard back. I don't take it personally when friends drop off for a bit, checking in again after time has passed. When my friend had a harrowing trip to Alaska with an ex-girlfriend, I helped her process it. When I found out my dad had gotten sick, my friend helped me process it.

Like me, most of us aren't just insecure or secure; we're insecure at times and secure in others. Growth is bending toward security even if total security eludes us. Lewis has created an online community to help people do so. He sees attachment as an asymptote, a line drawing closer to the X-axis of security but never touching it. Charlie, who is now secure except when he's highly stressed, says he has to "watch out for when I'm in my basement because then I'm avoidant again."

We'll be bending toward security in Part II of this book, where we explore six proven practices that lead us to make and keep friends as an adult. These include initiative, vulnerability, authenticity, anger, generosity, and affection. And to do them right, to allow them to make us into better friends rather than skilled schmoozers, each practice will require us to become more secure. If we do the internal work, if we face ourselves, then we won't just make friends by saying all the right things; we'll feel the right things deep inside us.

At our center, we are loving and courageous, empathic and kind. It is only our tragedies that unplug us from this core. When we're insecure, this core exists but is hidden, like sunlight radiating through a window scrambled by blinds. The blinds are there to protect from the sun, but they keep our world dark and may even darken the worlds of those beside us. Finding security is finding our core. Like I said at the start of this book, it's not about us transforming, but about us excavating, finding out who we are underneath the graves we've dug and pieces of us we've buried for self-protection.

It's a grueling journey to security because, as the poet W. H. Auden puts it, "We'd rather be ruined than be changed." But if you are lonely, or push people away, or use humor to hide uncomfortable feelings, or try to be strong all the time, or think everyone will reject you, or keep hurting those who love you, or are overcome with jealousy, or don't feel truly seen, or don't feel like enough, then stagnancy is its own agony.

Jared has an analogy for what it's like to evolve into security. While in the military, he took a trip to Saudi Arabia and arrived in an area dubbed the "empty quarter" because it's desert for miles. "We had a sandstorm that night, the first night we were there. And once it was over and the clouds cleared, I looked up, and for the first time in my life, I saw the Milky Way. It was breathtaking. I could not believe it. And I'm like, well, wow. This has been here the entire time. And I stayed up the rest of the night and I watched the galaxy." Connection is our galaxy, and it's waiting for us. Let's find our way there.

PART II

Looking Forward

Practices to Make and Keep Friends

CHAPTER 3

Taking Initiative

How to Turn Strangers into Friends

I showed up at New York University in a dressy green blouse that just covered my bum, leggings I passed off as pants, and one secret wish: to make friends. I grew up in New York City, so a couple of my high school friends would be at NYU with me, but I wanted to break out of my small circle and meet new people. *College is supposed to be the best four years of my life, and I'm supposed to meet the people who will be my best friends forever,* I thought to myself as I lugged my bags into my new dorm room.

NYU has a prolonged "Welcome Week" orientation, full of activities like a *Rocky Horror Picture Show* filming interspersed with live drag queen commentary, an improv show, a play put on by the illustrious students of NYU's Tisch School of the Arts, speed friending, and lunches with food from restaurants around campus. But despite all these opportunities to meet people, I stuck to my high school friends turned college friends, Krizia and Byron, throughout all of Welcome Week. I thought people would come up to me and introduce themselves. But somehow, they never did.

Luckily, however, Byron introduced me to a new person I liked. Lauri was a ball of joy and empathy, the kind of person who will give you a pity laugh if your joke falls flat. I loved Lauri's good vibes and whole attitude (and the fact that she laughed at all my terrible jokes). When Lauri, Byron, and I hung out, Lauri and I felt more drawn to each other than to Byron. Something was effortless, easy, familiar. The self-consciousness and flustering for words that typically coincide with new relationships weren't there. It was easy to be ourselves. But I only ever saw Lauri when Byron invited us to hang out.

As much as I liked Lauri, I had no idea that for us to become friends, one of us would have to be proactive. A part of me assumed that our friendship would somehow just happen. Asking Lauri to hang out felt like I was violating some sort of social script, wherein it was written that friendship should happen effortlessly. Shouldn't fate just bring friends together? Intentionality seemed to betray this magic.

Believing in the "magic" of friendship also protected me from the vulnerable feelings that arose when I thought about putting myself out there and asking to hang out with Lauri. It was much easier to walk through a world where people liked *me*, instead of *me* liking people. If they were the initiators, that freed me from the vulnerability of potential rejection. My strategy at the time was to make myself so irresistibly likable and interesting that people, including Lauri, would flock to me. It made me feel safe to build friendships via magnetism. But this grandiose friendship strategy was a cover-up for a deeper fear: that others didn't like me. Rejection would confirm that fear, and by expecting people to come to me, I could escape it.

One night, Byron had a party in his dorm—it was a small gathering with a 1:1 ratio of people to cheap bottles of alcohol. Lauri and I were sitting on the floor next to each other when Lauri said, "Marisa, I think you are really cool, and I really want to hang out with you." Look at that—I felt pure joy that the connection I felt to Lauri was palpable to her too. When I decided I liked Lauri, Lauri's opinion of me mattered more, and thus her affirmation did as well.

Lauri saved me from the loneliness of freshman year. My "I'll just be impressive and let 'em come to me" approach to friendship didn't pan out, but Lauri and I hung out nearly every day, overindulging at the campus dining halls together, buzzing through homework on caffeine highs, being each other's right-hand woman during many nights out that could only be characterized as horrifically college-esque, and even zoning out in front of the television in each other's company. Without Lauri, my freshman year would have felt empty.

On my end, it seemed as if the "magic" of friendship was at play between Lauri and me, that somehow we were caught in the divine chi that propelled us together. But the truth is that Lauri had been intentional about initiating our relationship. Now that Lauri is one of my best friends, I see how she is an intentional person in all aspects of her life, and it is something I deeply respect about her. I remember Lauri telling me about a discussion she had with her mom about a Chinese proverb. She said that some people wait for things to happen, and other people claw their way in to make space for themselves. Her mom and I agree that Lauri has the claws, and I am all the better for it.

In my reluctance to initiate with Lauri, I was assuming friendships should happen "naturally" (which looked like Lauri initiating with me). And the reason I thought this way was so I wouldn't have to face my fears of being disliked or rejected. But friendships require initiative, and that means we must confront our gravest fears.

It Shouldn't Be This Hard to Make Friends

Why is it so hard to make friends as an adult? It doesn't seem to happen organically like it used to. It's hard enough in high school or college. But for many, it gets exponentially more difficult after that. Sometimes, it feels as if once you've missed some sort of tiny window for friend-making earlier, you are at a loss. Where do you even meet people? It feels especially hard living in a new city, where everyone already seems to be hanging out with their established groups. How do you break in?

Before we blame ourselves for lacking friends, it's worth mentioning just how hard it is to make friends—a problem compounded in our modern age. While we tend to talk about loneliness as an inevitable feature of the human condition, it isn't. Before the 1800s, people lived among their families, farming and, more generally, living a more settled and locally based life. They had a community of extended family and friends and were involved in village life and their place of worship. Their community was built in, not sought after. Before 1800, there wasn't even a word for loneliness as we know it today. The word "lonely" described the state of *being* alone, rather than the exquisite pain of it.

With the rise of industrialization, and of parents leaving home to work in factories, community bonds tapered and the nuclear family became the center of people's world. People began to move for work, but increased residential mobility means friendship becomes more disposable, according to one study. And as people left their family for work, they lived alone for the first time, which magnified loneliness. John Bowlby, one of the fathers of attachment theory, said, "If people know each other and have long-term relationships, mutual help makes sense, because I can help you today and five years hence you can help me. But if you aren't going to be here in five years, and the community is constantly changing, it is by definition not mutually helpful." Increasing work demands, residential mobility, and single-person homes explain why *The Economist* called loneliness "the leprosy of the 21st century."

Outside of residential mobility, technology has some role to play in the rise of loneliness. In Robert D. Putnam's book *Bowling Alone,* he rigorously examines culprits that explain our increasing disengagement from civic life. One of the guiltiest, he finds, is the television. It not only gave us something else to do so we didn't have to knock on our neighbor's door to see what they were up to, but it also, according to Putnam, "seems to encourage lethargy and passivity," a phenomenon my friend Mikelann and I call "the plop effect"—plop on your couch, and you'll never get off. Putnam's book debuted before social media, but research since has found that the way social media affects loneliness is more complicated. One large study found that heavy social media users were either the least lonely or the most, depending on whether social media was used to schedule in-person interactions or replace them.

Because of this cauldron of factors, over the last few centuries, we have increasingly sacrificed community for work and convenience. We live in a society in which it is acceptable to cancel plans with friends for work, but never vice versa. One in which giving up a promotion to have free time for the people you love is wasted potential. In which mentioning you're lonely is still taboo—despite 61 percent of Americans admitting to it behind closed doors. In which increasing affluence means a one-way ticket to bigger homes, more land, and isolation. In which chitchat with our grocery store clerk has become a ring of the doorbell and the materializing of delivery boxes. In which our friend picking us up at the airport has been replaced by our Uber driver. Despite connection being a fundamental value of our species, it is not a fundamental value of Western society.

We are living in what sociologist Émile Durkheim calls "anomie," a disjuncture between the norms of society and what people need to thrive. Sharon Abramowitz, an anthropologist, concluded in the book *Tribe: On Homecoming and Belonging,* "We are an *antihuman* society. . . . Our society is alienating, technical, cold, and mystifying. Our fundamental desire, as human beings, is to be close to others, and our society does not allow for that." The result? A 2013 analysis of 177,653 participants across 277 studies found that friendship networks have been shrinking for the past thirty-five years. Some-one living in the 2000s has four fewer friends, on average, than someone living in the early 1980s. Another analysis found that four times as many people have no friends in 2021, compared to 1990. Circumstances are more dire for men, with five times as many men reporting no friends in 2021, compared to 1990.

Perhaps remnants of our evolutionary past lead us to assume that friendship happens organically. Because it once did. But it doesn't anymore. If we want to make and keep friends, we need to swim against the tides of disconnection that have been gradually contaminating us for centuries. It's not fair at all. It shouldn't be this hard. But I'm here to equip you with the tools to succeed, despite it being tougher to make friends now than it's ever been in human history.

Adult Friendships Don't Happen Organically

Here's a simple, sometimes surprising truth: making friends as an adult requires initiative. We have to put ourselves out there and try. It's a process of reaching out over and over again. It's meeting some-one we like and, instead of letting the moment pass, hoping they might ask for our phone number, seizing the moment and asking them for theirs. In Kat Vellos's book *We Should Get Together: The Secret to Cultivating Better Friendships,* she describes how she changed the course of her friendships through a continual process of initiat-ing. As she puts it, "A basic but critical part of nurturing relation-ships is the act of following up and checking in with people. I scheduled repeating reminders in my phone to reach out both to my old friends and new friends."

In fact, believing that friendships happen organically—that the cosmic energies will bestow a friend upon you—actually *hinders* people from making friends, because it stops them from being intentional about doing so. Nancy E. Newall, an associate professor in psychology at Brandon University, and her colleagues, surveyed older adults to determine differences in the social worlds of people who believed that friends were made based on effort and those who believed they were made based on luck. They found that those who believed that making friends was a matter of luck were lonelier five years later, whereas those who believed that friendship takes effort were less lonely. The reason? Believing it takes effort was related to engaging in more social activities, such as visiting friends and family or going to church. And it was engagement in these social activities that made people friends.

You have to initiate to make friends, but the good news is that you get to choose how you initiate. It may not be your style to show up to that networking event for urban farmers or that five-mile ride with the cycling club. But initiative doesn't just mean going to meetups and networking events. One introvert-friendly strategy is reaching out to old friends to reconnect. Another is getting in touch with an acquaintance you've been wanting to get to know better. I especially like these options because the friend is pre-vetted, and you know you have solid evidence of a connection with an acquaintance. Tara and Mika are friends who met just briefly at work before Mika quit, but they then followed each other on Instagram. They would comment on each other's stories, building up a rapport, until Tara asked if Mika wanted to get lunch sometime. With technology as a buffer, taking initiative can be even easier.

Initiative can even look like asking that co-worker for coffee, the one whose company you enjoy but whom you haven't yet seen outside of the workplace. It could mean taking the initiative to join a recreational sports league, enroll in a course, or get involved in an organization that you are passionate about so you can consistently place yourself in an environment wherein you can develop friendships. Newall's research pushes us to challenge the passive approach to making friends that most of us would admit to taking. It asks us to embrace what I call "unapologetic initiative." It forces us to recognize that even if the social landscape doesn't make friendship easy, we still have agency.

To ward off passivity and hopelessness, it's important to cultivate what's called an "internal locus of control," which is research jargon for taking responsibility for achieving your goals. People with an external locus of control, by contrast, believe their life is determined by forces outside of their control and thus have trouble taking initiative toward reaching their goals. Who do you think is the pilot of your airplane? People with an internal locus of control would say themselves, whereas people with an external locus would say something else—their horoscope, boss, spouse, or mercury being in retrograde. Someone with an internal locus who wants to make friends might join a hiking group and introduce themselves to their fellow hikers, whereas someone with an external locus will sit on the couch watching fabulous hiking destinations on TV.

One of my previous romantic partners reminded me of all my advice on initiative when we were walking in the hallway of our apartment building. A couple of other neighbors congregated there too. He knew that I wanted to befriend my neighbors, but as I saw them talking, I was too intimidated to say hello. As we entered our apartment, he asked me, "What advice would you give yourself?"

"Take initiative; introduce yourself," I muttered.

"Perfect," he responded as he pushed me back into the hallway. As awkward as I felt, I knew the responsibility to say hello, the locus of control, was in my hands.

"Hey. I moved in here recently. I just wanted to introduce myself." The neighbors were open and friendly, and we ended that interaction by exchanging numbers and chatting on a WhatsApp group. On that group, we started a weekly neighbor outdoor picnic. People think tiny acts, like saying hello, can't have colossal consequences for their life. But they can. One hello can be the difference between being lonely and finding your best friend.

Keeping your internal locus will benefit you not just at the initiation stage but at all stages of friendship. We can develop an internal locus of control by shifting our mindset to see friendship as something that happens when we make it happen. We can believe that we can get closer to people if we try. We can stop assuming that friendship should happen without any effort or that making friends requires us to wait until someone chooses us.

We do the choosing. We show up. We follow up. We ask to hang out when we want to hang out. We take ownership of the process. But to do so, we will have to explore and address a few underlying assumptions that might get in our way.

Love Is (Not) All You Need

Rob's life was going well in most ways.

He was a good-looking guy, muscular with thick chestnut hair and matching eyes, and wide square glasses that topped off his Clark Kent look. He'd recently moved to Chicago, where he landed a decent job as a paralegal at a high-powered law firm. The salary saved him from choking on his monthly student loan payments. He found a nice apartment for a decent price in a neighborhood that was accessible to all the city had to offer.

He lived with his girlfriend, Leila, and their relationship was going well enough. Leila worked at a daycare and would come home with stories from her tots: *Today a kid cried like a banshee because his friend had a fruit snack and his mom didn't pack him one. Poor thing.* They'd met just after college, and while they were different in many ways overall, they got along well.

A lot of their differences came down to personal communication style. Rob was naturally extroverted with an unmistakable vibrancy. His buoyancy contrasted with Leila's muted demeanor. Rob liked talking and hanging out, but Leila often desired to hole up in her room and read. Rob was interested in some things that Leila had no interest in—like video games, kung fu, and smoking weed. Meeting new people would help fulfill these interests, but he felt ambivalent about doing so. Sure, he could get out there and make awkward small talk with strangers about the rainy fall they were having, or the chewiness of the pizza bagel hors d'oeuvres, or he could stay at home and cuddle with Leila.

But as much as he enjoyed their nights in front of the TV, ingesting dumplings, General Tso's chicken, and Diet Cokes, Rob knew something was missing. He knew that it wasn't good for him to rely on Leila for all his social needs. But whereas he was intentional about most aspects of his life—reaching out to his connections to get a job, joining a gym (well, at least for a little while), and diligently calling his parents like a good son—he was never intentional about making friends. He'd never had to be.

In the past, friendships had just happened. He'd find himself in a class or a new dorm and people would gravitate toward one another. School settings provided him with the ingredients sociologists consider essential for connection: continuous unplanned interaction and shared vulnerability. Since moving to his new city, Rob assumed he didn't have to work to make friends; they would eventually just trickle into his life, as they always had before. But with each new day, he found himself disappointed.

There'd been a few exceptions over the last couple of years. He'd met one man, Mike, in a pickup basketball game and was delighted when Mike expressed interest in getting to know him more. They met up a couple of times and Rob enjoyed Mike's company, until Mike started to share about his fabulous knives, which could slice through the bones of a chicken in one swift cut. Mike asked Rob if he might be willing to host a knife party for his friends, which was when Rob realized that Mike was caught in a pyramid scheme and that their friendship had an agenda.

Then there was the colleague at work for whom Rob had high hopes. They'd hung out together and played tennis. It was pleasant enough, but not so pleasant that Rob felt compelled to call him again. After the game, no one reached out, and the friendship dropped. They returned to being just colleagues.

Rob's long drought in friendship started to affect how he acted around others. He began to feel insecure when he was interacting with people he didn't know well. When he met somebody new, his brain would chatter about how they were probably uninterested in him anyway, how he didn't have something substantive to add to the conversation, how if he tried to hang out with them, they'd certainly be put off, and why risk the inevitable rejection? The social world unfolding in his brain was far bleaker than reality could ever be, but he was buying into its scary stories. Loneliness had begun to warp his perception of the world.

Rob wanted to make friends, but he didn't know how. He craved deeper connections, yet he had no patience for the stumbling process of forming one. He felt anxious, sometimes even fearful, of others, but he also needed others to feel like himself. He was sure that if anything would improve his life, it was friends, and yet he embraced a passive approach to making them.

Sadly, Rob and Leila's relationship didn't last. It was a tough breakup, but Rob's heart would recover. What really floored him, however, was the abyss of loneliness he plummeted into. His recovery was made even more difficult by the vacuum of friends who could have helped him weather the blow. Instead of coming home to takeout and movies with Leila, he came home to an empty couch and a conspicuously uncrowded bed.

Looking back, Rob wished he hadn't waited until the breakup to start building a community. He felt like a shell of himself, in so much despair that the idea of putting himself out there made him recoil. But he wasn't going back to Leila, so that left him with two options: writhe in loneliness or make friends.

Rob enrolled in a kung fu class, followed up with a connection from college, and slowly started to build a community for himself. His new friends listened empathically as he shared about his relationship with Leila, his reluctance to go out and find someone new, his desire to soon be a dad, and how he felt like all of this had been robbed from him. Their empathy didn't cure him, but it helped.

Rob's situation reveals an impediment to friendship that I touched on in chapter 1: the idea that our romantic relationships are all we need. This belief leads people to neglect friendship, or even to actively shun it, so that they can spend more time with their romantic partners. Even single people embrace this idea. Their thumbs are sore from swiping on apps for love, and yet they don't lift their fingers to find friendship. They may not schedule time with friends for various nights of the week, on the off chance that their date ends up becoming free. I've been guilty of this behavior as well, and I share it as an observation rather than as a judgment. The exaltation of romantic relationships over friendship is a by-product of our larger cultural sphere. Prioritizing friendships requires unlearning this cultural message.

We can relearn an important truth, one that is based on the science of friends and romance: having close friends betters our romantic relationships. Conflict with our spouse, one study finds, makes us secrete an unhealthy pattern of stress hormones, but only if we lack quality friendship outside the marriage. Studies have found that even for men who feel as if they have found their romantic soul mates, good friendship is still linked to better self-esteem. This research, combined with another study that finds that people are more resilient to negative events within their romantic relationship when they have friends (particularly for women who tend to have stronger friendships), suggests that maintaining friendships while in a romantic relationship is a part of what healthy romance looks like, one that isn't crushed by the weight of each partner having to be everything to the other. Studies like these are evidence that making friends will help our romantic relationships thrive, and that one person can never complete us or fulfill us so deeply that we do not need or benefit from friendship.

If you're in a relationship, make sure you're making time for friends. If you've been relying on your partner to be your only friend, it's time to make some new ones. Find friends who share your interests that your partner doesn't. Set aside a time each week to catch up with them. Encourage your partner to spend time with friends too. If you're single and looking for a healthy romantic relationship, lay the foundations by developing strong friendships. Remember: friends will only make your romance better.

Assume People Like You

We already know that our attachment style—secure vs. insecure— affects how we make connections. We learned that the more secure someone is, the better they are at taking initiative in friendship. And insecure people are better at initiating in the moments when they feel secure. One study found that when insecure people were primed with security—through writing about someone who was loving, comforting, and supportive toward them—they then reported being better at taking initiative in friendship. "How bold one gets when one is sure of being loved," Freud once said.

But why? Research into romantic couples suggests that the more positively we feel about ourselves, the more likely we are to assume others like us. And the more unworthy we feel, the more likely we are to *underestimate* how much others like us. How people thought their romantic partner viewed them, the study found, was less a reflection of how their romantic partner actually viewed them and more of a reflection of how they viewed themselves. People say, "You have to love yourself before someone can love you," because if you don't love yourself, you won't notice when they do.

This study suggests that how we think others view us isn't fact. The same is true with platonic relationships. Humans are awful mind readers. When we meet someone new and, despite any evidence, think, *I don't think they're interested in hanging out with me,* we make this assumption not because we have some sort of telepathy about how that new person feels about us, but because *we* think we're uninteresting. If I love myself, I think the world is my social oyster. If I don't, I think the world is cruel and unforgiving. In either assumption, the world is the same, but my experience of it differs based on my inner world. This is so dangerous because people who feel bad about themselves need friends *the most,* and yet tend to be most defeatist.

Secure people know their worth, so they assume others do too. They *assume* people like them. Insecure people, however, assume the opposite. Rejection sensitivity—the tendency to project rejection onto ambiguity—is a key feature of anxious attachment, and it hurts anxious people and their relationships. Research finds that the rejection sensitive are more likely to be depressed, anxious, lonely, and unhappy in their relationships. They report that their romantic partner wants to leave them, even when their partner has no such intent. They are also more likely to respond to ambiguous social situations (like someone being quieter in an interaction) by becoming distant or cold. Since they think they're the ones being harmed, in relationships they're more likely to become jealous (for men) or hostile and emotionally unsupportive (for women), which ultimately makes their relationship partners more dissatisfied. This research suggests that when we project rejection, it is a self-fulfilling prophecy. We become the rejectors—hostile, withdrawn, and jealous—and then we will experience the rejection we fear.

When secure people assume others like them, this is a self-fulfilling prophecy termed "the acceptance prophecy." Danu Anthony Stinson, a psychology professor at the University of Waterloo, and her colleagues hypothesized that "if people expect acceptance, they will behave warmly, which in turn will lead other people to accept them; if they expect rejection, they will behave coldly, which will lead to less acceptance." To test this hypothesis, she told people they'd join an ongoing focus group, asked them to report on how much they thought the group members would like them, and then had them record a video to introduce themselves to the group. Observers then rated how likable the participant was in the video. The participants who assumed they'd be liked were, in fact, seen as more likable. This study built off a similar study conducted in the 1980s, which found that volunteers led to believe an interaction partner liked them shared more about themselves, disagreed less, and had a more positive attitude—ultimately making the premonition come true.

Much of friendship is defined by ambiguity; it's rare that people straight up tell us whether they like us or not. Thus, our projections end up playing a greater role in our understanding of how others feel about us than how others actually feel. Our attachment determines how we relate to ambiguity. When we don't have all the information, we fill in the gaps based on our security or lack thereof. Security leads us to navigate ambiguity with optimism. We value ourselves, so when we have limited data, we assume others value us too.

Overall, this research reveals one of the most important secrets to taking initiative in friendship. Assume people like you. Want to invite a friend on a coffee date? Assume they're interested. Tempted to ask a gym friend if they want to become a happy hour friend? Assume they do. Want to reconnect with a friend you're sad to have fallen out of touch with? Assume they're in. When we make this assumption, initiative isn't scary anymore. And this assumption not only makes us more likely to take initiative, but to navigate the friendship-making process, and life, with more peace, levity, and pleasure.

When we assume others will like us, we not only display behaviors that foreshadow our acceptance, we also become more accurate in our predictions of reality. In 2018, Dr. Erica J. Boothby, then a post-doctoral researcher at Cornell University, ran a study that had people interact in a number of settings—in a college dorm, in the lab, at a professional development workshop—and asked interaction partners how much they liked one another. Across all these settings, people evidenced what's called the "liking gap"—they systematically *under*estimated how much their interaction partner liked them. Assuming others like us corrects our bias to underestimate just how liked we are.

You may be thinking, *That may be true for most people, but not me. I'm a true-blue kooky weirdo. The Supreme Court appeal is unnecessary because my case is closed.* But even when we assume we're unlikable, and we are, consequently, withdrawn and cold, people *still* like us more than we think. Boothby's research finds that the people who have the most negative views about themselves are the *most* inaccurate about how they're perceived. Boothby asked people to report on prominent thoughts they had during their conversation with a stranger and the degree to which their thoughts were negative or positive. Maybe they thought they were a social champion who was building a winning connection (positive) or that their crusty social skills were disgusting to their interaction partner (negative). The more negative people's thoughts were, the more likely they were to underestimate how much they were liked. In other words, participants believed their self-critical thoughts when those thoughts were actually distorting the truth.

What this research shows is that many of us feel insecure and assume that others can sense our felt inadequacy—but feeling socially inadequate is not the same as *being* socially inadequate. If you spill wine on the party host's plush carpet at a fancy gathering (happened to me; the host was my PhD advisor), you'll probably end up being harder on yourself than other people are (I hope; thanks for being nice about it, Karen). You'll likely *think* others are judging, and when it comes to human psychology, thinking others are judging you has the same effect on you as others actually judging you. Our thoughts often hurt us more than our bullies do. The truth is, no one cares about your social clumsiness as much as you do. They're too busy worrying about their own.

When you think an interaction isn't going well, ask yourself if it is your thoughts that have given you that sense or if it is the other person's behavior. What behaviors has the person demonstrated that have indicated that they disapprove of you? If you cannot pinpoint any particular behaviors, then your anxious thoughts may be overly cynical in guessing what the other person is thinking.

Even if you put yourself out there and don't make any new friends, one or many times, it doesn't mean that you're no good at making friends. In fact, as a psychologist, I encourage my clients to reward themselves for the process rather than the outcome. I'm proud of you if you are able to initiate, no matter whether you make friends. You're still building a new skill either way. The effort confirms that you're positioning yourself to get the results you seek. You win no matter what.

Say Hello

When Clive, a mid-thirties Black male business analyst, was trying to make new friends, he went to a networking event hosted by LinkedIn. The event was for minority young professionals looking to start a small business. Clive showed up dressed to impress, in a snow-colored button-down shirt, silver dress pants, and a black-and-lime-green-striped bow tie that he hoped telegraphed: "I'm conventional, but also interesting." Plus, he figured the event was formal since it was in the Empire State Building.

When he got to the top of what seemed like an egregious number of floors, the elevators opened into a room that looked as if its floor plan had been stolen from Google headquarters. There were white smart boards, walls made of windows, and circular tables where everyone could sit together. The hosts seemed to remind the attendees, however, that this was not a tech huddle, and was indeed a networking event for minority professionals, by serving rice and beans, jerk chicken, and plantains.

After people finished eating, the brave attendees got up and started mingling. In the past, Clive would have sat at his table and waited for others to approach him—and if they didn't, he would have assumed the club was exclusive and unfriendly. But Clive eventually realized that a social context wasn't just something that was happening *to* him; it was something he could create. So instead of sitting at his table, Clive got up and introduced himself to a woman who looked like Alicia Keys. Their mothers were both real estate moguls. Clive had good vibes from her, but she seemed like she was in a rush to get somewhere. Before Clive could ask if they could exchange contact information to stay in touch, she had to leave.

Clive then started talking to Cameron, who worked for the United Nations and seemed eager to speak with him. Cameron had recently gone through a work training that had involved tucking and rolling out of a moving truck, to prepare him to work in dangerous areas. Clive was fascinated and asked, "Do you think you're actually going to work in a hazard area?"

"I'd love to!" Cameron shared. Clive found Cameron's adventurousness intriguing, and Cameron's engagement in the conversation helped him feel confident enough to ask if they could exchange information. His go-to line: "We should keep in touch. How can I contact you?"

There was another man at the networking event Clive thought he'd connect with, Adrian. He was doing diversity consulting and went to Clive's alma mater, the University of Michigan. Adrian had a grounded energy about him that made Clive feel comfortable. When Clive approached Adrian and asked for his contact information, Adrian put his LinkedIn in Clive's phone. *Am I being swerved?* Clive wondered. Or was this the millennial New York scene—LinkedIns before phone numbers? Or was it the assumed point of contact because they were at a LinkedIn event? Clive wasn't sure if he was being rejected.

Clive decided to assume he *wasn't* being rejected by Adrian. Generally, when it comes to making friends, we've learned this assumption is a good idea. Adrian must have just been used to sharing social media handles over digits. After the event, Clive messaged Adrian on LinkedIn asking if he might be willing to connect in person. Adrian was happy to.

Clive ended up connecting with two people from the networking event, a number that would have been zero if he hadn't initiated. Clive's story also reveals that initiative doesn't mean just showing up. It requires more than that. You must engage with people when you get there, sometimes multiple people. Persistence, it seems, pays off. If you are persistent, you'll likely have a more positive experience of your social environment. In a Finnish study, participants rated themselves and their classmates on their impressions of one another and they also rated the class's social climate. The study found a wide range in how people rated the same climate. It was seen as healthier by people who were intentional about engaging within it, whereas women in the study who were more disengaged saw the climate as chillier. Although we don't know which came first, whether people who were warmer experienced the climate as friendlier or vice versa, these findings may suggest that the social climate isn't a static reality. Our perception of it is linked to the actions we take within it.

Those who are more active in a social climate—waving hello to others, introducing themselves, sharing about their weekend, gossiping about their teacher's crooked toupee—have overcome not one but two types of social avoidance: overt and covert avoidance. Overt avoidance is when people don't show up to events because they are too uncomfortable. When people invite you out, and you don't show up, they're less likely to invite you out again; they don't know you might be anxious and instead will take your actions to mean that you're not interested in them (people assume rejection easily, we've found). For the Finnish students, overt avoidance looks like not showing up for class or social gatherings. People engage in this type of avoidance to reduce their anxiety in the short term, even though it perpetuates it in the long term.

In contrast, covert avoidance looks like showing up physically but checking out mentally. It is getting to the event but failing to engage with others, not making eye contact, talking really fast, messing with your phone, petting the dog, playing thumb war with the dog, and winning unjustly because the poor creature has no opposable thumbs. Initiative requires us to overcome overt and covert avoidance. You not only have to show up. You also have to introduce yourself and stay present and engaged.

It is important to recognize the types of covert behaviors you might display that feel like they're protecting you from others' judgments (but are actually pushing people away). So next time you go to that happy hour, don't just stand there—introduce yourself. When you start orientation for your next job, say hello to your new co-workers. When you get to your place of worship, arrive early to say hello. When you meet friends of friends, ask them questions and show interest.

Avoidance is the life-force behind social anxiety, and most of us experience social anxiety (or anxiety around others, coupled with fears that we're unlikable) to some degree. People overcome their anxiety by repeatedly exposing themselves to their fears and coming to realize that the lion they feared is actually a Shih Tzu with a shadow. When you no longer avoid that which you fear, eventually the anxiety dissipates, but consistent avoidance crystallizes the fear. Through experiences, you accumulate proof that the seedy voice in your head that says you are hideously unlikable isn't speaking the truth. You also prove your resilience, your ability to survive even the most egregiously uncomfortable of circumstances. So go for it!

The lesson we can learn from Clive is that to get good at initiating with others, we don't just have to get good at getting out of the house. We have to get good at saying hello, introducing ourselves, inviting people out to coffee. We must do it repeatedly too. We have to overcome overt avoidance by showing up and overcome covert avoidance by engaging with people when we get there. To do so, we may have to confront our inner voice telling us we'll be rejected and instead tell ourselves that others like us, that they'd be happy to connect, that we are likable.

How to Take Initiative

The barriers to taking initiative we've explored—focusing too much on romantic partnerships, assuming people will reject you, showing up but not engaging when you get there—are just part of the story. You may have other issues that you'll have to grapple with to get yourself to a place where you're ready to initiate.

- Maybe you still think you're too busy—you have your nine-to-five grind and are juggling both your kids (and three to five bowling pins, on account of that juggling class you signed up for at the local community center). You need physical therapy for jugglers' wrist before you can even think about making friends.

- Or perhaps you're convinced you don't really need friends, because you are somehow an outlier in the human experience.

- Or maybe—*far less likely* than either of these other scenarios, of course—you've recognized that you've been passive about making friends and are hoping to do better. You're ready to put in the work, and you're wondering, *Well, what now?*

Let's talk about what you can expect when you start to put yourself out there, and how you can most effectively navigate initiation.

Picture yourself at a social gathering. You're at a happy hour for people in your profession and don't know anybody else attending. At first, you notice a smattering of people who might be there for the networking event and you begin to feel sheepish. *Why do I push myself to go to these silly things?* you wonder to yourself. The woman standing adjacent to you shoots you a look, and you wonder if you said that out loud. You shoot her a look back, pretending to be confident that those were thoughts and not words. You hope that she doesn't keep shooting back because your face is out of ammo and you're starting to feel a bit anxious. Nervousness, reluctance, it's all to be expected when exposing yourself to a pack of unfamiliar hyenas, er—human beings.

You get a drink at the bar and chew on the plastic red straw to avoid finishing it prematurely. This drink is your liquid covert avoidance, and so is the prattle in your brain that's going on about how you shouldn't have used plastic because of the inevitable climate change apocalypse. But if it's inevitable, then why should you give up the luxury of the straw? You are percolating with discomfort right now; you deserve the damn straw. Ah, sweet, sweet covert avoidance. You have someone to talk to, even if it's your very own critical mind.

Someone hovers close to you, a rogue networker like yourself, also fascinated by his drink. He's wearing a gray blazer and some jeans. This is your chance, you think. But what if he rejects you? You make up a story about how he's probably waiting for someone, how you're probably the only loser here who didn't have a friend to bring with you. Self-critical thoughts, you recognize. What did that book say? Oh right! You're likely assuming others are rejecting you more than they actually are. Now you know that research says that when you're self-critical, you project that others don't like you, even though this isn't necessarily true. You repeat an affirmation to yourself: *May I assume that others like me.*

The rogue networker next to you probably thinks something's wrong with you now, a part of your brain whispers, as you continue mumbling your hokey mantra. But another part of you begins to feel more at ease, less threatened. Your shoulders relax, your forehead softens its furrow, and you approach Gray Blazer.

"Hey! I'm [insert your name here, or else the name you made up so people couldn't search you on social media until you wanted them to]. What brings you here?" you ask.

"Oh, I'm Obi. I work for such-and-such company," he responds. Such-and-such? Hmm, haven't heard of them, you ponder. You begin to chat. Luckily, Obi is an easy conversationalist and seems relieved rather than horrified that you approached him. You talk for about five minutes until the conversation begins to peter out, and Obi looks itchy to make his way around the room.

"Well, it was great talking to you," you offer.

"You as well," he responds.

Breaking the seal of initiating makes you more confident, and you find yourself approaching a bunch of people that evening. There's the bubbly woman in the evergreen dress, Keshia, who seems fascinated by you. You like her. There's the skittish stout man in suspenders who is fairly curt. A few others but you can't remember their names: one person who lives in your neighborhood, another who showed off pictures of his cute dog—a dalmatian/dachshund mix. How did that even happen?

There are moments when you are left alone, in the purgatory between conversational partners, but the record of non-abysmal interactions that you're building keeps you at ease. People even begin to approach you. Clark, the host of the networking event, comes by to ask you how you're enjoying yourself. You answer, but he seems distracted. You aren't sure what might be distracting him and hope that it's not your boring answer about wanting to expand your professional network.

You second-guess yourself: Were you supposed to tell him that you've been feeling a gnawing sense of loneliness, particularly during the long stretches of weekend, and how it was getting to the point where the pain of the loneliness eclipsed your fear of having to do something about it? Then you remember not to project rejection onto an ambiguous circumstance. Maybe Clark has other things on his mind. You were right, you think, as you peer at the clock, and realize that he was probably distracted because his networking event is ending. He pauses your conversation to make an announcement: "Thank you all so much for coming. This event was a great success, and that is because of all of you. Join us monthly for our happy hour. But before you go, make sure you exchange business cards liberally and link up."

And now you're left with a choice. Who exactly should you follow up with? You spent the longest time chatting with Obi, felt a connection with Keshia in the evergreen dress, and feel warmly toward that guy with the cute dog and its impossible mix.

Research has shown that it pays to be strategic about who we follow up with when we initiate. In a study conducted by Michael Sunnafrank from the University of Minnesota and his colleague Artemio Ramirez then at Ohio State, researchers followed college students as they interacted with one another for nine weeks. After their first encounter, the students were asked to predict their likelihood of becoming friends. The researchers found that students' ratings of each other's friendship potential after their first meeting predicted whether they were actually friends nine weeks later.

In other words, the spark is real. So trust yourself when you meet someone who feels familiar or comfortable, when there's chemistry, when you sense you might be experiencing a kindred spirit. Following up with these promising seeds of connection will lift your chances of finding the deep friendships you are looking for. Ding, ding, ding—your first winner is Keshia in the evergreen dress. My motto is that if I ever meet anyone I think is really cool, I'm going to follow up with them and ask them to meet up again. Those sparks are too precious to waste.

Keep Showing Up

An alternative means to get the biggest bang for your buck when you initiate is to rely on what researchers call "propinquity." Propinquity means that you are likely to build relationships with people to whom you are consistently physically closer. New Yorkers know this is true. When Amazon withdrew from building its headquarters relatively far into the borough of Queens, near JFK Airport in New York, I read a tweet that said, "In all fairness, they're not the first person who has pulled out after committing to going to Queens."

Mady Segal, a professor of sociology at the University of Maryland, discovered the power of propinquity during a study that aimed to predict which police officers would become friends. She found that the secret to friendship was last names. Those cadets with last names that started with the same letter—say, Carlton and Cassidy—had a higher likelihood of becoming friends. It actually wasn't about the last names, per se, but rather the implications of last names. Cadets were seated alphabetically, and Carltons and Cassidys were likely to sit next to each other. When each cadet was asked to nominate someone else in the academy as a close friend, a whopping 90 percent of cadets listed someone they sat beside.

Propinquity is proof that friendship isn't magical. It's overwhelmingly determined by the spaces we find or place ourselves in. If we're lucky, our job, school, or hobbies will already provide us with ample propinquity with others we might get along with. If we're not, then we'll have to create our own. That means that if we stay at home all day and watch television, then we may only ever achieve propinquity with late-night talk shows. It doesn't matter how many soul mate friends may be out there for us if we never achieve any sort of propinquity with any of them; they won't slink their way into our lives like fruit flies do to fruits unless we invite them. When we regularly place ourselves in physical proximity with others we can connect to, we are writing our own fate, acknowledging that we have control over our friendships, and upping our chances of connection.

One reason propinquity works so well is that it reduces the costs involved with seeing someone. When potential friends live far away, you have to go out of your way to get in your car or ride the bus to get to them, but when they're already in your vicinity, seeing each other is easy. According to a small study conducted by Robert Hayes at the University of California, Los Angeles, when you're building early relationships, costs diminish the likelihood of the relationship progressing. So, if you have to commute an hour to see each other, you may realize that even though you have a budding friendship, the commute isn't worth the bud.

Later in the relationship, costs are way less correlated with sustaining the relationship, so people will make the commute for the connection, but they won't just to figure out if they kinda maybe sorta will eventually become friends. That is why so many people have "locationships," or low-cost friendships that are sustained because friends live in the same location. Returning to our networking event, even if you chatted briefly with that person who lives in your neighborhood and forgot their name, they are someone to follow up with.

Another reason propinquity works is because if we know we might see someone again, we like them more. In an older study, conducted in the 1960s, women were presented with profiles of two women who were similar. They were told they'd be engaging in ongoing discussion groups with the woman in one of the profiles. They reported liking the profile of the woman more whom they'd presumedly see again. When we know we'll see someone again, we tend to be more invested.

One last reason why propinquity works is that we like people when we are exposed to them more and they become familiar to us. In the psychology world, this is called the "mere exposure effect," since through merely being exposed to someone continuously, we come to like them. In a study conducted out of the University of Pittsburgh, an experimenter chose four strangers to show up at a large psychology lecture, for a varying number of classes. One stranger infiltrated fifteen classes, another ten, another five, and the last zero. The strangers didn't interact with anyone in the class, and yet, students reported liking the most the stranger who showed up to the highest number of classes; this stranger was liked about 20 percent more than the stranger who never showed up to any. By and large, the students didn't even recognize that any of the strangers came to their class, demonstrating that the mere exposure effect happens unconsciously.

Mere exposure means that the people who end up building relationships are those who establish the most face time with the people around them. That is why research in college dorms has found that people who live at the ends of the hall develop fewer friendships than those who live in the dorm's center. Centrally located rooms offer face time with more of your fellow dorm residents and the gift of mere exposure.

You can harness the mere exposure effect by joining a continuous social event rather than a one-off one; it's choosing book clubs over happy hours, or a language class over a language workshop. Propinquity also tells us to befriend people we already see often, maybe our neighbors, or our co-workers, or someone who lives close by. You can also make both propinquity and mere exposure work in your favor by becoming a regular at your local coffee shop, bar, or gym. Achieving regularity will make it more likely that others will feel positively toward you. On the other hand, mere exposure means that to make friends, you have to show up again and again.

But mere exposure alone doesn't build relationships; initiation does. I suggest building up "spontaneous communication" with other regulars over time and seeing if these scatters of interactions build the foundation for friendship. Spontaneous communication is unplanned conversation that occurs because two people are in the same place at the same time. It is in fleeting moments of chitchat that relationships are sprouted.

We can initiate a conversation with strangers by using the insight and question method developed by David Hoffeld, CEO and chief sales trainer at Hoffeld Group. This involves simply sharing a statement or insight and asking a question to follow up. We might say, "I really loved the main character in the book we read for book club. What did you think about her?" or "This drink is so sweet and tastes so good. How do you like yours?" or "It's been so long since I've been to the beach and I'm so glad to be here. What do you like about the beach?"

It's truly scary to talk to strangers, and to do so, I have to rev myself up by reminding myself to assume that people will like me and be open to talking to me—the opposite of what we typically assume, but in fact, an assumption that is closer to the truth. A study by Nicholas Epley and Juliana Schroeder at the University of Chicago involved asking people to talk to a stranger on the train. Can you guess how many were shot down? None! According to Epley and Schroeder, "Commuters appeared to think that talking to a stranger posed a meaningful risk of social rejection. As far as we can tell, it posed no risk at all."

Talking to strangers has helped me turn my neighborhood into my community. As a graduate student, I spent many days at Starbucks at a communal table with strangers, writing and reading research articles. At first, the people around me would fade into the background, human wallpaper, but eventually, through "spontaneous conversation," as in "I've been working for so long. How's your work coming along?" I started to connect to them. I'd see their familiar faces all around the neighborhood—at the pool, a restaurant, or walking on the street. We'd say hi and the entire neighborhood started feeling far less anonymous. There was something about bumping into people I knew that made me feel like I belonged. Those days at Starbucks turned my neighborhood into my community.

This is how it has gone for me when I have wanted to make friends: I show up at some sort of gathering or meetup. I usually feel clumsy and uncomfortable as a new person showing up to a meetup of people who've already built connections, get discouraged, and never return. But mere exposure is my reminder to keep showing up if I'm at a new social club, soccer league, or co-working space and I'm tempted to leave when things feel awkward. It is why you should live out our networking scenario and keep showing up for those monthly events. Mere exposure means not just that people will warm up to you at the social group over time, but also that you'll come to like *them* more too. Initiate, unapologetically, and then do it again and again.

Mere exposure is justification for the value of persistence. Instead of committing to a single happy hour to make friends, commit to a group for at least three months before dropping out, otherwise you'll foil mere exposure. Then, take initiative by inviting your favorite person in the group to get smoothies. Mere exposure also leads us to expect that (1) making friends will be uncomfortable at first—all those unfamiliar faces that we're programmed to be wary of; and (2) it'll gradually begin to feel easier the more we show up.

HOW TO MAKE A FRIEND

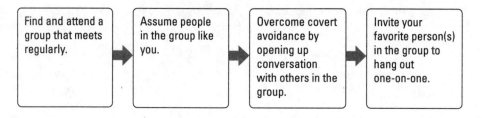

Be the Friend You Want

The lesson we've learned from this chapter is that to make friends, we need to take initiative. But the larger lesson is that to make a friend, we must *be* a friend. "Be the friend you want to see in the world," to mangle Gandhi's wisdom. Instead of waiting for someone to pluck us into their friendship worlds, we must do the plucking. I've noticed, and research supports, that insecure people (like me in college, and sometimes still now) often fail to do this. They wonder:

Why is no one approaching me? Why did no one invite me? Why didn't they say hello to me? Why didn't they check in on me? Don't they love me? If their answers to these questions aren't favorable, they'll leap into denial. *Screw them. I didn't like them anyway. I don't need anyone but myself and that one dog I liked at the party.*

But as I wish someone had told me in college, we must instead turn these questions on ourselves: Am *I* inviting people out? Am *I* saying hello? Am *I* engaging with them? Am *I* checking in? When we're so consumed by how others treat us, we desire to hold them accountable without holding ourselves accountable, demanding more from our friendships than we offer them. But the secret to making a friend is not expecting everyone to put in the effort and puncture our walls while we wait. That's just not fair. Not to us, nor to others.

Elizabeth Gilbert, the author of *Eat, Pray, Love,* put it best: "On social media, I've talked about incredible friends that I've had and I've shared stories of amazing acts of friendships and invariably, someone in the comments who's feeling very sorry for themselves will say, 'You're lucky. I don't have any friends like that.' And I always want to say, 'So be a friend like that.' Be a friend like that to someone. If you don't have anybody who's generous and loving and full of grace in your life, then go be that in somebody else's life. It's not about what you get. It's about what you can contribute to this relationship. What can you bring as an offering? And that's how community is built. It's built on the offerings of the generous and the loving." We'll learn this lesson over and over again.

TAKEAWAYS

- ▸ Friendship isn't based on luck. Embrace unapologetic initiating by putting yourself in settings that allow for continuous unplanned interaction and shared vulnerability to develop friendships.

▸ Try not to ignore friendship in favor of romance. Having friends will make your romantic relationship better.

▸ Assume people like you. When you are fearful of approaching someone new, remind yourself of the "liking gap"—you're likely underestimating how much you will be liked.

▸ When you think an interaction isn't going well, ask yourself if it is your thoughts that have given you that sense or if it is the other person's behaviors. What behaviors has the person demonstrated that have indicated that they disapprove of you? If you cannot pinpoint any particular behaviors, then remind yourself to assume they like you.

▸ Overcome covert and overt avoidance. Once you're in the door, don't hide in the corner. Initiate and follow up with those with whom you feel chemistry, those who live close to you, and those whom you already come in contact with from day to day.

▸ Join something that reoccurs to harness mere exposure. Sign up for the class instead of the workshop. Some options include improv classes, writing classes, work affinity groups, a book club, hiking groups, volunteering, etc.

CHAPTER 4

Expressing Vulnerability

How to Trust Friends Without Feeling Weak

Sam met other graduate students for a networking event at Busboys and Poets, a local coffee shop and restaurant in Hyattsville, Maryland. About twenty students showed up, and the night began with an open mic. Busboys and Poets is known for spoken word performances, and Sam listened to poems about love and racism and depression. It was evocative—only Sam couldn't focus on the poetry.

She was hoping for a message from a guy she had been dating for a few months. But with each check of her phone, she realized this was less and less likely. Still, she checked compulsively. But each check only left her with a blank phone screen and a surge of anxiety.

By the end of the night, the graduate school coordinator gathered the students for a picture. Sam was worried her sadness would be caught on record. She hovered at the edge of the photo and tried to look serious rather than sad. As people shouted and laughed around her, she realized she had made the wrong decision in coming. She was too distraught to enjoy herself, and other people's happiness felt like a dig, accentuating her isolation.

As she drove home that night, she couldn't help but feel pitiful. Here she was obsessing over someone who wouldn't even return her text messages. Sam reveled in being a strong woman, one who didn't require a man's affection, but her obsessiveness was revealing otherwise. Ashamed, she made the calculated decision to simply stop thinking of him. She'd block him on her phone like she would in her mind. Every time she thought of him, she'd push the thought away. No one would know of her shame, not even herself. Instead of being pitiful, she'd be invulnerable.

For about a week, Sam was happy with her decision. She wasn't mulling over the guy as much. She'd think about him and swat the thought away like a fly in her bedroom. In the past when she talked about this guy with friends, she'd usually express her worry. But now, when her friends asked, she told them it was over and she was fine.

For that week, Sam felt strong and in control, the opposite of what she felt before. Suppressing her emotions not only helped her feel less consumed by them but also bolstered her identity as a strong woman. She felt relieved to not have to pester her friends with more of her fears. Sam felt proud of her decision during her grief hiatus: Why admit to her feelings when she could control them? Why burden friends with her pain, let them see her as weak? Why be vulnerable?

Sam would soon find out why. We will too.

What Is Vulnerability?

Vulnerability is the deepest form of authenticity, and it involves sharing the true parts of ourselves that we fear may result in our rejection or alienation, the parts we feel most shame over. Shame is the sense that our secrets make us unworthy of human connection. It's why, when we're vulnerable, it doesn't just feel like our secrets are at stake, but our entire being.

"Vulnerability is a construct," explained Dr. Skyler Jackson, a

Yale University professor who studies concealment and disclosure of stigmatized identities. "There's nothing inherently vulnerable. It's a construction based on whether something empowers someone to have material or emotional power over you." What feels vulnerable to us reflects our unique psyche, culture, and history. What feels vulnerable to me may not mean anything to you. Understanding and feeling attuned to others' vulnerability is a key to developing and deepening friendships—and missing those cues can jeopardize them.

Sam felt shame over obsessing about a guy, likely because she adhered to an "ideal" of being a strong woman who didn't let men affect her. A friend told me about his shame over his divorce, and I didn't fully understand why until I realized he inhabits a strongly Christian community where people can be denied jobs if they are divorced. The Islamic Penal Code of Iran "stipulates that the penalty for fornication is flogging, that is 100 strokes of the lash, for unmarried male and female offenders," which means people in Iran probably feel, on average, more shame over premarital sex than people in the USA, birthplace of *Sex and the City*. Some people can talk about their bankruptcy, their chlamydia, their criminal history as if they're asking a waiter for some baguette. For others, the idea of sharing this sort of information makes them sprout hives. The truth is, what feels vulnerable for us reveals something deeper about what we've learned to be ashamed of.

Dr. Jackson also pointed out that we communicate vulnerability not just through the content of our words but through *how* we say them. "Does your voice shake? Are you emotional? Are you nervous? That's actually communicating to the person, 'This is important to me.' Me saying something that feels vulnerable, that's vulnerability. But even *more* vulnerable is for me to let them know, behaviorally or through nonverbal cues: it's our willingness to not just share something vulnerable, but to actually *be* vulnerable in the moment of sharing it," It's when there's a mismatch of the content (*this is me being vulnerable*) and the nonverbal cues (*this is no big deal*) that misunderstanding can arise. I call this mismatch "packaged vulnerability."

Dr. Jackson and I went to graduate school together, and we both know packaged vulnerability well—when the words seem vulnerable but the delivery doesn't. Since we were studying to be psychologists, leaking our guts in class was the norm. But many of us would package our stories about our past experiences or traumas in a way that *sounded* vulnerable but didn't *look* it. People would talk about their tumultuous relationship with their mother as if they were chatting about bringing their poodle to the dog park—not necessarily because they didn't care, but because they wanted to present a certain way to the class. They packaged their vulnerability to make it more palatable to the rest of us.

The issue with packaged vulnerability, Dr. Jackson shared, is that "emotions are the cues for other people, so they know how to respond." When we package our vulnerability to seem less helpless, we run a greater risk of receiving a flat response—not because people don't care, but because they don't sense that this is a moment when caring is important. In support of this, one study found that people who suppressed their emotions went on to receive *less* social support in their first year of college. They also reported feeling less close to others and less satisfied with their relationships.

On the other hand, if I am nervous, and I display that publicly, I will probably find that people soothe me and tell me whatever I'm worried about is going to be okay. If I'm sad or anxious, they may check up with me the next day and say, "Hey, how are you feeling about that?" In one study, college students were more likely to look up information to help a woman giving a speech when the speechgiver admitted to being nervous. And in that study, more generally, people who openly expressed negative emotions—regardless of their gender—had more social ties. Full-bodied vulnerability, aligning our actions with our words, gets us the connection and support we need.

Sam learned this lesson on packaged vulnerability when she let a friend know, in passing, that she felt stuck in getting over the guy. She didn't make a big deal about it—even though on the inside, she felt shattered. But even so, Sam was surprised by the flippant response from her friend. "You really need to get over him," her friend said. It was a small comment, maybe even well-intended, but it plummeted Sam deeper into shame. *Yeah, why can't I get over him? What's wrong with me? Why did I even say anything in the first place?* she agonized. It just confirmed that if she asked for help, it would only magnify her shame, reminding her of what she had lost.

But was Sam's error that she was too vulnerable—or maybe that she wasn't vulnerable enough? Perhaps, if she asked for help more wholly—not just in a passing comment, but with her full feelings— she *would* get the help she needed. Her friend would sense that this was a great crisis for her and be more tender. None of us wants to be misunderstood, but when we downplay our feelings, we invite misunderstanding.

Does Vulnerability Make Me Weak?

Just like Sam, you may feel reluctant to embrace full vulnerability. Full vulnerability is scary. If people fear sharing something vulnerable, they may fear *looking* vulnerable even more. It's one thing to admit weakness, another to embody it. But is vulnerability admitting weakness? Lately, we've been more critical of this view of vulnerability, thanks to thought leaders like Brené Brown.

"Vulnerability is not winning or losing; it's having the courage to show up and be seen when we have no control over the outcome. Vulnerability is not weakness; it's our greatest measure of courage,"

Brown said in her book *Rising Strong.* It takes bravery to reveal se-crets. It takes trust and optimism to assume that others won't cast you off. People who are vulnerable know they matter and are worth others' time and attention. So yes, there is strength in vulnerability.

But there's still weakness in it too.

William B. Stiles, professor emeritus in psychology at Miami University, used the metaphor of a fever to describe vulnerability. When we have a fever, our body is using its internal warriors to fend off sickness, boiling us up in the process, but we are still sick. A fever reflects our ability to contain multitudes—sickness and strength, distress and healing, disturbance and restoration. Similarly, vulner-ability captures these same multitudes. We are strong in taking the initiative to heal ourselves, in believing our pain matters enough to share, in being brave despite the risk of sharing, while our desire to share suggests our distress. When vulnerable, we embody the yin and yang of strength and weakness. Suppressing vulnerability doesn't abolish the weakness; it impedes us from practicing strength alongside it.

There's wisdom in letting ourselves acknowledge the weakness in vulnerability. "Feelings communicate information to you, and that's beneficial. They're not just a reaction. They give us data on ourselves, on how important things are," Dr. Jackson shared. And weakness communicates something powerful if we let it. Weakness tells us to slow down and be soft with ourselves, revealing the truth of our vincibility, the knowledge that we are mortal and must take care of ourselves. Our weakness is an invitation to experience our inherent worth, a worthiness that doesn't evaporate when we're too weary to sustain, create, or produce. There's no better opportunity for deep self-acceptance than that which we can practice when we are weak. When we're weak, we have a greater need for others' love and support, which deepens our relationships and highlights our fundamental interrelatedness. Our weakness reminds us to be more sensitive to our fellow humans, as our understanding of their turmoil is short-circuited when we ourselves are strong.

Lily Velez, a life coach and speaker, felt unraveled when her father died of colon cancer. At first, she hid her feelings, until they burst out like water cracking through a dam. When she finally acknowledged her despair, these feelings that made her feel so weak, she surprisingly felt peace and release. She also found that admitting to her weakness brought her closer to others: "An incredible bond is established between you and another person when you embrace your weakness. Transparency, honesty, and open communication win. I felt the flow of love between myself and those around me. It was uplifting and intoxicating; empowering and encouraging. It was love like I'd never seen it in action before—the type of love that can only be perfected in our very weaknesses."

Weakness is an inherent part of life for every one of us. We can't escape it, certainly not by denying it. The problem of weakness is not that there are moments when we are undone, frail, or need support and rest, but in the way we stigmatize weakness, so much so that we do not allow ourselves to reflect on what it reveals about ourselves, our relationships, and our human condition.

The Dangers of Avoiding Feelings

After a week of suppressing thoughts of the guy, Sam anticipated she'd blissfully coast on. In that week, she felt more relaxed and less upset than she had in months. But one day, while she sat in her apartment alone with nothing to distract her, her thoughts suddenly became harder to suppress. What once felt like swatting a fly away became more like slamming it with a mallet. The more she suppressed, the harder the effort got, and the more she did it, the more images of the guy would jackhammer themselves into her thoughts. Her mind felt invaded, and it gave her headaches.

One day, while she was walking to class, her advisor called her about her master's thesis. Her advisor's voice faded into the background, as all Sam could focus on was trying to avoid her distressing thoughts. As she continued to walk to class, she began to cry. She tried so hard to keep control over her thoughts and feelings, but she felt so out of control. It was like she was being terrorized by her own mind. She wiped her tears off her cheeks and put on her glasses, hoping none of her classmates would notice.

What happened to Sam? How did she go from coasting and relaxed to breaking down between classes? What went wrong? To figure this out, we need to understand the science of suppression, which Professor Mario Mikulincer at Bar-Ilan University and his colleagues set out to do. In their study, people came to the lab and were asked to think and write about a painful breakup. After, they were assigned to either a suppression condition, in which they were told to write about anything but the breakup, or a control condition, in which they wrote about whatever came up.

They then completed a Stroop task, where they had to name the ink color of a word as quickly as they could. If a word was presented in red ink, they had to say "red," or if one was presented in black ink, they had to say "black." The hiccup was that if the meaning of the word represented something they were preoccupied with, even on an unconscious level, they'd get more distracted by it, and it'd take them longer to name the color of the word. So if I am hungry and the word is "strudel," it might take me longer to say "blue." Or if I'm about to get evicted, and the word is "home," it'll take me longer to say "green." The words they were presented with in the task related to breaking up—"separation," "abandonment," "rejection," "leaving"—and if they took longer to name the color of the words, it would suggest they were more preoccupied with the breakup they had written about.

When people had to suppress their thoughts, a rebound effect occurred. Compared to those in the control condition, the suppressors took longer to name the color of separation words, signaling that they became more preoccupied with the breakup after suppressing thoughts of it. These striking findings frame Sam's experience. We hope that in suppressing our feelings, they evaporate. But the rebound effect reveals this isn't true. Our feelings survive in the cold backyard we leave them in, eventually prying open the back door to get into the house.

But Mikulincer's study went one step further. There's a group of people known for being masters at suppressing: the avoidantly attached. Because of earlier failures of loved ones to respond in times of need, they consistently inhibit emotions and aspire to invulnerability. With a lifetime of practice, would the avoidantly attached suppress successfully, without any rebound effects?

Two to three weeks before taking part in the study, the participants filled out a survey that assessed their attachment. The results indicated that people with anxious attachment were preoccupied with separation words in the Stroop task, whether they suppressed in the stream-of-consciousness activity or not, confirming what we know about anxious attachment. Relationship problems preoccupy them.

But for avoidant participants, the results were more complicated. To make things even harder, during the Stroop task, half of the participants were given a one-digit number they had to recite throughout the Stroop task (called the low cognitive load condition), and the other half were given a seven-digit number (high cognitive load condition). This add-on helped the researchers explore a vital question: Just how much can avoidants suppress? Since suppressing is thought to consume brainpower, could they suppress, even when their brainpower was all dried up, like when they were under high cognitive load?

For avoidant people, the rebound effect didn't occur. "Blue," "green," "yellow," "red," they recited rapidly. Even when they were told to suppress thoughts of the breakup, they could still quickly recite the color of separation words. Maybe suppression works, if you're really good at it, like avoidant people? The avoidants, however, had a breaking point. In the high cognitive load condition, when they did the Stroop task while reciting a seven-digit number in between, they could no longer suppress. Regardless of whether they were told to suppress earlier, it took them a longer time to read the color of separation words. Their rebound effect occurred only when the demand on them became high.*

Mikulincer conducted a follow-up study with methods that were, though similar, even crueler: people wrote about a breakup and were or were not told to suppress their thoughts afterward, and then did a Stroop task. Except in the follow-up study, people listed their negative qualities before coming to the lab, and these qualities comprised the Stroop task words. If they took longer to name the colors of words that represented their negative qualities, it would signify that these qualities preoccupied them.

Under high cognitive load, when avoidants did the negative quality Stroop task, they were slower at naming the colors of words representing their negative qualities, and so they were believed to be more preoccupied with these qualities. They were more thrown off by these negative words and less able to suppress than those low in avoidance, signaling that under high stress, avoidants' veneer of suppression not only cracks, but when they can't suppress, they also

---

* The authors explained that because avoidants are suppressing all the time, they were likely suppressing regardless of whether they were told to do so (in the suppression condition) or not (in the control condition). This explains why they experience a rebound effect even when not in the suppression condition.

become more preoccupied with negative aspects of themselves than secure people.

What do these results tell us? That the surest way to be consumed by our thoughts is to try to suppress them. Avoidance may have more mileage with suppression, but when it gets to be too much, avoidants are more susceptible to stress than the rest of us—because they not only have to deal with the stress but also with their self-imposed flagellation about being too weak to suppress it. For them, suppression may work for smaller, passing issues, but not for intense or prolonged stress. For example, for Israeli Jews enduring the chronic stress of living in a territory contested with Palestine, the more avoidant someone was, the more they experienced psychiatric symptoms. The secure were less vulnerable.

These results also suggest that people who chronically suppress their feelings—avoidants—may claim to feel "strong," but this claim rests on rickety foundations. It takes work for avoidant people to maintain their positive self-image as "strong" or "invincible." It taxes them. As soon as their brainpower is otherwise claimed, they become zapped of the resources to uphold their self-image. This isn't true for people low in avoidance or who are secure. Their susceptibility to negative qualities in themselves doesn't skyrocket when they are too mentally strained to prop them up. Their positive self-perception is steadier and more honest, less forced. According to the study's authors, "Not having to create a facade of extreme autonomy and self-worth, because they have generally been accepted by their attachment figures, the [secure] are free to look at themselves fairly realistically (i.e., moderately positively)." As Eric Micha'el Leventhal, a holistic educator and author of *A Light from the Shadows,* put it, "We are at our most powerful the moment we no longer need to be powerful."

We talk so much about the risks of vulnerability that we forget to acknowledge the risks of invulnerability, risks that plague avoidants, plagued Sam, and plague many of us. And it's not just suppressing our emotions that harms us, it's also refusing to share them with others. According to the research, if Sam continued down her path of keeping her problem to herself, she'd end up *more* preoccupied with it, more depressed, and mentally and physically sicker.

While we may worry that by being vulnerable we make our problems more real, Sam's story and Mikulincer's research reveal that the problem is *more* real when we conceal it, at least in its impact on our bodies and minds. In the documentary *Disclosure,* which explores depictions of transgender people in the media, Cheetah Girl actress Sandra Caldwell shared what it was like to worry about her trans identity getting out on set.

"Do you know what it's like to go on a set and be afraid? Your head is trying desperately to stay in the scene. You wake up afraid. You go to sleep afraid. You're trying to see if somebody is going to drop a bomb that day, the next day. When is it going to happen? So you're just afraid all the time," she said. What we suppress consumes us, which is further revealed by a study that finds that keeping secrets leads us to ruminate, and the more shame we feel about the secret, the more we ruminate.

Suppression also deteriorates our mental health. Self-concealment, the tendency to withhold negative information about ourselves, is related to psychological distress and even suicidality for younger adults. Our invulnerability exacts a hefty toll on our bodies. All the energy we spend thinking about what we're hiding means that, as research finds, secret-keeping makes us feel more isolated and fatigued. When people go through traumatic experiences and don't share them, they experience more health problems. Another study found that when people experienced the death of a spouse, the less they talked about it, the less healthy they were in the year following the death. Counter to what many might think, these studies signal that if Sam truly wanted to "get over" her grief—to think about it less and be less affected by it—she needed to open up.

Invulnerability can rob us of our lives: so much bandwidth is spent trying to cram our skeletons in the closet that we ignore the rest of the house. Only vulnerability can give us our lives back. But as a society, we're somehow only becoming more invulnerable. A longitudinal survey found that in 1985, people reported having three people to confide in, on average. By 2004, that number crept down to two, and three times as many people had *no one* to confide in. In an interview for NPR, the author of the study, Duke University professor of sociology Lynn Smith-Lovin, said, "We don't usually see big social changes like this over a ten- or twenty-year period. Most features of people's lives are fairly stable from year to year."

The cost of all this invulnerability is grave. What life-giving art have we been deprived of because the artist was too afraid to reveal their pain through their craft? How would the course of the opiate crises have been different in a pro-vulnerability world? What scientist could be solving climate change but is too debilitated by thoughts she tried to bury? All the shame, the rumination, the depression, the hospital visits, the suicides, that would never have happened if we could only be vulnerable.

How to Be Vulnerable

Dr. Anna Bruk is a paradox, just like the name of her blog on *Psychology Today,* "Beautiful Mess," suggests. A high achiever, she graduated from business school and then started a PhD program in social psychology, both at the University of Mannheim in Germany. She's now chair of the social psychology department there. Her dissertation on vulnerability was groundbreaking enough to be featured in *The Atlantic* before it was finished. But despite her polished résumé, if you met Bruk, the first words that would come to mind wouldn't be "intense" or "intimidating." You might instead think "kind" and "warm" as she smiles at you as you speak. Talking with her about her research felt like chatting with a friend. She preaches the importance of connection but also personifies it.

Bruk went through hard times to arrive at where she is today. In the same few months, she endured a tumultuous breakup, the death of her cat, and a surgery that left her stuck inside and lonely. She had faith in her ability to pass the time binging Netflix shows until that ability waned. Her faith extinguished, she turned to TED Talks. That's when she came across Brené Brown.

She was inspired by Brown's pro-vulnerability message and went on to buy all her books. Vulnerability is good? Perfectionism is bad because it reflects shame and keeps us from being vulnerable? Until then, Bruk had not only been perfectionistic but viewed this quality as an asset. Yet as she reflected on her past, she realized the ways in which her perfectionism was fueled by shame, like Brown said, and also weakened her friendships. "It used to be so hard for me to apologize," Bruk said. "My perfectionism made things black and white. It was as if, if I made a mistake, then that would make me a bad person, so I had to defend myself. To actually be able to say 'I'm sorry'—that was a big change for me."

As a graduate student in psychology, she decided to formally study vulnerability. She realized there was a long history of great thinkers who valued vulnerability. Sigmund Freud said, "Out of your vulnerabilities will come your strengths," and he was cynical of our ability to be invulnerable: "He that has eyes to see and ears to hear may convince himself that no mortal can keep a secret. If his lips are silent, he chatters with his fingertips; betrayal oozes out of him at every pore." Alain de Botton, the British Swiss philosopher, argued that if society were wiser, we all wouldn't try so hard to hide imperfections. David Whyte, the British poet, emphasized that vulnerability is part of our very nature, "the underlying, ever-present and abiding undercurrent of our natural state."

Bruk became a disciple of vulnerability, but she reasoned others were more reluctant to because they feared its consequences, like judgment and rejection. With her knowledge of psychology, and of the ways we are biased in understanding the effects of our behaviors, she wondered if these consequences were real. So she set out to study if our vulnerability is as negatively judged as we believe.

People Appreciate Vulnerability More Than We Think

In Bruk's dissertation study, she had people imagine disclosing personal things—like telling their friend they had romantic feelings for them or admitting they made a mistake at work or revealing the flaws in their body. People imagined that being that vulnerable would lead others to see them as weak or even repulsive, but when they imagined others in these situations, they actually viewed them more positively, seeing their vulnerability as desirable and good.

In another study, she divided people up into singers and judges. The singers were told they would improvise a song and the judges would evaluate it. While the participants, thank goodness for them, never actually had to sing, the assumptions they made about how they'd be viewed were telling. The singers assumed they'd be judged negatively, whereas the judges saw the singing more positively, as a sign of strength.

Bruk's research builds off other studies with similar findings: when we're vulnerable, people don't judge us as much as we think. And in fact, they may perceive us positively—as authentic and honest. In one study, people endorsed fears and insecurities like "I'm often overly critical of myself and often feel inadequate around others" that were later shared with a peer. They rated how much they thought the peer liked them as a result, while the peer rated how much they actually liked them. Just like what we learned about the liking gap, people underestimated how much their peer liked them when they disclosed their insecurity. This discrepancy occurred because the peers reported that the honesty and genuineness of the disclosure influenced how much they liked the discloser, while the discloser underestimated the impact of these factors.

This research suggests that while we often think of vulnerability as burdening our friendships, it can instead ignite or deepen them. That's because, as much of the research suggests, we're often cherished rather than devalued for our vulnerability. In one often-cited study that combined results from ninety-four different analyses linking intimate self-disclosure and liking, the results indicated that the more people self-disclosed, the more liked they were.

Contrary to popular belief, people like vulnerable people *more,* not less. Once when I was teaching a psychology class, one of my students asked me if I disliked any of my therapy patients.

"No," I answered, surprising myself. "Because when you come to know someone deeply, you understand how their unlikable parts are hurt parts, and then these parts endear you rather than repel you."

Dr. Arthur Aron (whom I spoke to in chapter 1) conducted a psychology study that opened our collective eyes to the ways that vulnerability nurtures bonds. In the study, he had strangers meet up and engage in small talk or else respond to increasingly intimate questions like "When did you last cry in front of another person?" and "How do you feel about your relationship with your mother?" The strangers who were vulnerable with each other reported feeling much closer than those who engaged in small talk. In fact, students who were vulnerable reported feeling closer to their interaction partner than 30 percent of students did to anyone at all. In a popular article in the *New York Times* called "To Fall in Love with Anyone, Do This," a woman goes through Aron's questions with an acquaintance. The two fell in love afterward, and she credits the study with giving them "a way into a relationship that feels deliberate."

Vulnerability cements connection, not just because it leads us to be perceived as more honest and genuine but also because it conveys that we like and trust the person we're interacting with. In an article by Julie Beck in *The Atlantic,* when Lincoln, a project director for a reproductive health nonprofit, described his friend Amina's vulnerability, he shared, "We didn't curate our personas for each other; we were just raw and honest. I took that really seriously because Amina didn't have to open up to me. Amina didn't have to share her struggles, or her anxiety, or her depression. So the fact that she was really open with me signaled to me that she valued our friendship."

Lincoln's response also highlights how our vulnerability may add something to our friends' lives, rather than detract from them. Giving our friends the opportunity to help us, research finds, improves their mental and physical health and adds meaning to their lives. One study found that when we share our secrets, it does burden others because they ruminate on our secrets, but they also feel closer to us. When I give talks with this information, I frequently hear audience members say, "It makes sense because even if I'm afraid to be vulnerable, I love when people are vulnerable with me." The benefits we bestow on others when we share our woes and welcome their support may explain why another study found that freshmen who were more willing to express negative emotions made more friends and received more support in their first semester of college. In times of crisis, our greatest fear may be burdening others, yet when we don't reach out, the biggest burden we place on our friends is often our silence.

Be Vulnerable, But Don't Overshare

But although many times others appreciate our vulnerability much more than we'd assume, Bruk is quick to add that there are no guarantees. Even if people are less likely to judge us than we might think, there's still a real possibility that they will. She admits that in the past, she's become so enthused with vulnerability, and so thirsty to counteract a culture that rejects it, that she's underplayed the risk.

This risk of rejection is heightened when we engage in the pseudo-vulnerability of oversharing. Oversharing is only "pseudo"-vulnerability because vulnerability is authentic and oversharing isn't. Oversharing is a defense mechanism, a concept we will also explore in the next chapter on authenticity. For now, we can say that it is a strategy to reduce our awareness of and distance ourselves from—rather than acknowledge—feelings we find threatening. When we overshare, it's a way to protect ourselves against anxieties of rejection. Instead of acknowledging these fears, we overshare, in the hopes that doing so will draw someone closer to us and allay our rejection fears. Oversharing is compensating for our insecurities, and that's not vulnerability. Vulnerability involves expressing our insecurities directly. Also, like most defense mechanisms, oversharing occurs compulsively, an automatic twitch to reduce our anxiety, whereas true vulnerability occurs deliberately after we discern we are safe with someone.

Daphne, a researcher who studied confession, knows the risk of oversharing well. She'd arrive at parties, have a few drinks, and tell strangers about her sexcapades. She figured it would be cathartic—she'd get it all off her chest, release it into the air, be liberated. Until one day, at one party, she confessed to two strangers, and one asked her, "Why do you do that?"

Frazzled, she mustered, "I do it to make it matter less."

But as she heard herself say these words, she realized that it never seemed to matter less. Her sense was further clarified when she read Michel Foucault, the French philosopher, who alerted us that while we think sharing is cathartic, it isn't always. Daphne said, "I thought by talking about these things, I would liberate myself. But on the contrary, I made something unimportant a more important part of my identity than it needed to be. It wasn't a relief. I'd think about how I told people and how that's how they see me. I'd regret it."

Daphne's story and Foucault's thinking highlight the risks of oversharing. When we overshare, people don't have the broader context of who we are, so our identity, in their eyes, becomes consumed by whatever we share. Rachel Bloom, the lead actress in the show *Crazy Ex-Girlfriend,* experienced this. As a kid, she divulged to her classmates that she had gotten a mole removed because it might have been cancerous, and they nicknamed her "Chemo." Kids are mean, y'all.

Instead of conveying that we like and trust the person we interact with, which occurs when we share gradually, oversharing often conveys instead that we need to get something off our chest, and any listener will do. This may explain why oversharing often backfires. In one study, women were told to imagine another woman disclosing to them at one of three levels of intimacy: low (where she shared her favorite TV show), medium (her greatest worry), or high (the most serious problem she had in the past year). The women reported liking the high discloser the least and saw her as more anxious and least well-adjusted. They liked the medium discloser the most. To keep from oversharing, we need to understand our motives when sharing, to ask ourselves, "Why am I sharing this?" Our sharing should reflect the safety we feel in a friendship, rather than the lack thereof that we are trying to compensate for.

But even when we don't overshare, vulnerability is still a risk. Sometimes people *do* judge us when we're vulnerable. But if they do, it may say more about them than it does about us. The avoidantly attached, for example, don't respond as well to vulnerability. Since they are more uncomfortable with emotion, when others are vulnerable, the intimacy, trust, and love inherent to the interaction may be eclipsed by their discomfort with feelings. Other people's feelings threaten what they repress in themselves. One study found that people were liked more when they disclosed, except when they disclosed to someone avoidant. In Aron's 36 Questions study, in which he paired strangers to answer increasingly intimate questions, avoidant pairs developed the least closeness after responding to the questions. These avoidant responses remind us that if we share and someone recoils, we weren't necessarily wrong to share. The person may just be the wrong container for our sharing.

Tony Stark in *Iron Man 3* exemplifies this dynamic. He meets a young boy, Harley Keener, when he breaks into the garage of Harley's home looking for food and shelter. Harley glumly tells Tony in one scene, "Dad went to 7-Eleven to get scratchers. I guess he won, 'cause that was six years ago." Tony's response? "Which happens, dads leave, no need to be a pussy about it."

Overall, despite the risks of vulnerability, which are real, Bruk and I agree that vulnerability is worth the risk. Its rewards are *even more* real. It makes us feel better mentally and physically, deepens our friendships, and helps us better understand ourselves. Without vulnerability, "there's a ceiling you reach in friendship that you can't exceed," Dr. Jackson said. And while vulnerability may give people the power to hurt us more deeply, it also gives them the power to love us more deeply. As Dr. Jackson shared, "If you're not vulnerable, all of your friends' love, support, and attention is not about all of you, as you know it. Their affirmation doesn't land in the same way. When you're vulnerable, and they really know you, it feels like you can trust their love for you more fully, because they are showing love for who you really are."

Practice Self-Compassion

Dr. Bruk also learned to be vulnerable through being kinder to herself. Before she read Brown's book, she read a book by Kristin Neff called *Self-Compassion,* which is practiced by showing ourselves the kindness and care that we would a good friend. When she decided to study vulnerability, she was advised not to because there wasn't much research on it (most of the research was on a related but distinct concept called self-disclosure). She'd have to come up with a way to define and study it, and as a pioneer who was new to the field, she might fail. But she pushed through because self-compassion helped her realize failure didn't define her worth as a person.

"Self-compassion creates a solid core of stable self-worth. And that gives us a safe place to land no matter where showing vulnerability leads us," she told me. One of Dr. Bruk's studies shows that while people usually evaluate other people's vulnerability more favorably than their own, this isn't true for people high in self-compassion. That's because they have a much more positive view of their vulnerability. If we can be kind to our vulnerabilities, we'll be less impacted when others aren't.

Self-compassion has three components:

1. Self-kindness: being kind and understanding toward oneself (*It's okay that you failed that test. It was really hard.*)
2. Mindfulness: having a balanced reaction to painful thoughts and feelings, not underreacting or overreacting (*I notice I'm feeling sad right now.*)
3. Common humanity: seeing one's experience as part of the larger human experience (*Everyone fails from time to time.*)

To practice self-compassion, next time you look in the mirror and want to criticize your stomach, tell yourself: *I know I'm feeling critical. It's okay that I'm not feeling great about my body today. Most people feel bad about their bodies from time to time.* Or if you feel upset that your child didn't call on your birthday, say: *I'm feeling upset. It's understandable that I feel that way. A lot of parents struggle with their kids.* If Sam practiced self-compassion, she might have said to herself: *I'm feeling out of control. It's okay to not be in control sometimes. Going through this connects me to everyone else who feels this way.*

Embrace Vulnerability as a Value

Self-compassion helps us accept ourselves, which makes vulnerability feel less risky because then others' acceptance matters less. But even if we can't muster all the love and gentleness toward ourselves in our vulnerable moments, that doesn't mean we can't be vulnerable. Vulnerability doesn't have to feel good. Often it feels scary—that's your self-protection reflex kicking in, which you can notice and honor. Even if vulnerability terrifies you, though, you don't need to avoid it. I'm sure there are many uncomfortable things you do for some larger purpose—you opt for cauliflower soup instead of Twizzlers for lunch, get pricked with needles, press your legs into squats even when no toilet is underneath them—because, like vulnerability, these instants of discomfort will protect you from much more sickness in the long run.

To get yourself to be vulnerable, it'll help if you remember that you're not practicing it because it's comfortable; you're doing so because it aligns with your values. If you value connection, well-being, intimacy, meaning, honesty, self-care, showing up in the world as your truest self, then being vulnerable expresses your values. You succeed, no matter the response, because in being vulnerable, you advocated for yourself and honored your values. Harriet Lerner frames this well in her book *The Dance of Connection:* "Let go of expectations of getting the response you want. We will always come from a more solid place if we speak to preserve our own well-being and integrity and refuse to be silenced by fear." Acting alongside values is also a tenet of a popular form of therapy, acceptance and commitment therapy, popularized by psychologists Steven Hayes, Kirk Strosahl, and Kelly Wilson. One principle of the therapy is that regardless of the amount of pain we have, we must accept it and commit to doing actions that align with our values to make our lives meaningful.

Be Vulnerable with the Right People

The tricky part of vulnerability is that it hinges on not just you, but also on whoever you are vulnerable with. It'll feel great and provide ample benefits if your vulnerability lands on an empathic ear, but if not, it backfires and you feel worse.

It may seem obvious to be discerning about who we're vulnerable to, but it's often something we forget. I remember getting a call from a friend around the same time that I was going through a difficult breakup. Because of the timing of the call, I ended up sharing the situation and my feelings about it. I didn't think about whether my friend would be compassionate, because if I did, I wouldn't have said anything. That friend is hyper-logical and doesn't speak the language of emotion. He tried to convince me that I had been exploited by the guy for sex. Of course, that only made me feel worse.

That experience also made me realize that part of practicing healthy vulnerability is also being comfortable with *not* being vulnerable. Sometimes, I've felt like some crisis is consuming me so much that if I don't share, it'll make me an imposter—a friend will be able to sniff it out and know I'm lying. But people are apparently really bad at knowing when we're lying, according to one meta-analysis. You're free to conceal things from people who you don't trust.

It's not easy to know who to trust, though, especially with all the research we've read about how we misjudge others' responses to our vulnerability. Perhaps the best sign that someone is trustworthy is if they've responded well to your vulnerability in the past. The liability is, of course, that by the time you give them this opportunity, it's too late to protect yourself if they end up dismissing you. To soften this risk, I sometimes "scaffold vulnerability." If I'm feeling really vulnerable, I'll talk to my friend Billy, who I know is amazing and empathic and wonderful and healing pretty much all the time. Talking to her will make me feel more secure, so that if I then go to a friend whose empathy isn't yet a sure bet, it won't hurt as much if they don't respond well, *and* it'll help me figure out whether they can handle my vulnerability in the future. If you don't yet have a confidante you can scaffold vulnerability with, start with a therapist or mental health hotline.

When we act or think in all-or-nothing ways—like never or always being vulnerable—our rigidity hides deeper scars. I hear these scars from friends who say things like, "You can't trust anyone," or "Everyone is going to let you down at the end of the day." If we assume one thing is always true, we aren't evaluating the situation to determine whether a behavior will or won't work; we're projecting. It's discernment, attention to the present moment and to the openness of the ears in front of us, that will allow us to carve out nourishing spaces for our vulnerability.

Without this discernment, we risk offering our vulnerability to the people who hurt us the most. Freud called this "repetition compulsion." We return to the site of our pain for our healing because what's more validating than validation from the person who hurt us? Repetition compulsion is why people return to a toxic friendship or turn to Tinder in the hopes that they'll be comforted by a new date to ease the pain of the last or keep trying to share with a friend who only ever cracks jokes in response. Unfortunately, this urge tends to leave us in even more pain because if a person hurt us once, they just might do so again.

If someone has a history of being rejecting in your moments of need, don't assume they'll change. Don't look for water in an empty well. Your vulnerability is too precious for that. Find people who will actually comfort and support you; turn toward them, rather than to the person you hoped would be different. How often do we expose ourselves to the wrong people because we wish to make them different when we could just accept who they are and be different ourselves?

Men and Vulnerability

Things seemed to be going well for Lucas Krump. He had spent many years abroad, hopping between places like Egypt, Thailand, Uganda, Aruba, Saint Kitts, and Singapore, eventually landing in New York City. He had a girlfriend, and the startup he worked for had been acquired, leaving him with a small fortune. By all outward appearances, he had it all.

But in the dark underbelly of his life, things weren't good. He was lonely and sad but didn't realize it. Since he suppressed his emotions, his best litmus test for whether he was living a good life was how good it appeared to others, so he thought he was fine. But the collective weight of these feelings still left him hollow and detached from everything, like he was watching his existence on a movie screen.

When he was out at dinner in Shanghai, China, where he attended business school classes, his BlackBerry vibrated. It was his sister: "dad dead." "Talk later. I'm finishing dinner," he responded. His father had always been cold and remote, and when he died, Lucas barely registered his pain at the loss, stuffing the emotions down and covering them with alcohol. While he was abroad, his grandmother and grandfather also died. Unlike his father, his grandparents had been the most important people in his life. But he didn't go to their funerals. He told himself that he knew people were going to die when he moved abroad and that he had to accept that and move on.

Eventually, all the unprocessed grief caught up with Lucas and landed him in a mental hospital. The emotion was intense and overwhelming, like nothing Lucas had ever felt. It was the residue of feelings suppressed but never extinguished. It was his body's revolution against a mind unknowingly using it as a repository to store the things it wasn't willing to see. And its revolution was a little bit effective. Lucas soon after moved back to the States, quit drinking for a while, and saw more of his family.

Lucas spent some time in Arizona with his mother, and she found him a therapist. He looks back at that first therapy session as divine intervention. As he imparted his struggles with drugs, alcohol, women, and isolation, the therapist told him, "There's no amount of money, drugs, or women that will fill the hole in your heart. You're going to have to grow. Because you didn't really have a father, you will need to create a community of men who will support you. It's all going to take some work." His problem was that he was lonely, not from a lack of people in his life, but from a lack of people with whom he could be truly vulnerable.

His therapist advised him to join Alcoholics Anonymous to find his community and change his drinking habits. He was in awe at the vulnerability, honesty, and community he found there. For the first time in his life, he felt surrounded by good men who wanted to help him. But he felt like an imposter. He couldn't quite relate to the experiences he heard because he was so functional even when drinking—holding down a job, paying his bills, getting himself home at the end of the night. "No one was going to save me," he said. "So I would drink thirty-seven beers and stop at thirty-seven and go to work the next day. I couldn't turn into a junkie because if I did, I knew I'd die." It wasn't just community he needed, Lucas realized, but a place where he felt like he could truly belong because he identified with the people around him. So, he left AA, but the experience made him hungry for spaces where vulnerability and authenticity were welcomed.

Lucas hopped around men's organizations, looking for authentic community, but nothing quite fit. They were religious or else full of spiritual mumbo jumbo. Where were the normal, everyday guys, the bearded, swearing, broad-shouldered dudes Lucas could see himself in? Then one day, in a moment of serendipity, Lucas met a man named Dan at a conference. Dan told him he was starting a retreat for men in an old barn in the Berkshires of Massachusetts.

That weekend changed Lucas's life forever. As men around him teared up and shared feelings, he realized it was normal for men, even more masculine dudes like him, to have feelings. Manhood, as he had known it, was a great charade. Men don't show emotion not because they don't have any but because they learn, early on, to fear what would happen if they did. "We're human beings. We were put on this earth to be vulnerable. We have that capacity within us and denying our evolutionary biology is the problem we face as a human race. As a man, I was given the ability to feel and be vulnerable for a reason. We can't deny our ability to be human," Lucas said.

That weekend, he realized the toll it took on men to stay silent. In something called an anger ceremony, the men went to the woods and spread out across the forest. All at once, they screamed, pouring out emotions churning inside them for years or even decades. First, Lucas heard the other men's rage, and then he heard their suffering, as, mid-scream, they broke down around him. Finally, he did too.

Society is starting to attend to the lacking state of Western men's friendships and the horrible effects this lack has on men's health, both mental and physical. Men's friendship crisis was explored in an episode of NPR's *Hidden Brain* podcast called "The Lonely American Man"; in a *Harper's Bazaar* article, "Men Have No Friends and Women Bear the Burden"; and in the book *The Lonely American: Drifting Apart in the Twenty-First Century,* where husband-and-wife authors Jacqueline Olds and Richard S. Schwartz highlight how men are intimate only with romantic partners while neglecting friends.

Lucas's story highlights how men's friendship struggles are, at their core, vulnerability struggles. An older meta-analysis, conducted in 1992, found men are less vulnerable than women in their friendships (and most of their other relationships). A 2021 survey found that women were approximately twice as likely to receive emotional support from a friend or share something personal with them within the span of a week. This dynamic was aptly put by a tweet from reporter Julia Reinstein: "They always say 'dudes rock.' ... They never ask if dudes have a rock."

Deep friendship is impossible without vulnerability. Without it, friendship deflates into companionship alone, which is nice but truncated, since friendship can offer us so much more. Friends are basketball buddies, drinking buddies, golf buddies, but they don't achieve the sort of depths of an *anam cara,* an Irish term for soul friend, the type of friend you confess to, sharing your innermost mind and heart.

An *Atlantic* article, "Games Boys Play," describes how men include a third object in their friendships to avoid the vulnerability that might otherwise bob up among idle friends: "When you're hunting, or working on a car, or shooting free throws, you can look together at the deer, or the transmission, or the basket, and talk. The common objective gives you something to talk *about,* and not having to face each other means you don't have to lay the full weight of your emotions on each other."

But if men aren't vulnerable in close relationships, where does their vulnerability go? An adage we learned in graduate school is "women internalize; men externalize." In broad strokes (and with exceptions), this means that when upset, women go inward, blaming themselves and feeling guilty and depressed. But men, instead, express their upset through how they interact with the world. This is evidenced by a study that found that women are more likely to suppress their anger, whereas men are more likely to act aggressively. They might yell, bully, punch a wall. Lucas is an example of this: "I was an asshole. I used dominant and selfish behavior with women."

We often choose to behave in ways that will make us feel more socially accepted, which frames why men may choose dominance or anger over vulnerability. When men act angrily, according to one study, they are viewed as higher status and more competent than women who do. Yet the more we reward men for dominance and aggression, the more we crush their vulnerability because dominance is a mask to evade vulnerability, to escape the acknowledgment of others' power. Vulnerability and dominance cannot co-exist. Vulnerability says explicitly, "I acknowledge you have power over me, and I'm hoping you'll use it kindly." Dominance says, "You have no power over me. I have power over you."

In being vulnerable, men relinquish their urge to dominate because vulnerability releases the threatening emotions masked through domination. Consider a story from actor and podcaster Dax Shepard. His wife was going to do charity work in a country in Africa. He protested, telling her he studied anthropology, and foreign charities create more problems than they solve. She didn't budge. He protested again, questioning the reputation of the charity. After dozens of arguments, Dax realized the vulnerability underneath his logic.

He shared: "I'm very afraid that this thing, helping people, will become more important than me."

Once he finally got vulnerable, she responded, "I will never pick anything over you." And Dax never again cared about the reputation of his wife's charities.

"I think I'm mounting some intellectual point, and it's not true," Dax said. Often our most spirited arguments aren't about logic, but about the drive to be dominant to avoid vulnerable emotions brewing underneath. It was only through vulnerability that Dax could get his *truest* need met and also heal his relationship.

The double-edged sword for men, however, is that even though dominance may undercut their relationships, so might vulnerability. Embracing it, particularly among other men, is risky. One 2013 study, for example, found that men, but not women, viewed men expressing vulnerability unfavorably. "Men police other men, so we keep our vulnerability in. Once men see weakness in other men, they go in. They become the butt of jokes and are teased and bullied," Christopher St. Vil, a professor of social work at the University at Buffalo who studies Black masculinity, told me. When I asked Adam, a social worker and founder of the Instagram account @dadswithwisdom, why he isn't more vulnerable with other men, he shared, "I know the other guy can't handle it. But it's not just that. I can be ostracized. Somebody's gonna call you a bitch. And that's it. Then you might get beat up twice as hard." With a response like that, it's no wonder men have told Adam that being shut down "helps us survive."

One night, when Lucas (who went on the men's retreat) was eleven, his father left in the middle of the night, and he woke up in the house alone. Afraid, he began to sob. His father got back and, seeing him cry, hit him openhanded across the face. Lucas looks back on that moment as part of his "conditioning." He said, "This moment fractured the safety that I believed my father was suppose to provide and taught me that my emotions were not accepted." By adulthood, this conditioning was complete. His emotions were choked down, invisibly undoing him like carbon monoxide.

But another man, Stephen, a doctor, argued that many men have discarded this dominance ideal in favor of vulnerability, realizing it hasn't worked for them. He said, "Yes, it's true that it happened when we were younger. A lot of men are frozen in time, thinking adult men will beat them up like their football-playing teammates would. But as adults, a lot of my friends realized trying to pretend you're always fine and don't have any problems, or emotions, doesn't work. Even the most masculine of them are in therapy and have begun to share." Dr. St. Vil has seen the same progress. He started a mentoring program to pair younger and older Black men. He credits older Black men, who have realized the hazards of invulnerability, with helping him become more vulnerable. "They told me, 'You aren't a pussy if you cry. How strong you are isn't based on how many people you beat up.'"

The assumption that male friends will shame you for your suffering was also challenged by Manny Argueta, a man profiled in the *Washington Post* article "No Game Days. No Bars. The Pandemic Is Forcing Some Men to Realize They Need Deeper Friendships." He had shallow friendships with his male friends, centered on going to bars and watching sports games. But after going through the pandemic, a breakup, and therapy, Manny finally told his male friends about his problems. He thought they'd roast him, but instead they asked about the breakup and how he was doing. In Dr. Bruk's study, men too underestimated how positively people would view their vulnerability.

Manny's story illustrates that spaces where men can be vulnerable exist, but finding them requires risks. Men who want to bring more vulnerability to their friendships will likely have to go first. Considering how deeply invulnerability is entrenched in Western notions of masculinity, men who wait for friends to go first will likely wither in waiting. Share something slightly more vulnerable than you usually might, and see where it lands.

Many men are embracing vulnerability and realizing that dominance doesn't make them happy, as evidenced by a study that finds that people who dominate others aren't as happy in their close relationships as those who build equal relationships. When men do not mask vulnerability through dominance, they gain a subtler power, one that allows them to love and connect. As Lori Gottlieb, therapist and author of *Maybe You Should Talk to Someone,* shares, "I know, for example, that people who are demanding, critical, and angry tend to suffer from intense loneliness. I know that a person who acts this way both wants to be seen and is terrified of being seen." We can't know ourselves fully if we're veiling our vulnerability to seem imposing. We can't know someone else fully if we're bent on stifling them to boost ourselves or, as actor Terry Crews puts it, "It's impossible to love and control someone at the same time."

Survival of the Most Vulnerable

Lucas Krump's men's retreat has grown and become a trademark of EVRYMAN, a company Lucas co-founded, marketed as "CrossFit for your emotions." EVRYMAN groups allow men to process their emotions among men. Some of their goals are to destigmatize men's vulnerability and help them make deep friendships. At the Brooklyn EVRYMAN group, men sat in a circle and talked about their "unspeakable" experiences. As Daniel, one participant in the group, shared, "I began to realize that my world doesn't collapse if someone else sees me have an emotion. It seems so simple now, but it came as a revelation." John, a sixty-seven-year-old, said after attending for just two months, "I actually finally feel like I'm alive."

Since learning to be vulnerable, Lucas has been doing so much better. Having language to express his feelings has allowed him to release them and feel mentally stronger and clearer. Knowing what he's actually feeling has allowed him to choose spaces and work that make him come alive. And perhaps, most important, revealing who he really is has allowed him to build an intimate community with, and feel supported by, other men. It's the community and their support that makes everything better. Lucas shared, "They tell you about suicide and anxiety and depression and addiction and all this shit that's happening with men. And they all want to frame that as a mental health issue. But all of these things come from a lack of intimate connection and community."

But why is being vulnerable with one's community so life-altering? Dr. Michael Slepian, a professor at Columbia University who studies secrets, helps us understand. In one of his studies, he examined what made people good at coping with the weight of their secrets. He had people fill out multiple questionnaires, one of which assessed their "coping efficacy" related to their secrets. Someone with high coping efficacy answered affirmatively to questions like "How capable do you feel in your ability to cope with the secret?" and "How much do you feel in control over the situation?" Coping efficacy had a strong and positive influence on overall well-being.

But the more important question here is—how did these well-adjusted secret-keepers become that way? Were they just innately strong, Chuck Norris types, applying their superior discipline or willpower to push through the burdens of their secrets? Or was there some extra magic that made them that way? The extra magic, the study revealed, was support. Those highest in coping efficacy had received the most support from others when they disclosed their secret. They were most likely to say others comforted them, were there for them, and gave them new insight when they shared their secret, like what happens to Lucas when he sits in an EVRY-MAN circle. Those least able to cope, by contrast, received the least support from others. "If there's one piece of advice I'd give to people who have secrets," Slepian told me, "it's to share them."

Slepian's study isn't the first to find that others' support makes us stronger. A study of men who had heart attacks found that they were most confident in their ability to adapt to the changes brought on by the heart attack when they were more dependent on their wives. They felt least able to cope when they instead attempted to hide their feelings to protect her. The core of attachment theory, supported by thousands of studies, is that we become secure only through being supported by our most foundational relationships. As we discussed in Part I, secure attachment is a "core feature of resilience" in part because, as research finds, the secure are better at seeking support. Dr. Skyler Jackson added, "For almost every aspect of well-being, social support is a critical part of what makes us endure and survive hardship." The only way we truly become strong is through being deeply supported by others.

This information on the power of vulnerability challenges our misconceptions of mental fortitude, misconceptions Lucas clung to until he couldn't anymore. We think of the strong-minded as contained and self-reliant. We assume strength is signaled by the popular phrase from eighties Gillette deodorant commercials: *Never let them see you sweat*. But this advice is better applied to armpits than to vulnerability. Never lettin' 'em see us sweat doesn't make us strong. It makes us suppress our weakness, so it is trapped inside us.

A friend's boyfriend once described this process to me. He feels like a waffle that keeps getting soaked with more syrup, becoming heavier and heavier but retaining its shape to the outside observer.

At first blush, the idea of strength derived from being vulnerable rather than solely gurgling from within runs counter to the US mainstream culture of rugged individualism. We love a rags-to-riches story of a self-made man (rarely ever not a man or not White) who never depended on anyone, who teaches us we can make it on our own, no matter how abysmal our surroundings.

But thinkers have been rightfully critical of these ideas for centuries. In his lecture on the self-made man in 1872, Frederick Douglass disclaimed, "It must in truth be said, though it may not accord well with self-conscious individuality and self-conceit, that no possible native force of character, and no depth of wealth and originality, can lift a man into absolute independence of his fellowmen." The French diplomat Alexis de Tocqueville feared that American individualism would lead to a situation where "each man is forever thrown back on himself alone, and there is danger that he may be shut up in the solitude of his own heart."

For some, it's tough to disavow individualism, because in the US, it seems like the natural order, but anthropologists Nick P. Winder and Isabelle C. Winder argue that so is vulnerability. They view vulnerability as an heirloom passed down from our primate ancestors. According to their "vulnerable ape hypothesis," as our ancestors siphoned into small groups to travel to isolated areas with less competition and more resources, their population was too small for only the most physically fit to survive. They didn't have enough genetic diversity for the physically "fittest" to surface, and the entire population could be wiped out in the meantime. Who survived, then, was not the strongest.

It was those most comfortable with vulnerability.

Those who could form relationships and call upon those relationships in times of need survived. They revealed when they were starving and needed food or got others to help them to build shelter. They didn't deny their needs. They communicated them. The survivors harvested the resources of a collective, and thus no individual had to be particularly fit or strong, but in doing so, each individual was stronger than any "fittest." If we are to be as successful as our ancestors, the vulnerable apes, we must do as Kathleen Dwyer, a social science research analyst who studied relationships, instructed me: "The goal of independence is not to be completely autonomous, but to recognize when you need somebody, and know how to reach out to them to get what you need."

Finding the Strength in Vulnerability

Vulnerability hasn't always been easy for me. I used to think people would love me more if I was invulnerable, that being invulnerable made me impressive and composed, and being vulnerable made me weak. These beliefs made me a worse friend and person. In middle school, a friend wanted me to go to an amusement park with her and her father every weekend. My parents didn't want to give me money to go, but this friend thought we were rich, so I would make up lies about having something else to do. Being invulnerable also led me to drop great friendships when conflict arose because it would take vulnerability to apologize. In middle school, I hung out with a group of boys. We had some big blowup over petty things that I hardly remember but know were my fault. Instead of admitting fault though, because that would be too vulnerable, I found a shiny new group of friends.

I've gotten better at vulnerability. While I was studying to be a psychologist, vulnerability was recast as desirable and healthy, rather than weak. That helped, but even as I understood this intellectually, it didn't mean that the prospect of being vulnerable didn't make me feel scared, or tense, or small. What do we do if our brain understands the importance of being vulnerable but our body understands only the danger of it?

I faced this discrepancy during one of my psychology courses. As I mentioned earlier, in these courses, it was normal for people to share revealing things and, sometimes, to break down and cry. It was maybe the third year of our PhD program, and I hadn't yet cried. But that day was my big day. I don't even remember what I was sharing, probably something about my childhood, but I distinctly remember my reluctant tears, tears I wanted to vacuum back up into my eyes. I had, until that moment, taken pride in myself for being one of the last few who hadn't cried, and I dreaded facing my actions and my cohort the next week.

During the next class, the teacher asked me what it was like to share the prior week. I remember saying I felt weak and worried everyone saw me as pathetic. My classmates chimed in to share the opposite—that they perceived me as brave and strong for coming to terms with and even sharing difficult experiences. To be honest, at the time, I didn't believe them. I thought they were saying that to make me feel better. But now I believe them.

Many of our fears of vulnerability are rooted in inaccurate assumptions of how others view us if we are vulnerable—assumptions I held on to even when *explicitly* told otherwise. Invulnerability dies hard. Now, I try to remind myself that if I'm vulnerable, others will appreciate my genuineness, my honesty, and feel closer to me. They won't judge me as much as I worry they will. Because I'm a research nerd, knowing all the research supports these assumptions helps because I know I'm not just telling myself lies to feel better. If you want to be more vulnerable, you'll need to make fresher and kinder assumptions about how others will respond to you (something we learned in the initiative chapter). *People will value my vulnerability, and it'll make us closer. They'll see me not as pathetic, but as brave and genuine.* This is a practice. You won't get over your fears by telling yourself this once. You have to remind yourself repeatedly.

From that experience, I also witnessed firsthand that a lot of what we assume others think about us is a projection of how *we* think about us. I feared people would perceive me as weak or pathetic if I was vulnerable because I felt weak or pathetic when vulnerable. We must undress our assumptions about vulnerability. If I could see my act of sharing as a sign of bravery and intimacy, then I'd be more likely to assume others would.

What became of Sam? Did she ever reach out to get the support she needed? She did. In fact, she ended up starting a wellness group with her friends, where every week they met up and focused on one aspect of wellness, which they practiced together. She led the week on vulnerability, during which she shared what she went through. She went on to write a book on friendship, with which she spread the good word of vulnerability to others. Sam is an invulnerable-in-recovery. Sam is me.

When I look back on the experience, the old me, the invulnerable me, feels so far away and in so much pain. I'm not sure I would have seen or, rather, admitted that in myself. I want to help her, but I'm not sure I'd be able to. She'd rebuff my help as an admission that she needed help, and thus, a sign of weakness, and in doing so, she would only entrench herself in more suffering. I wish I could have been gentler with myself, more forgiving of and honest about my weakness, and more willing to care for it by asking for support.

I attribute my invulnerability to a faulty internal algorithm. It read, "If I share my pain, I will be shamed." I put so much stake in that algorithm that it prevented me from living in the actuality of what others' responses would be, how they'd actually receive me. I wasn't leading a true life, because I was living based on my fears rather than in reality. I only found that out, of course, when I made myself vulnerable. Sometimes you just have to take the leap. And every time I'm vulnerable with those who love and accept me, my algorithm is debugged a little more. This is the power of vulnerability—it provides for the "sacred correction" of our internal algorithm. Opening up doesn't just heal us in the moment but careens us down a more healing course for the future. I carry a little less shame and fear of others. I'm a little more open, honest, and liberated. I said vulnerability can bring you your life back, and I am Exhibit A.

Now I know that times of great suffering, of great pain, of great crises, are a portal to deep connection, if we let them be, if we are vulnerable. If we are invulnerable, we may find ourselves stagnant, consumed, and alone, or, in the words of poet Mary Oliver, "breathing just a little and calling it a life." Nothing would have (eventually) motivated me to lean on my friends like my vulnerability. It brought us so much closer. As Morgan Jerkins, essayist and editor, put it, "Sometimes it's good to let people love you in moments when you're not strong so you can see their capacity for love." But this required me to accept that there is some peace that I cannot provide myself, that I need other people for. I'm still in process and it's been a hard pill to swallow, but the more the pill goes down, the more I find peace.

TAKEAWAYS

► Express vulnerability through not just the content of your words but your demeanor. If your voice shakes, let it. If it's scary for you to share, say so. If you start to tear up, let tears fall. Doing so communicates the magnitude of what you're sharing and lets others know to be sensitive.

► Go to your trusted friends for support when you need it. It'll make you feel stronger and deepen your friendships.

► To practice vulnerability:
- Don't overshare. Oversharing can drive people away and cause you harm. Your vulnerability should be a symbol of the trust and affection you share with someone. You're free to conceal things from people you don't trust.
- Be vulnerable first. Don't wait for friends.
- Remind yourself:
  - Others won't judge you for your vulnerability as much as you think, and in fact they might perceive you positively, as authentic and honest.
  - Being invulnerable doesn't abolish your weaknesses; it just keeps you from showing strength alongside it.
  - If you assume "if I share my pain, I will be shamed," your internal algorithm may be faulty. The best way to correct it is to be vulnerable with a trusted source.
- Practice self-compassion, which involves:
  - Self-kindness: being kind and understanding toward yourself. Ex: *It's okay that you failed that test. It was really hard.*
  - Mindfulness: having a balanced reaction to painful thoughts and feelings, not underreacting or overreacting. Ex: *I notice I'm feeling sad right now.*
  - Common humanity: seeing one's experience as part of the larger human experience. Ex: *Everyone fails from time to time.*

- Scaffold vulnerability by disclosing to someone you trust, and then being vulnerable with someone who you're less sure of.
- Be vulnerable even if it's scary. Remember that you're not practicing it because it's comfortable; you're doing so because it aligns with your values and your highest self.
- Don't keep being vulnerable with people who have hurt you when you're vulnerable.

CHAPTER 5

Pursuing Authenticity

*How to Deepen Friendships by
Showing Your True Self*

On a spring day in 2014, Hannah and Sarah decided to road trip across the country. The two had met at work at a graphic design firm, in a cramped office in Canarsie, Brooklyn. Hannah had immigrated from Hungary for the job, and Sarah was already at the firm when she arrived. On Hannah's first day, she wore a flowy white tunic that swayed as she walked over to Sarah to introduce herself. In contrast to Hannah's boho look, Sarah's tailored clothes resembled those of an Ann Taylor Loft model. Her beige skirt, freshly pressed, hugged her jet-black sweater at the waist. A jeweled necklace and hair coiffed back in a tight bun topped off the outfit. Very professional not just in her clothes but in her demeanor, Sarah said a curt hello and went back to work. Hannah, however, was not easily dissuaded. She invited Sarah out to lunch. To her half-surprise, Sarah said yes. After a few lunch dates, the two became fast friends.

Sarah, who was used to keeping people at a distance, enjoyed the intimacy she developed with Hannah. Her manicured appearance concealed the nervousness she felt around others. With Hannah, Sarah could wear her comfortable clothes and unpin her hair. The upcoming road trip they had planned would further deepen their bond, at least she hoped.

When the trip began, Hannah wasn't in the best headspace. Her recent breakup depressed her; she felt tired and hopeless about love. The road trip with Sarah was a welcome distraction, an opportunity to feel less alone. Driving south to Virginia on I-95, Hannah confessed to wanting to text her ex.

"You'll find someone new who's better than him," Sarah said.

"Maybe, but it's still hard to get him out of my head," Hannah insisted.

They went back and forth: Sarah encouraging Hannah to move on and look forward, Hannah shooting down her optimism.

Finally, Sarah snapped, "You have to face the truth. He doesn't want to talk to you. He doesn't want anything to do with you. And you need to get over it."

Hannah was hurt. The silence that followed was deafening. Sarah thumbed through their road trip playlist. "I'll Be There for You," by the Rembrandts vibrated from the speakers. Sarah clicked to another song.

For the rest of the day, they made small talk, but the incident loomed over them and threatened to derail the vacation. When they arrived at a motel in Chattanooga, Hannah asked for separate rooms. Arriving at her room, Hannah sat on her bed, and the bedframe heaved. Tears rolled down her cheeks and stained the flowery pillowcase. As she turned on the television, she heard a knock at the door. It was Sarah. Before opening the door, Hannah scrambled to wipe off her face with the comforter. Sarah came in and said, "I think we should talk about what's happened between us."

Sarah started: "I remember when you talked to Tamara [another co-worker] about your breakup and you said you felt better after, and I feel like you never say that after you talk to me. I try to help you and it doesn't go anywhere, and it makes me feel like I'm not a good friend."

"I don't expect you to fix me when I share," Hannah responded.

"I just want to feel heard." The two reached some sort of initial resolution, but the tear between them wasn't fully patched.

Another week into their trip, the two touched down in Chicago. They galivanted around the city, staring at their reflections in Chicago's famous arched mirror sculpture, the Bean; ascending on the Navy Pier's Ferris wheel; munching on Garrett Popcorn; and then expanding their bellies with slices of deep-dish pizza. It was a good day, and Hannah felt closer to Sarah than she had the entire trip.

As the day came to an end, the two were walking through a park, back to their Airbnb. Maybe it was a fresh feeling of safety, or maybe she was tired of censoring her grief, or maybe this was her way of sewing the final patch in the tear, but for some reason, Hannah brought up her recent breakup.

Sarah froze for a few seconds, took a deep breath, and then unloaded: "When you talk to me, it's almost like I don't matter at all." Hannah was confused and immediately regretted bringing the topic up. She glanced at the street sign and calculated how far they were from the Airbnb. She didn't want this to go down in public.

"All you think about is yourself and what you want to talk about, and you don't care if I'm overwhelmed," Sarah said. The two by that point had stopped walking and faced each other in the street adjacent to the park.

"That's pretty hurtful to say," Hannah responded.

"I don't understand why you can't see my perspective," Sarah said.

Hannah noticed a pedestrian wearing a sky-blue cap circling the park, eavesdropping on their fight. She worried that a crowd might gather, as Sarah's voice boomed.

"I'm sharing my honest thoughts and feelings with you. Do you want me to pretend? If you were really my friend, you would be proud of me for being honest and setting a boundary. But no. You just keep bringing up your ex over and over and over again. It's selfish," Sarah screamed. She had been processing in therapy how she was too much of a pushover, too passive, too willing to go along with others' needs while sacrificing her own. No more. The guy with the blue cap dawdled. He glanced over at the two of them, but when Hannah glared at him, he looked away.

Hannah could think of nothing else to do but walk away. She could hear the noise of insults being lobbed at her as she walked. The tear between the two of them, never fully patched, was split wide open. And their friendship would never fully recover.

Sarah learned a lesson that day. If you want to keep people close, you have to fake it. Being a pushover was better than being honest. Sharing how you really feel, and unleashing your anger, will make people flee. Authenticity is overrated. Or is it?

What Is Authenticity?

There's consistency in how authenticity was defined by the ancient Greeks and how social scientists define it today. The ancient Greeks referenced authenticity with the well-known phrase "To thine own self be true." A later definition by psychologist Susan Harter got more granular: "Owning one's personal experiences, be they thoughts, emotions, needs, wants, preferences, or beliefs" and "acting in accord with the true self, expressing oneself in ways that are consistent with inner thoughts and feelings."

But what is a "true self"? There is danger in centering authenticity around the "true self" without clearly defining what that is—after all, people can easily justify destructive behaviors as reflecting a "true self." It's the friend who tells you your haircut sucks and they're "just being blunt." It's the friend who, after your presentation, shares, unsolicited, that you "need to work on your public speaking." It's the friend who shrieks at you outside the park, while a pedestrian eavesdrops, and wonders why you aren't open to their honesty. People use authenticity as a cop-out for being mean.

How, then, should we define authenticity? When I dug into the research, I noticed a pattern. Research finds, for example, that people report being most authentic when they are around others who are open and accepting, and they feel inauthentic when others are judging them. They feel authentic when they feel good—joyful, calm, or loving—whereas they feel inauthentic when they feel lousy—anxious, stressed, or depressed. They feel most authentic when all their psychological needs are met, when they feel more competence, belonging, and self-esteem.

This research reveals what authenticity is and what it is not. It's not a knee-jerk reaction we indulge when we feel bruised. It's not wildly expressing our thoughts and feelings with wanton disregard for everyone else. Blaming, putting down, or attacking—these behaviors are more *raw* than they are authentic.

Instead, authenticity flourishes in safety. It is a state of presence we access when we aren't hijacked by our defense mechanisms. We're not authentic when we're distracted, multitasking, or saying things on autopilot, like compulsively responding "Fine" to a "How are you?" Authenticity occurs when we access feelings of safety—when we don't feel the need to activate our defenses—even in the face of threat, judgment, rejection, or neglect, among other things. It's who we are when we aren't triggered, when we can make intentional, rather than reactive, decisions about how we want to show up in the world.

Let me further flesh out this definition. We often distance ourselves from our true feelings for what feels like the sake of our relationships or our self-esteem, or as the father of attachment theory, John Bowlby, put it, "What cannot be communicated to the [m]other cannot be communicated to the self." Instead of admitting we yearn for a friend who abandoned us, we say we don't care that they left. Instead of sharing that we feel hurt by a friend's teasing, we tell ourselves we're being too sensitive. Instead of admitting we've outgrown a friend, we tell ourselves everything is fine. We contort our natural feelings and instead justify, rationalize, or dismiss. Authenticity, however, involves allowing ourselves to feel rejected by the friend who abandoned us, hurt by our friend's taunts, or incompatible with our childhood friend. It's a state of internal honesty. It's who we are underneath these defense mechanisms we've constructed for our self-protection.* And when we dislodge these defenses, we find we are loving creatures who value connection.

The authentic self, or "true self," referenced in the definitions I shared, then, isn't our everyday self. In precluding our primal defenses, when authentic, we access our highest self, rather than a triggered self. In a study called "The True Self: A Psychological Concept Distinct from the Self," researchers Nina Strohminger, Joshua Knobe, and George Newman evaluated research to identify how people view the true self. They found that people see true selves, both their own and others', as moral and good. When someone develops positive traits, for example, it's experienced as discovering one's true nature. According to the authors, "Though we are perfectly willing to conceive of other people as bad, we are unwilling to see them as bad deep down." This glowing sense of the true self is present across cultures—in the US, Russia, Japan, Singapore, and Colombia, among others.

We see the true and the higher self merge in our favorite movies. At the end of *A Christmas Carol*, when moneybags Ebenezer Scrooge sheds his miserly ways and agrees to pay Tiny Tim's father so Tiny

---

* Some psychologists disagree with my definition of authenticity and propose that authenticity doesn't really exist. For more on this, see Roy F. Baumeister's article "Stalking the True Self Through the Jungles of Authenticity: Problems, Contradictions, Inconsistencies, Disturbing Findings—and a Possible Way Forward."

Tim can get treatment, we watch with hearts warmed, sensing that this benevolent man was the real Scrooge all along. The Grinch steals the town's Christmas presents. And yet when he sees the townspeople still celebrating because Christmas isn't about presents, his heart triples in size. He risks his life to stop a sled, bursting with gifts he stole, from bowling off a mountain and returns the presents to the bereft townspeople. While sharing a Christmas dinner, he reveals he didn't really hate Christmas. He just hated being alone and neglected. We are left with the sense that these villains need only to confront their scars for their core of goodness to be unleashed.

Maybe villains *are* more like us than we think. Maybe if we felt loved and accepted, we, like the Grinch, would all be our "real selves," and our masks would fall to the floor like crunchy leaves from an autumn tree. What if insecurities, baggage, and trauma inhibited not just the villains' better nature, but the rest of us normal folks' too? Do our insecurities impede our authentic and highest self?

How to Be Authentic

You're in a room, having just finished a quick computer task. The researchers instruct you to watch a woman, Liat, on the television. Liat is engaged in a study in the room next door. She must complete a series of gruesome tasks, a la *Fear Factor.* You watch her recoil while viewing images of people who have been severely maimed, dunk her hand in ice water and keep it there as it shivers, and pet a live rat. Now the researcher instructs her to rub a live tarantula. He takes the eight-eyed creature outside of its glass, its legs shaggy with wisps of hair. The researcher prods it, and it moves a few of its legs. There's no doubt it's alive. Liat moves her hand closer to it, then pulls back. "I can't go on. Maybe the other person can do it," she says. By "the other person," she's referring to you.

The experimenter leaves Liat's room and returns to yours. He gives you surveys that assess how much compassion and empathy you feel for Liat, as well as asking whether you'd be willing to take her place. He then asks you face-to-face too: "Are you willing to take Liat's place?" You'd have to replace Liat not just for tarantula petting, but for the tasks she has in store, one of which involves plopping your hand into a black bag crawling with cockroaches. What do you do?

If you're anything like the participants in that study, your response depends on the computer task you endured at the start of the experiment. While you were doing the task, you were subconsciously primed with words that appeared on the screen for just twenty milliseconds. The words were the names of a person: either someone you feel most secure with, who you turn to in times of need, someone you're close to, or an acquaintance. The purpose of the prime was to induce feelings of security (with the name of the person you turn to in times of need) and to examine the effects of inducing security on your empathy, compassion, and willingness to sacrifice.

A similar security prime was used by researcher Omri Gillath at the University of Kansas and his colleagues, to determine whether security is linked to authenticity. Instead of subconsciously priming people engaged in an unrelated computer task with the name of someone they feel secure with, they flashed the word "love" for twenty-two milliseconds (or the word "chair" in a neutral condition). After being primed with love, the participants reported higher rates of authenticity. The researchers also asked participants to recall a time when someone close to them was available, supportive, and loving, or in the neutral condition, a trip to the grocery store. Even consciously remembering a secure experience led them to report higher rates of authenticity.

I've argued that authenticity summons our kindest and highest self, which makes it a worthy goal for us as we seek to make and keep friends. Gillath's study suggests that security activates this authentic self. If security breeds authenticity and authenticity springs kindness, then is security the secret to being kind?

Yes.

When it comes to Liat, those primed with security reported more compassion and empathy for her and were even more willing to take her place. It turns out that we're not so different from Scrooge and the Grinch. Our caring too is impeded by insecurity. In Scott Barry Kaufman's book *Transcend,* he delves deep into Abraham Maslow's concept of "self-actualization," which is akin to how I define authenticity. "Maslow argued that the Being-Realm of existence (or B-realm, for short) is like replacing a clouded lens with a clear one. Instead of being driven by fears, anxieties, suspicions, and the constant need to make demands on reality, one is more accepting and loving of oneself and others," Kaufman wrote. The secret to authenticity, then, is security.

When we're insecure, we're often so consumed by our own pain that we lack the resources to care. Sarah, so overwhelmed by Hannah's grief, struggled to acknowledge Hannah's pain. If I sliced my index finger while chopping parsley and my neighbor came by to complain about her headache, I'd tell her I was too busy bleeding to listen.

Our behaviors in relationships often lie on a continuum, from those that protect us on one side and those that protect the relationship on the other. To protect ourselves from rejection or harm, we withdraw, devalue the relationship (*It wasn't so great anyway*), or act competitive or dominant, but in doing so, we injure the relationship.

To protect the relationship, we accommodate the other person's needs, do things for them, or affirm them, but in doing so, we are left more vulnerable to exploitation or rejection. When we're in self-protection mode, we're in anti-relationship mode. When we're in relationship mode, we're defenseless. Insecure people hover in "self-protection" mode, which is why they struggle in relationships. When triggered, they're thinking about themselves and not the other person.

Mario Mikulincer, who conducted the study with Liat, said, "Only when relief is attained and a sense of security is restored [when the bloody finger is bandaged] can many people easily direct attention and energy to caregiving. Only a relatively secure person can easily perceive others not only as sources of security and support but also as suffering human beings who have important needs and therefore deserve support." In other words, secure people, less consumed by their pain, are better at considering others.

Unlocking authenticity is about becoming more secure. And authentic people, in feeling this bedrock of security, unearth the empathy and consideration that lie within us all. Research, for example, links authenticity to less moral disengagement—the ability to act badly without feeling bad (it's not the real us anyway). Authenticity, then, will make us friends, because when we're not so burdened by fear of judgment, when we're secure, our naturally true and good selves emerge. Consider a study in which socially anxious participants were told *not* to engage in their usual safety behaviors— behaviors they engaged in to avoid rejection, like shutting up so they don't say something awkward, or the opposite, blabbing to evade an awkward silence. When they dropped these behaviors, the people they interacted with reported being more interested in interacting with them and becoming their friends. This was because without flailing to avoid rejection, the participants were more present; they talked more openly, showed more interest, and were more engaged.

With these many benefits of authenticity, it's no wonder why research has linked it to greater satisfaction in friendship and less loneliness. Still, many of us are attached to the misconception that we need to be someone else to be liked. This is the implicit message in the mega-bestseller *How to Win Friends and Influence People*. The author, Dale Carnegie, encourages us to ingratiate. Smile at people, use their name, get people to talk about themselves, make them feel important. This isn't bad advice per se, but it is manipulative. Instead of ingratiating, we must do the internal work of building security so warm behaviors flow from us naturally.

What Carnegie missed when he sold us ingratiation as a means to relationship building is not only that inauthenticity sabotages our friendships by eclipsing our natural shine, but also that there's a psychological toll of faking. As author James Baldwin puts it, masks are something we "fear we cannot live without and know we cannot live within." Inauthenticity is linked to depression and lower self-esteem. Other studies find that the effects of inauthenticity are more grave, leading us to feel immoral and impure. After the participants in that study wrote about a time when they acted inauthentically, they reported a stronger desire for cleaning products like toothpaste, Windex, and Lysol, as a way to cleanse. Suppressing who we are is labor (as we explored in the vulnerability chapter). As one of my clients described it, it's like "trying to keep a balloon underwater." Eventually, our true selves leak out and confuse our friends, who thought they knew us.

But don't we need to be inauthentic? you may wonder. Isn't that what "getting along" is all about? Isn't inauthenticity necessary for our relationships' success. If we're depressed and meeting new people, we need to pep up. If we don't like our friend's friend, we need to be civil. If we're on a ski trip with friends but get freaked out by the slope and want to hide in the lodge, we need to ski anyway, for our friends' sakes.

But I would retort that accommodating others is not inauthentic. Authenticity doesn't mean always doing what we want or expressing what we think or feel (that's rawness). It means we are responsive, rather than reactive, intentional rather than primal. It's choosing behaviors that express who we are rather than being triggered to act in ways that don't. Doing so requires us to give ourselves the space to decide whether we want to accommodate others or ourselves, depending on the circumstance.

For example, let's say our friend's kid got into an Ivy League school, whereas our kid was rejected. We feel jealous. Acting inauthentically means jerking into a defense mechanism to protect ourselves from our jealousy—like telling our friend Brown is the lowest tier among the Ivies. Authenticity may look like expressing our jealousy (*I really want to be happy for him, but I'm having trouble because I'm still grieving my own kid's rejection*) or it might mean recognizing that the need to be happy for our friend is a greater priority than our jealousy, so we still congratulate and celebrate. Authenticity is acting with intention in a way that balances others' needs and ours. We'll unpack this more later.

When we aren't controlled by our defenses, when we're responsive rather than reactive, we develop more flexibility to adjust to other people, which is why authenticity helps us care for ourselves and others. Accommodating doesn't feel inauthentic when we are in touch with ourselves, our feelings and needs, and why we accommodate. We're less accommodating when we're inauthentic, as one study found inauthenticity makes it harder for us to regulate our emotions, which subsequently makes it more difficult for us to accommodate others. It's when we accommodate others out of fear or mindlessness that inauthentic feelings creep in.

At our most authentic core, we are kind, loving, charming, and considerate. We don't need to be anyone but ourselves to make friends. But I acknowledge this isn't easy. When I've received the stale advice to "be yourself," I instantly forget how to stand. Do I usually cross my arms or let them dangle? Thank goodness for pockets. To figure out how to be authentic, I'll go beyond telling you to be yourself and reveal what this entails. To do so, we'll gather clues from Adamma Johnson, a woman who endured a series of tragedies that helped her figure out who she really was.

Embrace Mutuality

Adamma Johnson's best friend dumped her: Victoria, the woman she never tired of, who road tripped with her to Disney World and flew beside her to Vegas. Victoria, who shared her love for vintage clothing and also obsessed over the movie *The Worst Witch* as a kid. The two were so close that, as Adamma put it, "I wanted to crawl under her skin." But therein lay the problem. Victoria felt like Adamma was trespassing on her life. Victoria's friends became Adamma's friends, her church became Adamma's—even the parents she babysat for hired Adamma. Victoria needed space.

Victoria's history made her sensitive to feeling consumed by another person. Adamma and Victoria hadn't always been close; in fact, they once hated each other. They dated the same jackass, Dennis, who claimed the other was just his clingy friend. He'd invite both over to watch *Buffy the Vampire Slayer,* while each pretended the other didn't exist. He promised each that they'd be his one and only someday. They were young, vulnerable, and wanting to be loved, so they gave and gave and gave: their time, their love, their self-respect.

Eventually, Adamma got suspicious. Was Victoria really Dennis's friend? Then why was she always around? She instant messaged Victoria. When the two shared notes, they realized they'd both been played. Dennis recycled the same lies to each of them, about his whereabouts, his vision for a shared future, his platonic relationship with the other.

That shared trauma of Dennis was the start of an intense bond. In Adamma's words, "She was the only person who knew what it was like to be in that toxic relationship because she was in it too. I don't use the term 'trauma bond' lightly. We both could see how going through this was important and formative, in this terrible time of life between eighteen and twenty-two, when you're just trying to figure out who and how you're supposed to be. We both could understand what we experienced and how it felt to leave a toxic, unhealthy relationship and also miss it, and also yearn for it, and also be so devastated that you weren't the one picked."

It took years of the friendship existing at this rickety intensity for it to buckle. It was tough to hear that Victoria needed space, but Adamma took it surprisingly well. "I was just like, I hear you, I understand where this is coming from. And I want to honor what you're asking of me. I will give you some space," she said. There were moments when Adamma felt the urge to call Victoria, getting as far as picking up the phone, until she remembered.

Many of us in Adamma's position wouldn't take the news so well. Adamma's ability to perspective take, to value Victoria's needs, even when they reflected negatively on her, is admirable. This style of relating, characterized by zooming out to consider others' needs alongside our own, is called *mutuality*, and it is a telltale sign of ego strength, secure attachment, and, thus, authenticity. One study found, for example, that when handling conflict, authenticity is linked to greater mutuality. Another study found that when people reported on their most authentic moments, these moments were high in both independence and connectedness to others, which is aligned with how M. Scott Peck, author of *The Different Drum: Community Making and Peace*, defines "community," as a group of people "who have learned how to communicate honestly with each other, whose relationships go deeper than their masks of composure, and who have developed some significant commitment to 'rejoice together, mourn together,' and to 'delight in each other, and make others' conditions our own.'"

For secure people, mutuality comes naturally. But for the insecure and triggered, my advice for accessing this authentic way of relating is to—plot twist—restrain from indulging in what comes most naturally, because it is likely a *defense mechanism,* and authenticity is who we are without defense mechanisms. Defense mechanisms are strategies we use to reduce our awareness of and distance ourselves from something we find threatening.

For example, Adamma likely felt rejected by Victoria. If she was anxiously attached, instead of acknowledging this feeling, she'd likely engage in the defense mechanisms of blame ("You're the one who invited me into your life") or playing the victim ("How could you do this to me?"). If she was avoidantly attached, she'd pretend she didn't care ("Well, screw you, then."). These defense mechanisms would guard against uncomfortable feelings of rejection. Defense mechanisms are found in the friend who dismisses his friend's success so as to not feel insecure himself, or the friend who always has to choose where her friend group eats so as to not feel invisible, or a friend who dips out on a longtime friend instead of addressing an issue to avoid anxiety. When we're not being fair to friends, our defense mechanisms are likely at play. We hurt others to escape our feelings. Authenticity means acknowledging what's truly there, feeling the feeling underneath the defense mechanism, so the defense isn't necessary. It's acknowledging the reality of the threatening emotion instead of acting inauthentically to protect ourselves from it.

Defense mechanisms may feel authentic because they happen reflexively, but, as the definition suggests, they're a way to fog reality to escape a threatening feeling. We have pain that needs attending, but when we chose defense mechanisms instead of acknowledging this pain, we choose a behavior to deny, minimize, or project it. These defensive impulses are destructive for our relationships because they implore us to not only solely consider ourselves but also to control others so they can forget their needs and pander to ours too. They tell us to protect ourselves, which is often antithetical to protecting the relationship. It's what Sarah did with Hannah. If our finger is bleeding, we lack the resources to consider others. So, if we need to elbow our way to the ambulance, we'll do it.

Practice Mindfulness

During a work training exercise, I was asked one of the most revelatory questions of my life: *What's the most uncomfortable emotion for you to feel?* I said powerlessness. My mind then pinballed through the defenses I used to avoid powerlessness. I overworked and underrested to feel productive. I got more stressed out than I should have over an unexpected bill because it felt overwhelmingly within my power to prevent. This fear also corroded my friendships. When my friend told me she was depressed, instead of letting her feel sad, I jumped straight to asking if I could find her a therapist. I judged a friend who hated her job but didn't try to change it because it poked my sense of powerlessness.

The things I did to avoid powerlessness exhausted me. But I had other options. We all do. We can allow ourselves to *feel* the dreaded emotion, to tolerate it . . . and it will pass, I promise. We can shed defense mechanisms and be more authentic by using mindfulness to feel what our defenses spring in to protect. In one study, the researchers assessed people's authenticity and mindfulness. Weeks later, these people were interviewed regarding threatening situations they'd experienced, like a time they acted unethically or felt sexually undesirable. Independent evaluators assessed their response for defensiveness, looking for behaviors that help us avoid our uncomfortable feelings, like blaming the situation on someone else, being evasive, or minimizing. It turned out that the more authentic people were, the less defensive they were. The reason? Authentic people were more mindful.

Our next step to achieving authenticity is to be mindful, aware of the emotions that propel us to self-protect. Like a hunger craving, when we feel an emotion, we don't have to respond. We should pause, breathe, and drop down into our bodies to feel where the trigger manifests. Noticing what these emotions feel like in our bodies will sharpen self-awareness and allow for self-soothing. Mine feel like a hot flash. When I'm really triggered, it feels like a hole has been blown in my heart. When it continues, it feels like my heart is a circuit breaker, with someone snatching all the wires out. In breathing and locating the trigger in our body, we calm ourselves so we can respond rather than react.

Without mindful awareness, we coast on autopilot and surrender to our uncomfortable feeling, allowing it to provoke us to attack, blame, criticize, or otherwise defy mutuality. With self-awareness, we can watch our emotions happen without "acting out," or expressing repressed feelings through behaviors instead of feeling them.

As we discussed, when we act on our uncomfortable emotions, we tend to act selfishly rather than mutually because pain prioritizes our protection over our relationship's. For example, when Sarah fought with Hannah, she was triggered by Hannah's grief. Her inability to make Hannah feel better made her feel like a bad friend. Without awareness of her trigger, she let it take control, and she yelled at and insulted Hannah.

With self-awareness, we notice when we feel insecure so we can restrain from engaging in defense mechanisms to coddle our insecurity. We can then shift our attention from defensiveness to openness. As psychotherapist Mařenka Cerny shares, our goal is to bring ourselves to a state where "rather than attempting to change or control anyone's experience in any way, we are asking how much can I get to know and appreciate this experience of being [with] you in this very moment?"

Here are some common uncomfortable feelings, as well as the defense mechanisms we might use to protect ourselves from them:

- If we can't tolerate feeling inadequate, we may get defensive in conflict.
- If we can't tolerate our anger, we may act passive-aggressively or aggressively.
- If we can't tolerate rejection, we may violate friends' boundaries.
- If we can't tolerate anxiety, we may try to control our friends.
- If we can't tolerate guilt, we may overextend ourselves with friends.
- If we can't tolerate feeling flawed, we may fail to apologize when warranted, blame others, or tell people they're sensitive or dramatic when they have an issue with us.
- If we can't tolerate feeling insignificant, we may dominate others.
- If we can't tolerate sadness, we may avoid friends who need support.
- If we can't tolerate tension, we may withdraw from friends instead of addressing problems.
- If we can't tolerate feeling insecure, we may brag about ourselves while putting down our friends.
- If we can't tolerate feeling unliked, we may act like someone we're not.

Avoid Projection

Another way we may enable our defense mechanisms is through projection. Projection occurs when we assume our feelings mean something about the person who provoked them, rather than reflecting our own psyche. On a vacation with a close friend, I spend an hour organizing the toiletries while my friend hangs out on the balcony, gazing at the ocean. I feel overworked, so she must be lazy. Or my roommate tells me, "Please wash the dishes." I feel condescended to, so she must be condescending. Another friend leaves my party early because he needs to finish up some work. I feel disregarded, so he must be uncaring. Projection muddles our feelings with our evaluation of the other person. Avoiding it requires us to own our feelings instead of shaping them into character judgments.

So what do we do, instead, when we notice ourselves projecting? Mindfulness! Our treasured practice of pausing, breathing, and dropping down into our body to feel where the trigger is located. After we pause, we might realize that our friend isn't doing anything wrong by relaxing on the balcony, or that it's fair that our roommate asked us to wash the dishes since they washed them last time, or that our friend leaving early wasn't to slight us. After a pause, we can then evaluate our own needs alongside the needs of others, to see the bigger picture. Our ultimate goal, as Cerny puts it, is to "tolerate hearing the effects we have on others [and the effect they have on us] because, on a fundamental level, we are more interested in being in relationship than in controlling the other's experience or controlling the way we are viewed."

Some people may be afraid to release their defense mechanisms. If they're not defending themselves, they think they will be, well, defenseless. Then, they'll end up exploited. But releasing defense mechanisms is not about deferring to the person in front of you— that sort of behavior can *also* be a defense mechanism, a compensation for our fears that standing up for ourselves will lead to alienation. When we're authentic, we can still bring up issues, but when we do, we do so intentionally because we value ourselves, rather than snarling like a dog backed into a corner.

It's not just when we're triggered that staying present can unlock our authenticity. It's all the time. One of the tips that psychologist Ellen Hendriksen, author of *How to Be Yourself: Quiet Your Inner Critic and Rise Above Social Anxiety,* gives to clients to stave off social anxiety is to focus on the person in front of them. When we're self-conscious, we focus on ourselves: *Did I say the right thing? Do they notice my one curly chin hair? Does my breath reek of the low-carb keto sausage balls and onion cream cheese that I had for a midafternoon snack?* All this self-conscious chatter overwhelms our attention, making us appear awkward. If we can, instead, give our full attention to the other person, then our organic selves emerge.

Adamma helped us unlock our first steps to being authentic. Self-awareness, presence, pausing, and breathing and feeling the trigger in your body, focusing your attention on the unfolding moment: all of these are examples of how to use mindfulness to be your authentic instead of your triggered self. But even as we figure out who we are, underneath the defense mechanisms, there's still the possibility that others may reject us for it. To figure out what to do when that happens, let's return to Adamma's story.

Don't Take Rejection Personally

In a period of a few months, Adamma faced a series of deaths. Her grandfather passed away at the start of the year. Her high school boyfriend died. Her other grandfather suffered a massive heart attack and pulled through, but her father, who had colon cancer, didn't. He went to Palo Alto to see her brother, Timothy, graduate from Stanford, but he felt sick and rushed back to his doctor in St.

Louis before the ceremony began. He never made it out of the hospital.

In the aftermath of his death, Adamma's friends showed up and reached out to give support, but Adamma preferred solitude. She prayed, meditated, and journaled. She reflected deeply on what she wanted out of life, which now seemed more fragile and ephemeral than it ever had. She thought about Victoria and about Dennis, the way she had clung to those relationships, even though they ultimately crumbled. She thought about her father and how she had taken for granted that he would forever be on earth.

And out of this, she realized that there needed to be a way to survive, as her relationships came and went like the moon. "I consciously made the decision that I am not going to let my relationship with people prevent me from living for myself," she said. "Relationships sever, and that has to be okay. If I can come out of this death and be full and capable, there's no relationship loss that I can't survive." With so many relationships ending in ways that had nothing to do with her, she came to see loss not as a condemnation of her but as an inevitable part of life.

This resilience, this ability to look loss in the face and still be whole, fuels Adamma's authenticity. Her experiences with Victoria, Dennis, and her father showed her she could balance being close to others with keeping a healthy distance so that her identity wasn't dependent on how they related to her. This is the epitome of security. The anxiously attached come in too close, their sense of themselves crushed when others don't accept them. Avoidants pull away too far, unaffected by others' judgments but also by their love. Tapping into security and authenticity doesn't mean you'll never be rejected; it just means there's enough distance between your self-worth and others' judgments so that it won't sting so bad. Authenticity, then, isn't about avoiding rejection. It's about lightening its weight.

Adamma's experience reveals another reason why authenticity nourishes friendship. It allows us to withstand the inevitable nicks that happen when we're intimate with others. Issues in friendship don't lead to destruction like they did between Sarah and Hannah. When others' actions don't feel like our undoing, we find grace for them, which Adamma practices. As she has gotten older and people have peeled off to marry and have kids, her friends don't reach out as often. In her words, "I definitely don't count absence as rejection. I just think that that is a natural occurrence. A lot of the friendships in my life right now have certainly evolved over time, and I just want to hold them loosely enough to allow that to happen and not let that mar the friendship as a whole."

Adamma showed us how authenticity makes us resilient, buying us enough room between our self-worth and other people's judgments that we don't have to succumb to them. In a series of studies, researchers Francesca Gino at Harvard University and Maryam Kouchaki at Northwestern University confirmed the link between authenticity and resilience. In one study, a group of participants was told to recall a time when they were authentic, while another group recalled a neutral event. All participants were then asked to empathize with someone going through a breakup. Those who recalled an authentic experience reported feeling less rejected after. In another study, participants were told to wear a wristband for a sports team they either supported or disliked, to make them feel authentic or inauthentic, respectively. They were then involved in a cyberball task, designed to make them feel rejected. It's virtual catch where no one throws you the ball. The study found that when people were more authentic—that is, when the apparel they were wearing represented their true affiliations—they felt less rejected. Their authenticity even altered their perception. When authentic, they estimated that they got thrown the ball more. In a final study, when employees were told to think of a time when they felt authentic at work (as opposed to thinking about something neutral), they reported feeling less excluded and rejected at work.

This research reveals that when we're authentic, rejection isn't as piercing. Adamma's insights reveal that we can achieve this resilience by decoupling rejection from its baggage of self-condemnation. Don't take it personally. When our friend brings up an issue, when we invite a new friend out and they turn us down, when we haven't heard from a friend in a while, it doesn't mean that we're unworthy, wrong, or unlovable. As Adamma puts it, "I don't take a lot of things personally. I take people's opinions or critiques or feedback as valid, so I can do something about it, but I try hard not to let that make me feel bad about myself."

Another way to achieve resilience is to retain the optimism of the secure, embracing that a moment of rejection doesn't foreshadow a lifetime of it. Studies find that authenticity, like security, is correlated with optimism. Optimism makes us resilient because, as author Rebecca Solnit shared, "To hope is to give yourself to the future—and that commitment to the future is what makes the present inhabitable." We must view rejection as something we can recover from, an instant rather than an eternity. For Adamma, that means, "I just believe that my relationships will survive and can withstand a little bit of turbulence. I believe that everything will be all right in the end. I am a tragically optimistic person."

People are going to reject us. We can crook ourselves into a pretzel to avoid it, but it'll happen anyway. We can wear a mask, but it'll happen anyway. And then we will have labored in inauthenticity for nothing. If instead of focusing our energy on an impossibility— avoiding rejection through inauthenticity—we focus our energy on softening rejection's bitterness, then we can access authenticity alongside connection. We can even reframe rejection as a symbol of pride, a collateral for us making every effort to curate the life and the relationships we truly want. It's a ticket to a life lived without regret.

We've learned the keys to unlocking authenticity. We've explored how self-awareness can help us parse whether we're reacting or responding, as well as how to take rejection with aplomb by seeing it as impersonal and temporary. Yet this is only a piece of the puzzle. Achieving authenticity is not just about who we are; it's also about how the world responds to us.

Being "Authentic" in an Unequal World

In a perfect world, we would all be loved in our most authentic form, but in the real world, privilege plays into whose authentic self is welcomed and whose is rejected. When people from disadvantaged groups act as their true selves, their behaviors are often misinterpreted through the filter of devaluing stereotypes. Research finds, for example, that students in training to be teachers (a large majority of whom are White) are generally more likely to accurately interpret White students' expressions and are more likely to misinterpret anger in the neutral face of a Black student compared with a White one—four times as likely, in fact. The study also found that Black children were viewed as more hostile when engaging in the same behaviors as White children. In another study, participants rated Arabs as less fully human, or more ape-like, than the average American. A meta-analysis found that women who assert their ideas, make direct requests, and advocate for themselves are liked less. Privilege is the latitude to be your authentic self, and to have people receive you that way, rather than through the caricature of stereotypes. Privilege means access to authenticity.

In being seen as threatening when authentic, people from

disadvantaged groups often feel pressure to act inauthentically to file down these misperceptions. A colleague of mine, Aubrey, a Black male, smiles so often, his mouth throbs. "I smile all the time to try to disarm people," Aubrey told me. A study of Black college students found that they code switched (altered their language to escape stereotypes) so they wouldn't come off as a "stupid Black kid." One participant shared: "I never wanna be seen as the angry black woman. So if I'm upset at a student during a group project, I would not be like, *Damn, like, get it together,* as I would with people of color. I'd be like, *Okay well, Sam or Emma, do you guys think that this is a better way of doing it?,* approaching in a more gentle manner so I don't fit the stereotypes."

"Burdened virtues" is a term sociologist Lisa Tessman developed for traits that allow one to resist oppression but at personal cost. Code switching is an example, and its costs are akin to those of inauthenticity. Participants in the study described it as "active" and "tiring" and like "putting on a mask." The researchers labeled code switching as *sociolinguistic labor,* "the physical, emotional, and psychological effort put into deploying sociolinguistic resources in a way that is meant to satisfy others." Chandra Arthur, founder of the Friendish app, discussed the effects of code switching in her TEDx Talk: "The cost of code switching is immense, as it causes minorities to spend time worrying about cultural compatibility, rather than dwelling on things that do matter."

As laborious as assimilating is, it works, often opening up people from privileged groups to being less judgmental of people from disadvantaged groups. Research finds, for example, that White participants evaluated a Black person who assimilated into White norms—by, for example, straightening their hair or altering their names—more favorably. One White participant reported, "Her name La'Keisha sounds obviously 'black' and some may even think 'ghetto,' but Renee is more conservative." Women who dressed provocatively were less likely to be objectified when they were pictured winning a swim competition or solving a math problem. Another study found that when Black men were depicted wearing formal clothing, rather than showing swagger (via sweatpants and sweatshirts) through their outfits, they were viewed as more intelligent, trustworthy, and warm. In contrast, Asian people who don't assimilate and retain accents are viewed as lower-status, less appealing and intelligent, and more insecure.

In building friendships across privilege, people from disadvantaged groups often face a dilemma—to be themselves and be misjudged, or to censor themselves and be more accepted. Some solve this dilemma by choosing to find spaces where they can belong as they are, among others from their group. When I asked Adamma whether she had White friends, after a long pause, she named one White woman who grew up around Black people and had a Black husband.

"I don't need to take accountability for someone perceiving my natural tone as threatening," Adamma shared. For her, having to act inauthentically to get along is too great a price. "Just by showing up, there's all these assumptions that will color the friendship that you didn't actively bring to the party. They're just projected onto your body. And there's nothing you can do about that."

We all deserve friendships where we can show up as our rich, true, textured selves. But too often, the privilege of authenticity is afforded to groups that have the most power. It's why our boss sends us blank emails at 3:00 a.m. with the entire message written in the subject line, and yet, when we respond, we reread our emails seven times, opening with a *Dear* and ending with a *Sincerely,* or rather a *Best* or perhaps a *With appreciation.* In his book *Give and Take,* Adam Grant writes, "As people gain power, they feel large and in charge: less constrained and freer to express their natural tendencies."

As Adamma's story reveals, people may eject from friendship

across lines of privilege because they are rejected, or even punished, when being their true selves. In Adamma's words, "I look for ease. My desire is to be in spaces where I just have to show up, and I don't have to perform or practice and say this is how I'm going to be when I get there. I don't have to accommodate myself for people's misconceptions."

Building Friendship Across Differences

I have a friend I met while studying in Haiti whom I'll call Paula. Paula is a White woman and a race scholar. Often when I have befriended White people, I have downplayed my experiences as a person of color because I worry I won't be understood. But because Paula studied race, I was honest. I shared with her when I thought my colleagues were employing racial tropes when evaluating students. I told her when I was yelled at by a man in a pickup truck for wearing my Haitian flag as a cape. She listened to me complain about the time when a White lady accused me and a Black friend of breaking into our White friend's apartment when we came by for a visit.

In other words, I practiced some of the three V's around Paula. The three V's comprise components of healthy and intimate relationships across levels of privilege: vet, vulnerability, and voice. Vetting involves choosing friends who believe in the worth and dignity of the disadvantaged group you identify with; vulnerability involves bringing your full self to the friendship, which includes freely expressing your experiences related to being a member of a disadvantaged group; and voicing involves expressing concerns related to your group as they arise in friendship.

I vetted Paula and even practiced vulnerability around her. I shared experiences with her I felt tempted to censor from other White people. She shared her vicarious rage and made me feel like she could truly understand how awful these things felt. But in other moments, I realized, as interracial friends Aminatou Sow and Ann Friedman report in their memoir, *Big Friendship,* there are "unbridgeable gaps in even the closest of interracial friendships."

One summer day, in a lovely apartment in Harlem, I gathered with Paula and her gaggle of quirky intellectual friends. It was her graduation party. These friends, like Paula, spoke all types of languages and referenced Marxism in conversation as often as other millennials might reference Beyoncé. With mostly everyone in the room having or pursuing a PhD we started to talk about the tribulations of academia. That was when Paula disclosed that I was in fact a "professor and diversity hire" who was leaving my institution.

I resented her insinuating I was hired solely because I am not White. It wasn't just that, though. Her words triggered many other experiences I had when I was assumed to be unintelligent and unworthy, my achievements chalked up to handouts rather than accomplishments. She brought me back to the moment in high school when I shared with my White friend that I got into Cornell, and he responded, "You got in? Where's my acceptance letter, then? Where's mine?" It brought me back to the moment in middle school when my English teacher told me I shouldn't get my hopes up of getting into the highly selective high school I applied to and eventually enrolled in, because "only really smart people" got in. It sent me to that moment at a faculty party, held in another professor's backyard, when someone brought up that our department lacked diversity and the host said, "We need to focus on applicants who are qualified."

What people with privilege may not realize—when they get confused that a friend from a disadvantaged group is triggered by a passing comment—is that prejudice feels appallingly cumulative. Each instance of it invokes the weight of every instance of prejudice experienced in the past. When voicing concerns, people from disadvantaged groups contend not just with an instance of prejudice, but what it represents about how they've been treated their whole lives, what it says about their larger value in the world in which we live.

I did address the comment with Paula. I remember fearing a backlash—that she'd counter that my suggesting that she did something racist was worse than my receiving the racism. *Is this even worth it?* I wondered. I talked about it with my romantic partner at the time, who suggested I bring it up because clearly I couldn't let it go. I wanted to swallow it, both for Paula's feelings and my own, since I'd likely get even more upset if this didn't go well. But also, I realized that bringing this up was in the service of our friendship, a way to shovel out muck between us. As Sow and Friedman put it, "Interracial intimacy is the only context in which 'broken windows' theory is actually relevant: any visible signs of crime encourage further crime! You have to call it out or it will erode your relationship."

As politely as I possibly could, I said, "Hey, Paula. I know you didn't mean this, but when you introduced me to your friends, you called me a 'professor and diversity hire.' That hurt because it's something I've heard before and I have worked really hard to get to this point." Paula had apparently been oblivious to saying this, but she said sorry, admitted to being wrong, and appreciated that I brought it up.

My experience demonstrates that bringing up pain points around identity in friendship isn't a way to attack, beat down, or reduce the friendship. It's a way to save it. It creates space for healing and, hopefully, precludes the problem from happening again. When these issues aren't brought up, they crust and rankle and begin to crack the friendship. That's why voice is so important. Voice has helped Paula and me remain close.

Following the three V's is not easy, but doing so is necessary for people from disadvantaged groups to be fully authentic in their friendships with more privileged people. And committing to friendship across levels of privilege isn't just about committing to engaging in the three V's for a moment; prejudice will inevitably flare up again over time.

Experiences like these reveal our collective misconceptions about authenticity. "Stop caring what people think," others might tell us, as well-intentioned advice to help us unlock our true selves. But this advice denies our deep humanity, a humanity that is concerned with others' judgments and criticisms. We cannot simply achieve authenticity by being calloused against others. That's avoidance. Authenticity implicates both the actor and their surroundings. When we become more secure, we build up some armor to criticism, but sometimes bullets penetrate armor. We can also choose to stay out of the gun range. That's why authenticity isn't just about becoming secure; it's about placing ourselves in spaces that nurture our security, places we vet, where we voice our concerns and practice vulnerability. This is easier for some than for others.

Adjusting Mutuality

People with privilege can also work to welcome the authenticity of their friends from disadvantaged groups. Up to now, we've discussed the importance of mutuality in friendship, considering not just friends' needs, or our own, but both people's. But in friendship across differences in privilege, we face a snag. Our friendship is no blank slate; the zeitgeist shapes power dynamics between friends. If one friend is more privileged, then the power dynamic of the friendship is inherently tilted, through no effort of either party. One person inherently feels freer to express their perspective. One person has allotted much more time to understanding the life experience of the other. One person is inherently more triggered when prejudiced comments spring up. And they're more preoccupied with them afterward. Because subjugated groups consistently have to take the perspective of the privileged group to function, but not vice versa, mutuality that doesn't correct for power dynamics is inherently non-mutual. So, we need *adjusted* mutuality instead.

So how is adjusted mutuality achieved? Emile Bruneau, a professor at the University of Pennsylvania who studied peace and conflict between groups, argued, "If one group is silenced the rest of the time, perhaps they should be given greater status when the groups come together, a chance to be heard by the more powerful side. Instead of perspective taking, they might benefit from perspective giving." In his study, he had Mexican Americans and White people share short essays about hardships facing their groups. After reading about and summarizing each other's hardships, White participants felt better about Mexican Americans, whereas Mexican Americans felt worse about White people. Mexican Americans felt better about White people only when a White person listened to and summarized their stories of hardship. A similar pattern of results was true for Palestinians sharing with Israelis. Jamil Zaki, a Stanford professor and empathy researcher, argued, "Contact worked best when it reversed the existing power structure rather than ignored it." Bruneau's research suggests that simply making friends from disadvantaged groups *feel heard* when they express issues is vital. Instead of disagreeing, counterattacking, playing devil's advocate, or justifying our actions, we can listen to and repeat back what they say.

What does adjusted mutuality look like in practice? Catarina Rivera, a disability public speaker and diversity, equity, and inclusion consultant, who has progressive vision loss and is hard of hearing, argued with her friend Rita. Rita accused Catarina of ignoring her and the rest of their friends and disappearing whenever they went out dancing. But what actually happened was, because of her disabilities, Catarina was getting lost. The dance floor was dark and noisy and she couldn't see her friends, "So when somebody has stopped dancing with me I stand there and I'm looking around because I've been twirling and I'm disoriented. I'm trying to find the group, but then the next song begins. It's easier to keep dancing."

Rita's judgments about Catarina were based on ableist assumptions. She needed to perspective take more, ask questions rather than assume the worst. Instead of relying on her version of reality, which was limited because she is non-disabled, she might have asked questions that invited Catarina to share her experience: "Hey, Catarina. I notice sometimes we lose you on the dance floor. I was wondering what might be going on for you when that happens?"

To achieve adjusted mutuality, we must compensate for an inequitable status quo. When disagreements arise related to race, ability, gender identity, sexual orientation, or any identity group divided on axes of privilege, the more privileged friend must listen and empathize *more* to achieve true mutuality, because in the words of Black feminist scholar Kimberlé Crenshaw, "Treating different things the same can generate as much an inequality as treating the same things differently."

When Is It Most Authentic to Say Goodbye?

I often get asked: At what point is it most authentic to dump our privileged friends if they seem oppressive? I typically hear two trains of thought in response. Some assume it's a duty for people from disadvantaged groups to endure friendship with their more privileged counterparts. "It's not worth ending the friendship. If only you could be the bigger person and get over it," they argue, as if exposing yourself to pain marks maturity. People who push these points are unaware of how brutal it can be to stay connected to someone whose words, sometimes even well-intentioned, ultimately convey that they see you as lesser.

Then others won't accept anything less than excommunicating friends who say something problematic. They've been so hurt when they've tried to build relationships with people more privileged than themselves that telling them to make friends across differences feels like the emotional equivalent of telling them to fling themselves in front of a speeding Ferrari.

What I've landed on when people ask me whether we should make or keep more privileged friends who do something harmful is that we should step back and weigh the larger pros and cons of the friendship to determine whether to maintain it. Instead of *always* embracing or avoiding these friends, we should be discerning: assessing what we personally gain and lose from the friendship and determining whether the friendship is overall doing more harm than good (because all friendships should do more good than harm). It will be a different calculus when deciding whether to dump a friend who says something problematic when we have known and loved them since childhood, versus when a new acquaintance does.

This weighing process is subjective and requires us to know ourselves, our values, our triggers, and our needs. For some, even a single instance of prejudice will always eclipse any friendship benefits. For Adamma, for example, the con of having to be inauthentic in order to be friends with White people is too great a price. For others, having to adjust to friends across differences might be worth it if their privileged friends are great listeners, or share a unique interest they can't express elsewhere, like painting mini-figurines or foraging for fungi. When it comes to deciding whether to maintain friends across differences, we need to know ourselves, our desires, capacity, and values, to make the right choice for us.

This discernment process became real to me when I became a professor and I experienced an onslaught of racism. A friend from college, whom I'll call Rob, became a professor at a prestigious university and suffered through the same. When we commiserated, I shared that I was thinking about leaving my job. He shared that he'd thought he'd stay. "You grew up in New York City and you were surrounded by people of different races, and White people who wouldn't act *blatantly* racist. I grew up Black in Germany. People would call me all types of slurs. This is something I've seen before," he told me. He's still at his university, and I'm gone from mine. It wasn't worth it for me to stay, but it was for him.

The decision of whether to maintain friends across differences will involve a different calculus during moments when we feel particularly triggered by racism, sexism, homophobia, ableism, or other isms. After the #MeToo movement, the attack at Pulse nightclub in Orlando, the increasingly publicized murders of Black people at the hands of the police, and attacks on Asian people during the COVID-19 pandemic, people from disadvantaged groups may feel particularly wary of being friends with people from privileged groups. This is normal. In theories of identity development, people from stigmatized groups who experience an episode of oppression hibernate among people from their group in order to feel safe. They need time to recuperate before potentially exposing themselves to more harm when they're at their most vulnerable. It doesn't mean they'll never be friends with people from privileged groups again, but they may need time to honor this need for self-protection, just like when we pause to recover after injury.

In chapter 1, I discussed research on how making friends across race is the most scientifically backed method we've uncovered to dismantle prejudice. Reading this research makes me want to cheer—go for it! Make friends with everyone! Be the change! But I can't cheerlead this message when I realize its implications: the most vulnerable among us must consistently potentially expose themselves to pain. Instead, I think there are some who, because of their unique histories, strengths, and weaknesses, will find themselves at the front lines, making friends with people who only ever saw someone like them on television. There are others of us who, because of our histories, would crumble if we did so. Not all of us have to be on the front lines. An authentic decision means honoring our capacity to make friends across differences in privilege and how this capacity evolves.

The following are questions for reflection for people from disadvantaged groups making friends across differences:

- In what ways do I benefit from this friendship?
- In what ways does this friendship harm me?
- Is there something I can do to make this friendship less harmful (e.g., have a difficult conversation, see this friend less often)? Do I want to do that?
- Do I view the benefits of the friendship as outweighing the harm?

Finding True Authenticity

A few months after Sarah and Hannah's dysfunctional road trip, Sarah approached Hannah while she was cleaning out her Tupperware in the office sink. Hannah saw Sarah enter the kitchen and turned away, suddenly absorbed by the distraction of the suds. "Hannah?" Sarah said. Hannah felt her body heat up and then chill. "Yes?" she said, now the curt one in the friendship.

"I've been doing some thinking, and I now know there's a way to share my needs without attacking. I'm sorry, and I hope we can move forward." Hannah kept scrubbing, not sure what to say, before finally mumbling an "Okay. Thanks," and exiting the kitchen.

Sarah and Hannah's interactions are now confined to the offhand social media comment. Sarah looks back and sees how the ordeal was her misguided attempt at intimacy, a desire to build a relationship based on raw honesty.

Like Sarah, I used to think authenticity was about rawness, boldly sharing whatever is on your mind. But now I see that it's about listening, listening to yourself, not being afraid to experience what's going on inside you, to acknowledge what you truly think and feel and fear and love, without covering it up with defenses. It's not just about having the bravery to admit your opinions to others, but in having the bravery to admit them within. It's only in this listening that we can sense which friends feel most safe for our authenticity and share our truest internal world. Because when we do this internal work, we don't ask others to do it for us. We don't dominate, control, bash, deflect, ignore, ghost, discriminate, or otherwise mistreat because we need them to relieve us from whatever discomfort is warbling inside. And with what's left, we can love others more deeply, cherish them in their truest form, and find friendship.

TAKEAWAYS

- ► Authenticity is a state of presence we access when we aren't hijacked by threat. It's who we are underneath our defense mechanisms.

- ► Authenticity nurtures friendship because humans are social beings, which means when we're authentic, we unleash our nature of empathy and compassion.

- ► To be more authentic in threatening situations, restrain from indulging in what comes reflexively, because it is likely a defense mechanism. Be mindful and aware of the triggers that propel you to self-protect without indulging them. Pause and breathe. Shift your attention from defensiveness to openness. Access your higher self.

► To stave off social anxiety that impedes authenticity, focus on the person in front of you instead of yourself.

► Don't take negative events in friendship to mean something bad about you. Decouple rejection from self-condemnation. To achieve this, keep a healthy distance from others so your identity isn't dependent on how they see you.

► View rejection as something you can bounce back from, an instant rather than an eternity.

► For people from disadvantaged groups to achieve authentic friendships across levels of privilege, practice the three V's:
  ▪ Vet friends so as to befriend only people who believe in the worth and dignity of your identity group.
  ▪ Be vulnerable by bringing your full self to the friendship, which includes freely expressing your experiences related to your identity group.
  ▪ Voice any concerns related to your identity group.

► People with privilege can welcome the authenticity of their friends from disadvantaged groups by practicing *adjusted* mutuality: recognizing they need to compensate for the inherent power dynamic within their friendship by actively taking their friend's perspective. Instead of disagreeing, counterattacking, playing devil's advocate, or justifying, listen more, repeat back what your friend says, and ask questions rather than make assumptions.

► People from disadvantaged groups deciding whether to maintain a friendship with a more privileged person who acts in problematic ways should ask themselves:

- *In what ways do I benefit from this friendship?*
- *In what ways does this friendship harm me?*
- *Is there something I can do to make this friendship less harmful (e.g., have a difficult conversation, see this friend less often)? Do I want to do that?*
- *Do I view the benefits of the friendship as outweighing the harm?*

CHAPTER 6

Harmonizing with Anger

How to Take the Chaos Out of Conflict

In a course in graduate school, my classmates and I took a questionnaire called the Minnesota Multiphasic Personality Inventory. Because we'd eventually administer it to our therapy clients, we took it ourselves first to better understand it. It's quite extensive: 567 questions, demanding over an hour to complete. Your answers suggest what mental malady you're suffering from: hypochondria, depression, psychopathy, etc. It's sophisticated, with questions embedded to detect if you fake it. So I didn't fake it.

When I got my results, I was relieved to find that I wasn't suffering from most of the issues the questionnaire assessed for, except one. The results told me I suppressed my anger. I was surprised it assessed for this. To me, suppressing anger seemed more like a strength than a problem. What's the point of anger? Angry people yell, curse, throw things, and harm people. Anger suppression was protecting my relationships, I concluded.

And I'm not the only one to think so. According to American essayist Ralph Waldo Emerson, "For every minute you remain angry, you give up sixty seconds of peace of mind." And in the words of Roman emperor Marcus Aurelius: "How much more grievous are the consequences of anger than the cause of it." More graphically, American author Mark Twain once said, "Anger is an acid that can do more harm to the vessel in which it is stored than to anything on which it is poured." The message is clear: Anger is bad. Avoid it at all costs.

When I met with Alejandro he further proved my point. Alejandro didn't seem like an angry person at first. He was quite charming. He told me how he dazzled in interviews, left every job he ever had with lifelong friends, and taught his daughter charisma like other parents teach their kids to share. He's the kind of person who jokes with you like he knows you, until finally he does. He smiles often, listens well, and once he likes you, he'll invite you to happy hour and dinner the very same day. And you'll go.

As an immigrant to the US from Peru, Alejandro had a savviness in connecting that was part talent and part survival strategy. His family first moved from Peru to a farm town in Texas before moving to a high-crime neighborhood in Houston. As a seven-year-old in Houston, he'd bawl every time he went to school. His big sister stayed with him until he calmed down. The family later moved up north to Manassas, Virginia, where he watched his older siblings achieve renown—his sister for her smarts, his brother for his athleticism. Eventually, he found his place as the social butterfly. Every day at lunch, he sat with a different group of people, transcending race by springing from the Black kids' table to the White kids', and then hopscotching between the jocks and the nerds.

Alejandro's only stumbling block when it came to friendship was his anger. But the issue was serious. "I'll feel it coming, and then it takes over. It's almost like I'm not in control," he reported. Alejandro could be downright vicious when he was angry, zeroing in to knead his friends' greatest insecurities. Once, he confronted a friend he'd perceived as "putting [him] down" when Alejandro announced a promotion he'd received at work. The friend refused to acknowledge the slight, and the conversation escalated until Alejandro was ready to say something cruel about his friend's kid. Luckily, the friend stopped the conversation, realizing it was careening down the wrong path. Another time, a childhood friend was supposed to accompany him to see his favorite deejay. When the friend bailed last minute with no excuse other than "I don't feel like it," Alejandro texted him, "You're a dick and you're dead to me." They didn't talk for three years.

In the research world, lashing out is called "anger out," and suppressing anger is called "anger in." Alejandro and I seemed to be on opposite ends of this anger spectrum, but the two strategies have more in common than it seems. They easily evolve into each other. Anger held in too long can gush out. Researchers theorize that each strategy likely increases resentment, making us brew in our anger, which might explain why they are each correlated with hostility, depression, and anxiety. They also each harm our relationships, scholars argue, because these anger strategies keep us from productively addressing the underlying issues that drive anger and impede intimacy.

As an anger-in, it may *seem* as if I have more control over my anger than Alejandro. But by suppressing my anger, I was controlled. When something made me angry, my reflex was to stuff it down, over-mmhmm, nod vigorously, concede a point I didn't agree with. It's those lousy defense mechanisms. When I was upset, instead of communicating, I'd offer a plastered smile, my upset fearful of upsetting another with itself. These behaviors overtook me, like cursing or screaming overtook Alejandro. I wasn't controlled by the expression of anger but by the negation of it.

Here's our dilemma. Alejandro's story (and Sarah and Hannah's story in the authenticity chapter) reveal that aggression doesn't work. My experience reveals that repression doesn't either. If anger harms us when it balls itself into a rage, as well as when it lulls itself into silence, then what should we do with it? How can we best get the need met that's nestled within our anger? And is there a way to express anger that doesn't harm our friendships or ourselves?

Anger Can Strengthen Friendships

In *Attachment and Loss,* the father of attachment theory, John Bowlby, describes two toddlers, Laura and Reggie. Each of them experienced an episode of abandonment, but they reacted in strikingly different ways. Laura, a two-year-old, went to the hospital for a minor operation. Her hospital stay was recorded on video, including an instance when she called out for her mother, who wasn't there. After she returned home, Laura watched the video with her mother. While watching, she turned to her mother and said, "Where was you, Mummy? Where was you?" Two-year-old Reggie was an orphan, raised by a chain of nurses, most recently a nurse named Mary-Ann. After Mary-Ann departed for weeks to get married, Reggie said to her upon her return, "My very own Mary-Ann! But I don't like her."

Bowlby uses Laura and Reggie to illustrate two types of anger: anger of hope and anger of despair, respectively. Anger of hope energizes us, indicating that we need to heal an issue wedged between us to be close again. It is less of an overpowering emotion and more of a signal that something needs to change. It primes us to reflect on what our unmet needs are and how to act to fulfill them. It admits that we care for the other, even while we're upset, and thus preserves the inherent worth of the other. We don't punish or blame, but instead reveal our unmet need and ask for change, just like Laura did when she said, "Where was you, Mummy? Where was you?"

Anger of despair, however, occurs when we have lost hope of healing a relationship. It confuses conflict with combat and sets out to defend, offend, punish, destroy, or incite revenge. Whereas anger of hope drives a pause for reflection on deeper needs and values, anger of despair blindly impinges. It's impulsive, highlighting, according to researchers, "insufficiently processed emotions." Anger of despair masquerades as protecting the self but is also about damning the other, just like Reggie did when he said, "I don't like her."

Anger of despair is the destructive force we typically associate with anger. Anger of hope, however, is a healing force that can deepen friendships, one that we should embrace. Psychoanalyst Virginia Goldner distinguishes between two types of safety in relationships: "the flaccid safety of permanent coziness," which is maintained by ignoring anger and conflict and pretending problems don't exist, and the "dynamic safety whose robustness is established via . . . risk-taking and its resolution—the never-ending cycle of breakdown and repair, separation and reunion." Dynamic safety, Goldner suggests, invites trust and fosters true intimacy. Anger of hope can bring dynamic safety to our friendships.

Research also reveals the benefits of expressing anger of hope. One study found that when a betrayal occurred, confronting the perpetrator in an open, non-blaming way *deepened* the relationship. People who are good at conflict (e.g., by listening, admitting fault, de-escalating, and taking the other person's perspective), another study found, were more popular and less depressed and lonely. Their roommates saw them as more socially competent, and their friends were more satisfied with their friendship. A study with romantic couples found that addressing an issue, rather than forgiving and forgetting, benefited the relationship and made resolution more likely, whereas minimizing the problem, while comfortable in the moment, did not incite change. James Averill, an emeritus psychology professor at the University of Massachusetts Amherst who studies anger, said, "When you look at everyday episodes of anger as opposed to more dramatic ones, the results are usually positive." His and other studies have found that expressing anger is more likely to benefit a relationship than destroy it.

In a 2005 study, conducted by Dr. Catherine A. Sanderson and her colleagues at Amherst College, researchers sought to examine how people who value intimate friendships work through conflict. Do they stay silent, or do they discuss their issues? She gave a survey to college students that assessed how much they valued intimacy in friendships, how they handled conflict, and how happy they were with their friendships. Results indicated that these kinds of friends voice their concerns constructively instead of avoiding issues or simply ending the relationship, which led to their friendships being more satisfying.

These studies suggest that anger of hope is something we should embrace, as it allows us to illuminate each other on how to be better for each other, forever enhancing a friendship. Sharing anger conveys that we're trustworthy enough to be up front and invested enough to confront. Conflict with friends can restore and even deepen our friendships. So why do we avoid it?

To Break Up or Open Up?

When it comes to friendship, most of us hold in anger and anger's siblings: upset, annoyance, frustration, rage. Studies suggest that people are more likely to avoid problems with friends than with romantic partners. Compared to romantic relationships, we see friendship as lighthearted, so when issues arise, we figure we don't have the right to our anger, hurt, or expectations. Underpinning these assumptions is the idea that friendship is trivial. As Dr. Skyler Jackson, whom we met in the vulnerability chapter, put it, "Many people think, *Oh, it's a friend, it doesn't matter.* Who gets in fights with your friends? But I feel very able to be hurt by friends, and not because things are super egregious—just because friendships are just another type of relationship."

In friendship too we can choose to confront issues instead of letting them fester until they're beyond repair. The problem is we too often dismiss gripes with friends, hoping we'll get over them instead. We think we're too sensitive or making a hubbub out of nothing. But the only litmus test for whether an issue is worthy of being addressed is if it continues to bother you. You can tell a friend you're upset about anything—their being chronically late, or mispronouncing your name, or making an offhand comment. There are no objective criteria for whether something is worth bringing up aside from that it upsets you.

Your friends may be happier to hear about your issue than you think. While we slurped noodles on my porch, my friend Ginnie lamented friendships that deteriorated without any direct conversation. In her marriage, she was used to problems arising and nipping them in the bud with her husband. They both even subscribed to the weekly newsletter from the famous couples' therapists John and Julie Gottman and used language like "You're not attuned to me," or "I was making a bid for connection and you didn't realize." As Ginnie put it, "There are a lot of stories society tells us about marriage being hard and full of conflict. Are there any stories about friendship being hard and full of conflict? No. We hear friends are supposed to make you feel good, to lift you up. So when we're mad at each other, we don't know how to handle it."

If friends are angry at us, often they express it indirectly, through distancing. Lydia Denworth's friend tried to break up with her by unsubscribing from her newsletter—and Lydia is a friendship expert! One of my friends only realized a friend was canceling her when the friend created a second Instagram account and blocked her from it. Other times, instead of backing away altogether, our anger leads us to demote our friend. They were once the first person we texted to share good news, but some mysterious problem occurred, and now we pipe a stilted "Hello. How are you?" at the yearly

Friendsgiving while we ogle the corn bread and scoop the cranberry sauce. According to Dr. Jackson, in friendship, we too often choose to "endure a lifelong ache rather than getting surgery, dealing with four weeks of recovery, and moving on, being happier, and getting your life back. You can deal with the hard part, but we instead let the friendship droop for the rest of our lives." To be clear, ignoring our upset isn't always bad. If it's a passing issue, we can let it go. When it's chronic, or we can't get over it, or when the friendship starts to droop, then we must face the problem.

Still, sometimes breaking up makes more sense than opening up. Conflict is a way to address problems to maintain friendships, and not all friendships should be maintained. With people who love you, it's good to work through, forgive, and give the benefit of the doubt, but with people who don't, it's not. No behavior is universally good. We must understand the relationship to know how to act within it.

Before we decide to work through conflict, we should assess whether a friendship is healthy. There's no reason to cling to malicious friends. Deborah, whom I interviewed, is a divorcée who frequently slept over at her new boyfriend's house. Her friend Mel, who was religiously devout, gathered their mutual friends to convince them to shun Deborah for tainting the community's morals by sleeping over at her boyfriend's. Considering Mel's disregard for her, Deborah was better off dropping the friendship. Other red flags are when a friend isn't rooting for our success. One friend gets a new job and instead of celebrating, the other says, "Wow! I hope you do better than you did at the last one." A friend may also be self-centered. They expect us to drive two hours in traffic to see them, but they won't drive to come to see us on our birthday. We may feel exhausted after talking to them, perhaps because they never showed any interest in us, or we fear their judgment if we share. Overall, our friendships should make us feel more good than bad. Problems arise in any friendship, but if we step back to take stock of the larger dynamic and realize it's more harmful than helpful, then we may need to end instead of mend.

However, when problems arise in an otherwise great friendship—one in which the other person has our best interests, considers our needs, and generally treats us well—then, as Priya Parker, author of *The Art of Gathering,* put it, "Connection is threatened as much by unhealthy peace as it is by unhealthy conflict." We need to express our anger, because after socking it away for too long, we may awake with the powerful urge to leave even the best of friendships. If we had allowed ourselves anger earlier, we'd have noticed the junctures where we could have acted so it wouldn't have come to this. If we had allowed our anger, we would experience an opening to repair and recalibrate the friendship and it could achieve new depths of dynamic safety. When we suppress our anger, we don't tend to the problem until it's doomed, leaving the cancer cells to metastasize and spread through the friendship's body.

I can speak to this process firsthand. My best friend Billy had committed a series of small offenses—I thought she forgot to respond when I asked her for feedback on a critical document, she agreed on my behalf that we'd show up for a friend's dinner I couldn't attend, and she yelled at me for putting too much pressure on her while we played Jenga. It sounds silly now, but at the time, I was upset. I noticed I wasn't reaching out to her as much, and when she reached out, I was less responsive. I thought I was helping the friendship by trying to get over these problems on my own. But as I watched myself withdraw, I realized how treating my anger with passivity was destructive for both of us.

Jeff Simpson, a professor at the University of Minnesota who has studied attachment and conflict, recommends that when problems arise with friends, we should "think about what a friend brings to our life that no one else does." This reflection challenges our tendency to trivialize friendship. It makes us realize what we stand to lose, which will help us face problems with friends instead of peacing out. With Billy, what I stood to lose was insurmountable. Billy is as vital to me as my kidneys. She makes me feel more understood than nearly anyone else. She's the person I call to share what's really going on. Because of her quiet empathy and wisdom, I've become more of myself. It was bonkers for me to sacrifice this relationship because of my accumulated grudges.

As an anger-in, here was my pickle, though: I knew by ignoring conflict, I was harming the friendship, but I wasn't sure addressing it would help either. If I lounged on Freud's couch and he asked me to reveal my unconscious associations with conflict, I'd say attacks, accusations, raised voices, fists clenched, burst arteries, Monopoly games toppled. Anger and conflict, based on what I knew at the time, destroyed rather than cured.

I agonized over whether I should talk to Billy, discussed it with Ginnie, and role-played the argument at a professional development session at work. Then, I finally texted Billy to mention we should talk. She said she was nervous. I said I was too. It calmed me to hear her say that since nervousness isn't aggressive; it's vulnerable, and vulnerability triumphing over aggression was what I prayed for in the conversation. I expressed what I was upset about. She apologized. She started crying. She wasn't upset. She was touched. Never before had conflict felt so loving for her. Me neither. We both mentioned that we felt closer than ever.

My experience with Billy taught me that there are some things we don't get over unless we talk about them and that acknowledging anger can lead to a conversation that allows for the release of the residue of past hurts that haunt our otherwise beloved friendship. Anger can spur positive change in our friendships, but only if we know how to use it.

How to Communicate Anger in Our Friendships

Our ability to offer anger of hope depends on our attachment style. Insecure people struggle with anger of despair. People have failed them in the past, so they enter conflict in survival mode. Their go-to conflict tactics—aggression or withdrawal—damage relationships, studies find. They fail to see their friend's perspective, zeroing in on how they've been wronged rather than how they've wronged. In *Why Won't You Apologize?*, Harriet Lerner discusses flying in to attend her friend Sheila's book launch. Harriet spent the launch sitting in the corner to catch up with an old colleague. Later, Sheila was furious at Harriet for not mingling because, unbeknownst to Harriet, many attendees wanted to meet her, a renowned author. Sheila demanded an apology, refusing to acknowledge that she never communicated her expectations or that Harriet flew across the country to attend. She called Harriet "self-absorbed" and "reprehensible," signifying that Sheila's priority was to blame and punish Harriet rather than repair the relationship. Her words also suggest that she assumed Harriet, rather than being oblivious, had malicious intent, which is an assumption insecure people make.

Insecure people become overwhelmed by emotion during conflict because they confuse it with combat instead of reconciliation. They approach conflict reactively, moving in whatever direction their frazzled emotions tell them (although avoidant people are less aware that this is happening). If they feel angry, they yell. If they feel threatened, they shut down. They also try to *win* at conflict, to get their needs met at the expense of the other person. Dr. Paula Pietromonaco, a psychology professor emerita at the University of Massachusetts Amherst who studies relationship dynamics, told me, "We live in a very individualistic, a very competitive, society. We bring that to our relationships so arguments become about winning, but that is not good in the long run for a friendship. A focus on winning is a red flag."

Secure people are collaborative, approaching conflict as a way to get both parties' needs met. They don't yell or blame but instead acknowledge their anger as signaling a need and voice the *need* conveyed by the emotion. Dr. Simpson told me secure people "put aside their negative feelings and think about what they need to do to solve the problem and move the relationship forward. They think more broadly about where they want to end up in the long term, what they want to achieve, how they want the relationship to be better at the end of the conflict."

If Sheila approached the conflict securely, she may have realized that her goal was to express her hurt to repair her friendship with Harriet and that attacking wasn't the best strategy. As Harriet Lerner says, when we over-accuse, we make it difficult for the offending party to offer the apology we seek. She would have, instead, relied on beneficial conflict resolution tactics of the secure, which include sharing feelings and needs without blaming, assuming the other has positive intent, taking their perspective, and admitting one's role in the problem. Sheila might have said, "Hey. I realize part of this is my fault because I didn't communicate this [admitting fault], but I was hurt that you didn't interact with others more at the book launch [non-blaming expression of feelings]. I know you probably didn't realize I wanted this [assuming positive intent], and I appreciate that you flew across the country to attend [perspective taking], but I would have loved it if you got to know other people there [non-blaming expression of need]."

"Secure people make insecure people look good during conflict," Dr. Simpson told me. They engage in co-regulation, where they soothe not only their own feelings but also those of the other party. We already learned how to manage our triggers in the authenticity chapter, but conflict requires us to take things one step further and manage our friend's. When secure people sense the other person escalating, they de-escalate. For some of us, especially those of us with trauma histories, this will seem impossible. Trauma makes it exponentially tougher to manage our triggers, forget about another person's. It may be more of a long-term goal to embrace co-regulation rather than something we can enact immediately, and that's okay.

Even while co-regulating, secure people don't back down from their needs. They don't apologize for something they shouldn't, as anxious people might. If a friend says, "You're being too sensitive," they might say, "No. This is important to me." They advocate for themselves, while also considering the other's perspective. They embrace mutuality, asking themselves, *If we are a team, and both our needs are equally important, how do we solve this problem in a way that honors both our needs?*

Calm Your Feelings

To succeed at conflict, you'll have to share your perspective while taking on the other person's. If you're too angry, you'll fail at this. Take some time to calm your emotions. Self-compassion helps. Label your feelings, validate them (*It's okay that I feel this way*), and acknowledge that everyone feels the way you do sometimes. Tell a trusted third party who will let you vent. Meditate. Don't tell yourself you're too sensitive or that the way you feel is wrong. Your anger is important because it indicates you need change, so honor it by feeling it.

Once your emotions simmer and you're ready to broach the issue, remind yourself to be collaborative rather than adversarial. You're not creating problems in the friendship by talking about them because whatever hurts you hurts your friendship because you're a participant in it. You're opening up dialogue, then, to address your hurt, but also to make the friendship better.

Before you approach your friend, you should ask yourself these questions:

1. What do I hope to achieve through this conflict?
2. What's my role in this problem, and what's my friend's?
3. Do I see the conflict as a way to make the friendship better?
4. Can I calmly approach my friend?
5. Am I ready to balance sharing my perspective with taking my friend's?

Prime Your Friend for Constructive Conflict

Text your friend to set a time to talk through the issue in person, so they'll be emotionally prepared. Set the right tone by signaling that you're bringing up an issue because you're invested in the friendship. Here are some useful opening lines.

- "Our friendship means so much to me, which is why I want to talk openly about something on my mind so we can work through it. And I'd like to get your thoughts too."
- "I love our friendship, and I want to make sure I bring up some things that have weighed on me so none of it affects our friendship."

Share Your World

When you meet up with your friend, share your feelings, but don't criticize or blame your friend. When sharing your concerns, replace "You are . . ." with "I felt . . ." Focus on how your friend's behavior impacted you, rather than blaming them. On Brené Brown's podcast *Unlocking Us,* she described blame as coping with discomfort by

185

transferring it to someone else. How much you desire to cause pain is proportional to how much you are *in* pain. Let your thirst for revenge clue you in to what you need to attend to in your own life. And once you figure out what's bothering you, share it. Sharing your world is also more likely to incite change in your friend. As Brown reminds us, when we instead label someone as a "bad friend" or "toxic," we simultaneously tell them we want them to change but they can't because their transgression fundamentally defines them.

- Instead of saying, "You're ungrateful. Every Friday, I pick up your daughter from soccer practice, and never once do you say thank you," say, "I feel upset when I pick your daughter up from soccer and you don't say thank you. It'd mean a whole lot if you did."

- Instead of saying, "It is awful that you missed my son's bar mitzvah. I thought you were a better friend than that," say, "I felt so hurt that you didn't come to Archie's bar mitzvah. It would have meant so much to me to have you there."

Ask for Your Friend's Perspective

After you share your side, ask, "What was going on for you at that time?" Understanding your friend's perspective isn't a way to weaken your stance or allow your friend to weasel their way out of accountability. It allows for mutual understanding, and we take things less personally when we understand how broader factors impact our friend's behavior. You might realize, for example, that your friend missed Archie's bar mitzvah because they broke their tibia.

Your friend might also reveal ways your behavior contributed to the problem. Be open to this. Owning your part doesn't minimize your concerns or make the issue your fault. It acknowledges multiple truths—that you can be upset by a problem *and* unknowingly add to it. Relationships (sans abusive ones) are often a dance—no one person is to blame, but each person's behavior ricochets off each other's until a larger problem materializes. If you think their rebuttal is fair, take accountability and apologize. If it's unfair, then don't.

For example, when a friend declined to help me out when I was in a bind, I told her I felt unsupported. I said something like, "I know you're great at providing emotional support, but maybe tangible support isn't your thing." The conflict escalated. Later, I revisited the conflict. She said she resented that I took a single instance to make a broader assumption about how she shows up as a friend. I thought she had a point, so I apologized.

Soothe Your Triggers

It's normal to get triggered during conflict. As we learned in the authenticity chapter, if you ignore your triggers, they'll control you, and you'll lash out or get defensive. Instead, during the conflict, you need to constantly monitor and soothe them so they don't assume control. You can use the same strategies we learned in the authenticity chapter: pause, breathe, feel the uncomfortable feeling beneath the trigger, and locate where the trigger manifests in your body.

One additional way to self-soothe involves picturing yourself splitting into two selves during conflict, one to experience yourself and the other to observe yourself. You can experience your urge to fight and observe it and wonder if your boxing gloves are helpful. You may feel the urge to get defensive or lash out, but realizing this won't solve the issue, you choose an approach that will. You can't neglect the urge either, though, because it contains a message—that there is something inside you that you need to protect. You acknowledge the anger in the cockpit, respond to it over the inter-com, while your highest self pilots the plane.

As you soothe yourself, you'll be better able to de-escalate.

De-escalate

Conflict is hard, especially in friendship, where people aren't used to it. You can do everything right, but your friend might still be on their anger of despair energy. Their past experiences lead them to assume you're attacking them, even if you've stated otherwise. Your goal is to heal the friendship, but their defensiveness isn't helping. But you're a team here, so where one person lacks, the other steps up. You need to be strategic and de-escalate, because your goal isn't to win. It's to resolve. Here are a few options:

- Put the conflict in front of you instead of between you. If your friend is getting defensive, they see you as their ad-versary. Either they win or you do. Remind them that you're in this together by stating your perspective and theirs and by asking what can be done to satisfy both of you. Include ample "we" or "our" statements: "So I felt up-set when you said that after I lost my well-paying job, I needed to swallow my pride and sign up for minimum-wage work. You said you were trying to be helpful. How can we communicate better so that we agree on what's helpful?"

- Admit when they have a point. Conflict escalates when we ignore what we agree on and zero in on where we dis-agree. Don't apologize for something you're not sorry for, but look for the tiny shred of truth that you can acknowl-edge within your friend's defensiveness. What is some small nugget you can take ownership of? "I told you it hurts my feelings when I talk about my divorce and you tell me it's time for me to get over it. You told me that I talk about it too much and it drains you. And I realized I can be better about reaching out to different friends for support instead of putting all the pressure on you."

- Ask questions. When our friend gets defensive, instead of drilling our point until they listen, pause and ask about their perspective. For example, if after telling our friend we feel angry when they're chronically late, they say, "Here I am trying to take care of three kids *and* make time to see you and you don't appreciate any of it," we can respond, "Okay, I hear you are overwhelmed. Tell me more about what's going on for you that makes it hard to show up."

- Take a break. If you or your friend is wound up, neither of you has the capacity to take each other's perspective, so ask to take a break: "Hey. I know it's hard to work through problems. Why don't we take a break and talk about this later, when we've cooled down?"

Ask for the Behavior You Want to See in the Future

Sometimes, venting your concerns and receiving an apology mends the problem. But other times, the conflict stems from a chronic issue you'd like to address. If so, be sure to ask for the behavior you want to see in the future.

- "In the future, I'd appreciate it if, instead of distancing yourself, you could bring up any issues you have in our friendship."

- "Next time be explicit about when something is important to you, and I'll make sure to show up."

How to Receive Your Friend's Anger

We've learned how to communicate our anger. But what about when we're on the receiving end of a friend's anger? How do we respond in a way that will enhance rather than harm the friendship? Njambi's story provides a cautionary tale.

It had been five years since Njambi and Makenna's friendship ended, but Njambi still broke down when she saw photos of Makenna on Instagram. Makenna shared pictures of her and her friends on trips, eating out, or meeting one another's babies, all things Njambi and Makenna once planned to do together. Friendship breakups can be especially isolating because there's no space to breathe through the grief. As we minimize the significance of friends, we minimize the grief of losing them. But for Njambi, the loss was devastating: "I realized that soul mates aren't always romantic. Makenna was my soul mate."

The two had met through a mutual friend in Kenya, where they were both from. They each immigrated to the US for college. Njambi attended a university in Arkansas, and Makenna one in Texas. When Njambi arrived, Makenna called to welcome her. They became each other's lifelines as they struggled to adjust to the frustrations of living in the US, like daylight saving and the dreaded imperial system. By the end of Njambi's first month stateside, they were talking every day.

In the summer before Makenna's senior year, Njambi moved in with her in Texas. The two became inseparable, often barging into each other's room with fresh gossip and life updates. Every day was their slumber party. This ease was especially important to Njambi, a self-described overthinker who was often tortured by social inter-action. She would replay her faux pas in her head for days, some-times months. But with Makenna, she felt unconditionally loved, and her self-consciousness evaporated. "I knew when I said some-thing off the wall, she'd charge it to my mouth instead of my heart," she said.

The two would also frequently discuss their relationship woes. Makenna had been dating her boyfriend for a few years and was antsy for him to propose. The next spring, he reached out to Njambi to ask about Makenna's ring size. Njambi was excited for Makenna but, as her best friend, expected to be alerted of the exact date when the proposal would occur.

One weekend, Makenna went to Washington DC for a trip with her boyfriend. When Makenna returned, she was engaged. Njambi was offended she wasn't told beforehand, even if perhaps this anger was misplaced (one could argue she should have been ticked off at Makenna's boyfriend rather than at Makenna. But anger, like love, isn't always rational). When Makenna returned from her engage-ment trip, Njambi expressed her anger by locking herself in her room without muttering so much as a "Congratulations." For Makenna, Njambi prioritizing herself over Makenna's joy was inex-cusable.

Makenna could have told Njambi how hurt she was, how much she needed Njambi to feel happy for her. But she didn't. She shut her out instead, hibernating in her room and scurrying out of the apart-ment before Njambi returned from work. They lived together for an-other eight months, avoiding each other the whole way.

It may appear as if Njambi's botched response to the engagement destroyed their friendship. But there was something more niggling that happened before the event in question that teetered the friend-ship onto its doomed trajectory. Njambi was a blunt, sometimes crass person. When Makenna once asked her how her outfit looked, Njambi replied, "Did you get dressed in the dark?" When Makenna got her eyebrows threaded, Njambi remarked, "Looks like you drew them on with a pencil." When Makenna received these responses, she'd say she was hurt and then go quiet, and her shoulders would sag. Njambi would justify herself, saying, "I'm an honest person. This is how I am."

Not only were Njambi's words harmful, but her response to Makenna's upset over them was even more damaging. The response convinced Makenna that if she addressed problems, she'd be dismissed. This assumption was slow poison for the friendship, as it meant the two could never resolve problems, that they'd only fester and bloat. The memory of this response assured Makenna that when new problems arose, she had only two options: endure or walk away. She chose to endure until she had to walk away. Once their lease ended, so did their friendship.

In healthy relationships, we desire to fulfill one another's needs. When one friend has a problem, the other tries to adapt to alleviate it (in the generosity chapter, we'll learn to do this without losing ourselves). A response like "This is how I am" not only dismisses friends' needs but also foretells their needs will never be met—as long as we are who we are.

Still, it's normal for our reflex to be to respond as Njambi did: to deny we did anything wrong, or even tell our friend how they are wrong for being upset: *You are asking too much, You think you're so perfect, You've done the same thing!* But, as we learned in the authenticity chapter, we have to be mindful instead of primal to avoid these responses, because they harm not only the friendship but also ourselves.

If we get defensive during conflict, we also miss out on an opportunity for enlightenment. Conflict is one of the only times we get honest feedback about ourselves. Without it, we obliviously cause harm. Most people silently back away when we do, leaving us to repeat our offending behavior in a carousel of self-sabotage. We're left in a déjà vu, with a sense that friends keep leaving, while the reasons remain fuzzy. When someone tells us how we impact them, they help us escape the carousel. Eventually, Njambi became friends with another woman who went through an awful friendship breakup. When the two dissected what went wrong in their friendships, her friend told her that her honesty with Makenna didn't have to hurt. Njambi is no longer a blunt person.

If we view a friend's feedback not as a putdown but as an enlightenment opportunity, we can respond to their concern by appreciating their feedback, taking responsibility, and growing. Practically, this looks like being responsive when our friend is upset. Many studies find that responsiveness improves relationships. It has three parts: showing understanding (rephrasing what our friend said back to them), validation (telling them their concern is valid and understandable), and care (sharing what we will do to improve). Here are some examples:

- "I hear that you are sad that I was so late to your birthday because I'm a really important friend in your life [understanding]. I get why you feel that way, and it's even nice to know how important I am to you [validation]. Next time, I'm going to try harder to show up on time, especially for times when it's important [care]."

- "You felt left out in the cold when you asked me to pick up some medicine for you and I didn't make time for it [understanding]. It makes sense that that felt isolating for you [validation]. I realize this is important, and next time I'll try harder to help [care]."

- "So you felt uncomfortable when I spent so much time talking to your wife at the party [understanding]. I understand why you might feel that way, and I'd probably feel that way too [validation]. Maybe next time, we can stick to talking in a group [care]."

You don't have to agree with your friend's feelings to be responsive. You might think they're totally off base in reading into your conversation with their wife at the party. But you never said you agreed; you said you understood. You said that their feelings are legitimate, not that you feel the same way. Agreeing isn't necessary for responsiveness. Your friend's views and feelings are important, whether you agree or not. Njambi eventually learned this lesson. Initially, she thought Makenna was being too sensitive in response to her bluntness since Njambi wouldn't have cared if Makenna communicated like she did, but then she realized "that I have to treat people how they want to be treated and not how I want to be treated, because we're not the same. So, if I'm friends with somebody and they want this thing of me and it's not over the top, then why not do it?"

To be responsive, don't offer care you can't give. You may feel the urge to play all-star friend and give in to whatever your friend asks: "Yes, I will fly to Marrakesh to visit you when you start your new job while my wife gives birth to our third child." Jeff Simpson recommends that instead we "figure out what drives their need and propose a concrete plan that fulfills their need in a way that is reasonable to you." So if your friend wants to call you every day on your lunch break, care might look like "I get that you feel alone at work at lunch. How about I give you a call on Wednesdays?"

Being responsive requires us to normalize screwing up. Just because you've *done* wrong doesn't mean you *are* wrong as a person. If you fuse your mistakes with your worth, then you'll never admit fault. Doing so will feel too much like throwing yourself in the garbage. To blunder is human. When one of my colleagues erred multiple times in a day, missing meetings and deadlines, she described herself as having a "human day." We all have human days.

"It sounds like a lot of work," a friend told me when I shared these tips for healthy conflict. "Like all of a sudden I have to be a conflict mediator even when I'm upset?" When you're used to being brutally honest, being deliberate sounds exhausting. And it is. Let's disabuse ourselves of the notion that conflict should be easy. Our relationships are the most important aspects of our lives. They deserve our painstaking effort, our highest selves.

We'll still probably screw up, though. I often do, even though I know the steps to do it right. It's one thing to understand how to have conflict intellectually and another to say the right thing when you are having conflict-induced hot flashes. Still, we can all get better at conflict if we try. The more we do it, the easier it gets. And in the long run, it's much less work than finding new friends. As Alejandro reflected on the falling-out with his friend over the deejay event, he said, "That was a three-year hiatus with that friend. Who knows all the fun things we could have done, the memories we could have had in that period, that we never will?"

Salvaging the Friendship

I want to be honest and acknowledge that conflict can be a shit show, even when we do it well. I've heard many stories of destructive conflict among friends. One person asked her friend to stop gossiping about their mutual friend, to which the friend responded, "You're not so great yourself." Another person told his friend he didn't want to talk about his recent date because said friend gets jealous. "I always used to talk to my therapist about how great and supportive you are, and now I know that's not true," the friend responded. One person confronted his friend for sharing something said in confidence. The response? "I don't give a fuck." While the research we've sifted through signals that conflict can save and deepen friendship, it won't always. It's a risk.

So what happens when conflict fails? Should the friendship end? Not necessarily. Sometimes the failure means the conflict needs revisiting. That's what Ginnie told me when I divulged that a conflict with a friend went badly and I had felt awkward around the friend since. She told me maybe the conflict wasn't over and encouraged me to reach out to this friend again. She was right. The sign that a conflict is over isn't that you've spoken about it once. It's that you've reached some sort of mutual understanding and resolution, and each party no longer harbors resentment, which may take a few go-arounds.

While I understand this all intellectually, when Ginnie gave me the advice to revisit the conflict, I bristled. *Are you really telling me to hurl myself back into the fire when I still feel burned?* It seemed absurd, but I had to admit that the logic behind her words made sense. If it was still awkward, the conflict wasn't over. I reached out to my friend and said, "Hey! I have felt things have been a bit off since we had conflict. I value your friendship and would love to get things back on track. I wanted to open up the conversation to see if there's any more air we can clear." The revisiting went better, in part because I approached it better. I was more ready to listen, and apologize, and show gratitude for what my friend did right.

Let's say you revisit the conflict and it still blisters into hostility. What then? Before you divorce your friend, I want you to consider something. We have this sense that people's truest selves are revealed during conflict. When endings are explosive, we rewrite the friendship, see it as perpetually defunct, our friend as treacherous all along, ourselves as naïve parties. This tendency is driven by a negativity bias, our tendency to weigh negative information more heavily than positive. I caution against this because, building off what I shared in the authenticity chapter, our truest selves are not revealed during conflict. Often our most triggered selves are.

To counteract the negativity bias, we need to rehumanize our friend after bungled conflict, to consider them more broadly rather than filing them down to whatever appendage of them materialized in conflict. We can remember what Oprah Winfrey and Bruce Perry remind us of in their book, *What Happened to You?*, that regulation is a privilege since dysregulation often comes from trauma. Thinking of regulation this way helps me to have more compassion for myself and my friends when conflict escalates.

Before cutting ties, zoom out to consider the larger dynamic of the friendship, the good and the bad. Perhaps the botched conflict reflects a larger dynamic of a friend being shoddy, in which case you have my full permission to machete the connection. But perhaps not. And if not, there might be something worth salvaging.

Salvaging a friendship means rejecting absolutes. It requires us to consider the degree to which we want a friend in our lives, rather than *if* we want them in it at all. It disabuses us of the polarized options of ending or enduring the friendship. It acknowledges there are gray areas of closeness that might fit better. Salvaging is reflected in the words of author Cheryl Strayed: "The answer to most problems is more often than not outside of the right-wrong binary that we tend to cling to when we're angry or scared or in pain. We are a complicated people. Our lives do not play out in absolutes."

If our friend is radioactive during conflict, we might resign ourselves to the fact that the friendship won't plunge into the dynamic safety that accompanies honest communication. But there are lower rungs of intimacy that may be apropos. Not every friend has to be a best friend. Maybe we expect less from them, share less of ourselves, and compartmentalize the friendship to what feels most fulfilling about it. "Sometimes the best way to manage a relationship is to have less of it," Jeff Simpson told me. I've coined the term "low-dose friend" to acknowledge that, like medicine, some friends are wonderful at a certain dose, though at high doses, they make us queasy. Distance isn't always bad for friendship; with certain friends, it can actually save it.

Even if the conflict didn't bring you the intimacy and healing you dreamed of, you still did right. Sleep easy knowing you acted within your integrity, instead of ghosting or gossiping, and that you can access the personal growth that comes with tough conversation, no matter how your friend responded.

Finding Catharsis

As we've learned throughout this chapter, the purpose of anger is to drive reflection, to sharpen our sense of our needs. If we can confess our anger instead of suppressing it, it'll convey vital information that reveals how we define fair treatment. And if conflict escalates, perhaps it tells us something about our triggers or our friends'. Perhaps we better understand our expectations and how they can be honored. Perhaps we reflect on what was missing to access something surer about what we want from friends to come. Then, no matter what happens during conflict, we gain a clearer picture of ourselves.

Reflecting on the need beneath our anger and expressing it strategically does not necessarily produce the catharsis we associate with anger. You won't hear shrieking or see food flinging or walls pummeled or pillows battered. You may not climax to what researchers call the "anger orgasm." But anger of hope can still bring us catharsis if we reframe what that means. The most common translation of the ancient Greek word for catharsis is "purgation," but another translation is "education." Catharsis doesn't have to be found by unleashing what's bad. It can be reached by adding what's good.

TAKEAWAYS

► Conflict is normal in friendship. We should bring up issues with close friends instead of distancing ourselves. To get yourself to do so, think about what the friendship brings you that no other relationship does.

► Some friendships aren't worth our conflict. To decide whether to end or mend a friendship, take a step back and think about the broader pros and cons of the friendship. Evaluate whether it's more helpful or harmful overall.

► To do conflict well:
  - Soothe your feelings.
  - Prime for constructive conflict by expressing how much you value the friendship and how this leads you to work through problems.
  - Share your world using the stem "I feel . . ." Don't blame your friend.
  - Ask for your friend's perspective.
  - Soothe your triggers:
    - Pause and breathe.
    - Split into two selves so you can observe yourself wanting to counterattack and choose to de-escalate instead.
  - De-escalate as needed by:
    - Putting the conflict in front of you instead of between you.
    - Admitting fault.
    - Asking questions.
    - Taking a break.
  - Ask for the behavior you want to see in the future.

- Respond to your friends' concerns with:
  - Understanding: rephrasing what your friend said back to them
  - Validation: telling them their concern is valid and understandable
  - Care: sharing what you will do to improve. Make sure you commit to something you will follow through with.

- To get better at admitting fault, unglue your mistakes from your self-worth, see screwing up as normal and inevitable, and recognize that feedback is an opportunity for enlightenment on how to be a better friend.

- If conflict ends badly:
  - Consider revisiting the issue. The sign that a conflict is over isn't that you've spoken about it once. It's that you've reached a mutual understanding and resolution, and no one harbors resentment, which may take a few go-arounds.
  - Before cutting ties, zoom out to consider the larger dynamic of the friendship, the good and the bad. If the conflict reflects a larger harmful dynamic, consider cutting ties.
    - If the friendship is great, aside from the instance of conflict, salvage the friendship by considering the degree to which you want a friend in your life, rather than *if* you want them in it at all.
  - Remember that even if conflict goes wrong, you did right by acting with integrity.

CHAPTER 7

Offering Generosity

How to Give to Your Friends
Without Losing Yourself

Melody's mother worked for the UN, so she grew up in Nepal, Morocco, France, and a smorgasbord of other countries. Her best friend was an American whose parents immigrated to Nepal for the Peace Corps and never left. A self-described third-culture kid, her wardrobe was styled with trinkets from her travels: a Moroccan leather satchel here, a beaded Cambodian top there. In her college essay, she wrote about how travel raised her, turning her into the eclectic, open-minded citizen that any college would love to have croon about epistemology in one of its seminars. It was effective in unexpected ways. Her top-choice college offered her the opportunity to spend her freshman year in Florence, Italy. Thrilled, she said yes. She pictured herself galivanting through Europe, learning how to say things like "Can I have some pizza?" in Italian and making some of the best friends of her life.

She arrived at her Florence campus on a steamy August day. It was peppered with olive trees and steeped in marble. There were gussied, flowery, outdoor areas to hang out in. A huge hill separated the dorms from the classrooms, affording students the opportunity to soak up the Tuscan sun each day. Stick-thin trees with oval-shaped treetops flanked the main classroom building. It was idyllic, exactly what she had dreamed of . . . until she met her roommates.

Her roommates were all wealthy, attractive women who could double as Lululemon models. They were more interested in the boys in the room next door than they were in her. Every night, they would blast music and welcome the boys over for parties, as Melody struggled to sleep. Melody is Laotian, and her roommates were White. One of them told a story about their cousin's roommate, a Korean woman, who smeared poop on the wall in the shape of a cross. "I think she did it because she's Christian and Korean," her roommate commented. "But you're not that kind of Asian," she said, peering at Melody.

"What exactly does smearing poop on the wall have to do with being Asian?" Melody asked.

Things continued to deteriorate. Her roommates and the boys next door started a fight club in her room. Every few nights or so, they would box one another, spewing blood on her sheets. At another one of their parties, someone spilled water on her laptop. When she brought this up, her roommate said, "Well, you shouldn't have left your laptop on your desk."

Melody, a people pleaser, handled the mistreatment by becoming kinder. She entered her freshman year with a reasonable idea about friendship: if you are nice, people will like you. So, as her roommates and the boys bullied and neglected her, Melody was giving. When the boys were hungry, she'd offer to make them paninis with fresh prosciutto and mozzarella. She'd help them with their homework, invite them to comedy shows she put on with friends, offer them croissants she hoarded from the cafeteria. She tried to make peace, to (metaphorically) extend one of those olive branches from the campus grounds.

None of it worked. The boxing matches in Melody's room continued, as did the rude comments and general neglect. If generosity is good for friendships, then why did it fail? You catch more flies with honey than you do with vinegar, as they say, but Melody was making honey and winning no flies. As we'll find in this chapter, generosity is complicated. It can make us friends, but it can also reopen our wounds, turn us sour, or overwhelm us. It can feel like an expression of love, or one of desperation, like it did for Melody. It can bring us closer to others, but it can dissolve us in the process. It is different from many of our other friendship skills, because it's especially finite. The more we give, the less we have left. It's love on a seesaw. And to handle its schism, we have to work with generosity's contours: to learn when, how, and whom to do it with, so we can make friends without losing ourselves.

The Benefits of Generosity for Friendship

Generosity is giving to others without expectation of anything in return. We can give material objects—gift cards, dinner dates, Swedish meatballs from IKEA—or our time and attention—by, for example, showing up at a friend's mom's funeral, babysitting their kids, or helping them move.

According to a flurry of studies, Melody wasn't wrong when she assumed generosity nurtured friendship. It does. The investment company Motley Fool conducted a survey with over one thousand Americans that found that generous people have closer relationships, more friends, and more support during difficult times. Other studies find that generous kids are more liked and accepted by their peers. Researchers found that best-friendless fifth graders were more likely to gain a best friend by sixth grade when they became more prosocial, or helpful and caring.

Being generous is also the key to maintaining friendships. One study tracked 2,803 high schoolers over time and found that prosocial people were most likely to maintain a high number of friends over time and experienced the greatest well-being. Participants who received help from a confederate after a computer mishap were more likely to report wanting to work with the confederate again. People want to be and stay friends with people who value them, and generosity is a way to express that.

An unfortunate misconception is that being popular is about being crass, self-serving, or mean. I used to think so. I went to middle school at the Michael J. Petrides School on Staten Island, where the popular kids weren't known for their kindness. The popular girls mostly ignored me, and the popular boys could be downright bullies. As a chubby tomboy, I still remember how an equally chubby bully would whisper "Earthquake" as I passed by. And even now, we see that many universally known celebrities, CEOs, and political leaders are known for their narcissism more than for their generosity.

But the truth is that while being mean can occasionally bring us status or lead others to view us as charming, fun leaders, it won't make us friends. One study pitted aggressive people and prosocial people against each other and compared their friendship trajectories. In it, the prosocial people developed higher-quality friendships. When we assume that being mean will win us friends, we conflate what it means to have status and what it means to make friends. In *Mean Girls,* the whole school cheered when a classmate confessed her plan to destroy the alpha, albeit popular, mean girl, Regina. They also didn't seem terribly sad when she got hit by a bus.

With all this research illuminating the merits of generosity for friendship, it's no wonder we see it as a virtue. Thomas Aquinas believed so deeply in generosity that he argued it elevated man closer to God. According to him, we mirror the love God has for us in how we treat others. Generosity also marks our greatest heroes—from

Mother Teresa to Martin Luther King Jr. Nearly all religions extol generosity, from Christianity to Judaism to Islam to Sikhism. According to early Jewish teachings, "Charity is equal in importance to all the other commandments in the Torah combined."

It's great that we value generosity. Doing so guides us to be more successful at making and keeping friends. We should all be more thoughtful about the ways we can be more generous toward others. Want to befriend a co-worker who lives close? Offer to drive them to work. You and a new friend going to a potluck? Save them some dumplings if they're late. Got an extra bag of Cool Ranch Doritos from wrestling the vending machine? Offer it to a friend. My best friend Billy told me early in our friendship, when we traveled to Portugal together, she knew I was something special when I helped her haul her heavy duffel bag across the airport.*

The following are some other examples of how to be generous with friends:

- Bake for friends.
- Send friends cards.
- Teach friends a skill.
- Offer to connect friends with someone who might be helpful to them.
- Offer to help friends reach a goal (e.g., to walk with them if they are trying to exercise more).
- Spend more time with friends.
- Buy friends gifts when you see something they might like.
- Cook for friends.
- Offer to run errands for friends (walk their dog, pick up groceries).

---

* Of course, though rare, there will be times when friends do not appreciate our generosity. We'll learn more about why in the affection chapter.

- Venmo friends money for coffee or a meal to treat themselves.
- Drive friends to the airport.
- Let friends borrow clothes or books.
- Babysit friends' kids.
- Share helpful information with friends.
- Get friends gifts when you travel.

The Downsides of Generosity

Recognizing Toxic Generosity

While generosity is wonderful and necessary for friendship, problems abound when we confuse it with self-sacrifice, proclaiming that to be truly generous, we must give away every last drop of ourselves. This conflation is the vestige of the Protestant work ethic that birthed the US: Do until you have nothing left, deny yourself rest, bury your needs. Asking for anything is self-indulgent. The martyr became our generosity role model. This martyring of self takes a toll on us, as Virginia Woolf described in her speech to the National Society for Women's Service on January 12, 1931:

> She was intensely sympathetic. She was immensely charming. She was utterly unselfish. She excelled in the difficult arts of family life. She sacrificed herself daily. If there was chicken, she took the leg; if there was a draft she sat in it—in short she was so constituted that she never had a mind or wish of her own, but preferred to sympathize always with the minds and wishes of others . . . I did my best to kill her. My excuse, if I were to be had up in a court of law, would be that I acted in self-defense. Had I not killed her, she would have killed me.

We are taught to sacrifice ourselves for others at a young age. In his *New York Times* article "We Need to Talk About 'The Giving Tree,'" Adam Grant, who wrote *Give and Take,* and his wife, Allison Sweet Grant, point out that the popular children's book *The Giving Tree* valorizes martyrdom rather than healthy generosity. As the story goes, a tree loved a boy, so she gave to him. The boy took her leaves to make his crown, climbed her trunk to eat her apples, and slept in her shade. When the boy got older, he rarely visited the tree, but when he did, he didn't want to play with her. He wanted to make money. So the tree shook off all her apples so the boy could sell them. When he returned, he wanted a house. The tree offered her branches for the house. Old and sad now, he wanted a boat to go far away. The tree offered her trunk for a boat. When the no-longer-a-boy returned for the last time, the tree said, "I wish I could give you something. I have nothing left. I am an old stump." The man just needed a quiet place to sit, and the tree invited him to sit on her stump, "and the boy did, and the tree was happy."

When the giving tree is our paragon of generosity, we learn the right way to give is to give to the brink of ruin. We feel bad, morally bankrupt even, when we erect boundaries. When we eke out a no, we are racked with guilt and shame, wondering whether we're defective because our will to give is finite. When boundaries trigger this guilt-trodden monsoon, it feels easier to just say yes. Anything is better than the agony of guilt.

From Selfless to Self-Absorbed

As these extreme forms of generosity have left us burnt out and resentful, the pendulum has swung in the other direction. In the 1980s, the self-esteem movement took hold, and we rocked from selfless to self-absorbed. In 1986, California assemblyman John Vasconcellos started California's Task Force to Promote Self-Esteem and Personal and Social Responsibility, believing low self-esteem was a "social vaccine" against social ills. He hired professors from the University of California system to write *Towards a State of Esteem,* a report linking low self-esteem to child abuse, teen pregnancy, and substance use, among other social problems. The report was a hit, with over sixty thousand readers. Vasconcellos went on *Oprah* to proselytize self-esteem. Even though the data was later challenged for being correlational but not causal, by 1995, thirty states had enacted over 170 statutes to promote self-esteem.

Towards a State of Esteem defined self-esteem as a responsibility to self and others, but the "responsibility to others" part has gotten lost along the way. Schools have radically changed since the self-esteem movement began, offering inflated grades and trophies for twelfth place. Promoting high self-esteem without accountability to others has been a recipe for narcissism, which has been ascending for decades, according to a meta-analysis. As Roy Baumeister, a researcher who studies self-esteem, put it: "Hitler had very high self-esteem and plenty of initiative, too, but those were hardly guarantees of ethical behavior," and "the costs of high self-esteem are born by other people."

With this upswing in narcissism, we've normalized prioritizing self over others, and it has trickled down into our friendships. In what I call "new age generosity," we aren't willing to give our friends a drop. Melissa A. Fabello wrote a viral tweet thread in which she referred to providing emotional support to friends as "emotional labor" and provided a template for how to say no to a friend in need: "I'm at capacity . . . Could we connect [later time and date]? Do you have someone else you could reach out to?" The tweet struck a cultural chord, triggering think pieces in *Vice, TIME, HuffPost,* and *The Guardian.*

New age generosity conflates generosity not with selflessness but with being taken advantage of. If your neighbor asks for a cup of sugar, be assertive and tell them you buy sugar in the raw and can't part with sugar of this caliber. If your friend calls you at 3:00 a.m. suicidal, tell them it's not appropriate to call at this hour and that you'll be reachable between the window of 10:00 and 10:19 a.m. If a friend needs to pick your brain, make sure you send them your Cash App handle because anything less means you're not valuing yourself.

These trends have all been compounded by the internet. Fay Bound Alberti, in *A Biography of Loneliness: The History of an Emotion,* argues the internet has given us relationships built on shared interests without accountability to one another. You can join the seltzer Facebook group, geek out on your shared love of carbon dioxide, but no one has to drive you to the hospital when the SodaStream rolls off the counter and clubs your foot. Fay writes, "A defining characteristic of community has historically been not only shared characteristics, which is the modern usage . . . , but also a sense of responsibility for others." Internet culture has led us to splinter friendship—to invite its joys but to dip out on its work. We're caught up in positive vibes only, where every request is an imposition, a friend in need is a friend to leave, and our bonds are more fragile than ever.

So where do we go from here? We've vacillated from an all-or-none inheritance of giving tree generosity to a reactive sucker punch against it. Along the way, we've failed to ask ourselves deeper questions about what generosity means to us, how we can intentionally invite it into our lives. We need to heal our relationship with generosity. But to do that, we'll still need to dig deeper into the source of our unhealthy relationship with it.

Is It Generosity, or Is It Fawning?

There are childhood memories that haunt Melody. Her dad trying to tutor her in math, calling her a stupid failure when she couldn't understand. Her mom stepping in to help her and her dad scream-ing at her too. Fights where she told him to stop yelling and he said, "Who do you think you are to speak to me that way?" Her breaking his cooking utensil and supergluing it in the bathroom so he wouldn't yell at her for being clumsy. Him finding her, screaming, and accusing her of huffing superglue. From these early experiences, she learned she was inadequate, that advocating for herself would lead to more put-downs, and that problems in relationships were her fault.

It was this same energy that she brought to her roommates in Florence. If they were mean, she must have deserved it. She brought it upon herself by not being thin enough to unself-consciously wear a bikini, or chill enough to let it go when they watered her laptop like a dracaena. If they were mean, the solution was to compensate for her flaws, go the extra kilometer (since it was Europe) to earn their love, feed them croissants and paninis and her soul, like she prac-ticed with her father.

According to trauma expert Bessel van der Kolk, "Being treated by family members as irrelevant . . . creates another kind of psycho-logical pattern. People's identity is formed around questions like 'What did I do wrong?' or 'What could I have done differently?' That becomes the central preoccupation of their lives." Wounds lead us to believe we can control people, change them, if only we contort ourselves just right—it's a problem of mistaken omnipotence. We've heard of fight, flight, or freeze reactions in response to trauma, but the last response is fawn: try to get people to like you so they'll stop harming you. We also call it people pleasing.

Fawning is a survival strategy. Fawners, like Melody, learned that the way to be safe or valued is to accommodate. And what other choice do they have? As kids, we can't walk away. Melody couldn't quit her family. She could resist, but that would amplify her dad's ire. Fawning softened her father's wrath.

The problem with fawning, however, is that it muddles our clarity on whether we give because we love or because we want to earn love. When we fawn, we often give to people we don't even like but who we want to like us. Secure people give because they care about people. Anxious people do too, but they also often give because they want people to care about them, research finds. Anxious attachment is related to something called "egoistic giving," giving not because of pure altruism or love for the other person but because you have an ulterior motive. In one study on volunteering, with samples from the Netherlands, Israel, and the US, the anxious volunteered not out of pure altruism but to feel better about themselves. As Melody put it, "I was scared of no one liking me and not fitting in. I felt like I had to compensate for my existence, to prove my worth. I wanted to be the smartest, the funniest, the most entertaining—to make people laugh or give them things so they wouldn't leave." This type of anxious giving is related to poorer psychological health, suggesting that our generosity may hurt us when it is propelled by insecurity.

A similar dynamic to that of her childhood played out between Melody and her high school friend Milly. Melody would pay for dinners, dote with attention, relinquish her time. Milly would take it all for granted. They were out for lunch once when Milly's boyfriend called to ask if she was busy. Milly left mid-lunch, as Melody footed the bill and finished her half-eaten hamburger alone.

But it wasn't all Milly's fault, Melody said. She gave to Milly, not out of love but out of what Milly represented to her: her salvation. If she got Milly to show her love, "It would mean something profound about me that I desperately wanted to be true—that I was enough. The love was shrouded in ego." She didn't love when Milly became the captain of the soccer team or got into her top choice of college. "If it were real love, I would have loved to see her thrive when it had nothing to do with me. But instead, I was most fed by her accomplishments when they related to our friendship. The biggest triumph she could achieve, in my eyes, was to be my best friend." When we lack in love for ourselves, sometimes our love for others is a Trojan horse, a tactic to get others to compensate for our feelings of unworthiness by loving us.

While generosity is a feature of great friendships, Melody's story reveals it is also a feature of toxic ones. One person dissolves themselves through giving, and another person dominates through taking. As Melody put it, "The giving came from fear rather than from love. When it comes from fear, I look for something in return, usually for someone to like me. I'm thinking that I have to give to people for me to be enough for them. So, I'd give even if it killed me because I didn't value myself." When we give to earn love, we lack self-love, and so we'll give until we collapse.

The problem is if you're not giving to express love but to earn it, then you'll give to the wrong people, as Melody did. Give yourself a break, though. The urge to earn love from those who mistreat you doesn't materialize from thin air. It likely helped you survive in the environment you grew up in, just like it did for Melody.

But now, you don't just need to survive. You need to thrive. Thriving means you don't invite destructive people into your life because they give you the opportunity to earn love. It means people who love you freely are no longer suspicious and those who withhold are no longer motivating. It means you are generous because you love someone and want to show it, not because someone doesn't love you and you want to change that. When someone withholds love, you thrive when you walk away instead of working harder. Because it's not your fault they don't love you and it doesn't mean anything is wrong with you. You deserve relationships of mutual generosity, but for Melody to realize this, "I had to let go of this identity as a broken person. I had to realize I could change my life."

Using Healthy Generosity to Build Friendship

We should avoid being generous to people who mistreat us and know how to discern whether we are generous to show love or cope with feeling unloved. Now that we know generosity's pitfalls, let's explore how to do generosity right, through Derrick and Park's story.

When Derrick first moved to New York for graduate school, he was often alone—alone on subway cars, alone while sipping black coffee at Café Grumpy, alone while scrutinizing the man in the tin-foil hat in Washington Square Park. He yearned for humans, and he eventually found one—a girlfriend, Dina. Then more humans came. Dina invited Derrick; her best friend, Che; and Che's boyfriend, Park, to her uptown New York shoebox of an apartment. At first, Park didn't make a strong impression on Derrick, whom he described as "quiet and chill with some swagger to him." The couples kept hanging out, and Park and Derrick began to like each other in that I'd-be-excited-if-I-bumped-into-you kind of way.

But graduate school is lonely and isolating—especially in the summer, when people scatter home to wherever they're from. Dina stayed with her father on Long Island (they call it that, she laughed, because it's a *long* way away from the rest of the city). Derrick's other New York friends never seemed to make it out to his tiny apartment in a remote part of the city, except for Park, who showed up all the way from the Bronx. He endured hour-and-a-half-long train rides full of buskers begging for cash he didn't have, just to see Derrick.

Park, a native New Yorker, became Derrick's New York mentor. He was obsessed with transportation, so as the two skateboarded to parks and bars and dollar-pizza joints, Park would explain why a street was fat or skinny, toothy with cars or bald without them. Park introduced him to others in the skate park: "Derrick's my man. He's new to the neighborhood." "I don't think I would have ever assimilated into New York City, made it my home like I did, if I never met Park," Derrick said.

It will surprise no one who has lived through their young twenties in New York City that eventually Derrick and Dina broke up, but around that time, to Derrick's surprise, Park vanished too. Derrick's texts to Park went unanswered for months, and Park's social media was conspicuously without update. His eventual update explained why no one had heard from him. He was in jail.

Derrick felt like he had to do something. So Derrick; his new girlfriend, Tasha; and her father (who was a pastor) huddled together to pray for Park, "a good-hearted man, who acted in desperation" to receive a second chance. Park prayed for himself too. Park's judge must have heard their prayers, because all charges were dropped. The outcome felt profound and spiritual, "as if our prayer had shifted the momentum of the universe," Derrick said.

You know what else will surprise no one who has lived through their young twenties in New York? Derrick signed a lease to live in a one-bedroom in Harlem with Tasha, but Tasha broke up with him before she moved in. The apartment reeked of his grief and the takeout cartons he used to run away from it. It reeked of Park's grief too, as he came over to play video games to escape worries over his own breakup, his chronic underemployment, and the recent news that his grandmother had cancer.

One night, when Park returned to his grandmother's apartment, where he lived, he couldn't get inside. His grandmother had moved to a nursing home for continuous care, and his uncle had apparently changed her locks. Derrick was the first person Park turned to. "I'm helping you, bro. I was praying for you, and it feels metaphysical that I'm in a position to help," Derrick told Park. "You can stay with me. Sometimes things align in certain ways, like it's the workings of the universe acted out through you."

But if Derrick was completely honest, his decision to help Park wasn't just metaphysical. It was practical. After the breakup, Derrick, depressed and lonely in his empty one-bedroom, decided to get a dog, Sheen, for company. And as he got to know his energetic new pup, Derrick realized that his frantic work schedule didn't give him time to take care of Sheen properly. He needed help.

And he knew who to ask.

"I really, *really* needed help to care for Sheen," Derrick said. And he knew Park would be there for him, because "though Park isn't going to pay for your trips or buy you food, he'll show up for you. He'll offer his hands, his feet, his mind, whatever he has."

Cultivate "Enlightened Self-Interest"

If we embrace giving tree generosity, we will assume Derrick's generosity was tainted by self-interest. We question if his behavior was truly generous. We'd reserve our praise, instead, for someone like Evan Leedy, a college student who raised money to buy a car for a man who trudged twenty-one miles to get to and from work. We'd save it for Robin Emmons, who turned her backyard into a garden to grow food for hungry people. We'd save it for Estella Pyfrom, who created a mobile computer lab used to tutor low-income kids. We'd save it for the winners of the Caring Canadian Award, who are described as "caring people who give so much to their fellow citizens, the unsung heroes who volunteer their time, their efforts and a great deal of their lives to helping others, and who ask for nothing in return." These winners are awarded a lapel pin depicting a hand "outstretched to represent boundless generosity." Boundless generosity, nothing in return. That's what we've been taught marks true generosity.

But when researchers interviewed the winners of the Caring Canadian Award, as well as a control group of average people from similar demographics, they found something interesting. The award winners weren't just more likely to give. They were more likely to give in ways that benefited others *and* themselves, to, as the researchers put it, "advance their own interest by advancing the interest of others." A winner might, for example, put on a boxing match to raise money for charity, but they would also be motivated to get an award for it.

Giving tree generosity, martyr generosity, it seems, has taught us wrong. The most generous people in Canada can attest to this. To live a virtuous life, the researchers of the study concluded, our goal should not be selflessness, but "enlightened self-interest," where our "own interests become aligned with the interests of others." In other words, we must let our friend stay on our couch, but we must also ask for help with our dog.

Why can't we just be selfless, though? Why does there have to be something in it for us? We're social creatures—don't we like giving? It's true. We do. In fact, research finds that when people are given money and told to spend it on themselves versus on others, they are happier when spending it on others. This finding holds all over the world—in the US, Canada, South Africa, and Vanuatu. Spending on others looked different in certain places—in Uganda, when people were asked the last time they spent the equivalent of $20 Canadian on others, they said they spent it on shoes for a barefoot little brother or medicine for a friend's aching ulcers. In Canada, people spent it on roses at Costco for their mom's birthday. But in nearly every country, people experienced joy from giving. The Gallup World Poll asked people how satisfied they were with their lives and whether they'd donated money in the past month. Spending on others contributed to well-being in every region in the world.

Giving feels good and benefits us. When a friend needs something from us, and it doesn't require a lot from us, helping benefits us and them. But when we sacrifice ourselves to give, the impact of giving twists. A meta-analysis combining data from 32,053 people found that people who self-sacrifice in their romantic relationships experience slightly poorer well-being. But people who self-sacrificed in especially costly ways not only experienced less well-being, their romantic relationship also suffered.

When we're chronically giving and receiving nothing in return, we become "unmitigated givers." Unmitigated givers embrace statements like "I always place the needs of others above my own," "It is impossible for me to satisfy my own needs when they interfere with the needs of others," and "Even when exhausted, I will help other people." These selfless individuals, these sweet little giving trees, are more stressed and depressed, studies find. And their behavior costs—rather than benefits—their relationships. A meta-analysis found that people who were motivated to give experienced higher well-being, and so did their relationship partners. This wasn't true for unmitigated givers or their relationship partners. Selflessness grants us a one-way ticket to Burnout City, where everyone is depressed, overwhelmed, and sucking it up.

But self-sacrifice can also be seductive. When we are absorbed by others, we shed the parts of ourselves we want to escape—the troubles, the depression, the low self-esteem. We're so consumed by people we forget, for a moment, the heaviness of being a person. This momentary lapse, this tiny death, of course, doesn't solve our problems; it only temporarily heaves sand over them. The only way the self-sacrificer can solve their problem is by understanding what they are trying to run away from through sacrifice.

Because self-sacrifice will not save us from our troubles but compound them. Even if it provides temporary highs, it also has withdrawal symptoms. Emotions like resentment or bitterness gurgle up to remind us not to give away the pie unless we get a piece of it. We feel downright exhausted when we chronically self-sacrifice, which reveals that unmitigated giving is not what our bodies crave. And the people we're giving to too often feel uncomfortable that we're resenting them for something we chose to give.

Madoka Kumashiro, a lecturer at Goldsmiths, University of London, calls the process of balancing our generosity "equilibrium." Her research finds that on days when we're too focused on our relationships, we naturally desire to focus on ourselves. But also, when we're too focused on ourselves, we naturally desire to focus on our relationships. We are creatures of balance. This is a good thing. Participants who experienced equilibrium—who answered affirmatively to the statement "I make my relational needs *and* my personal needs a major priority in life," the people who found win-wins—were less depressed and anxious and more satisfied with their lives six months later. You know what else? Their relationships didn't suffer because they focused on themselves either. In fact, the study found, as Derrick can attest, that the more people maintained equilibrium, the healthier their relationships.

Kumashiro's research suggests that although we may think enlightened self-interest pollutes generosity, it actually sustains it. Derrick let Park stay on his couch for an entire year, and he was less resentful, more willing to give, because Park gave too. His asking for help from Park was in not only his best interests but also Park's, because when the setup served Derrick, Park got to stay longer. Derrick is a natural giver, but his advice for people looking to be more generous is to ask friends for things too. This is part of what differentiates healthy generosity from unmitigated giving. Unmitigated givers, one study found, were more depressed because they were uncomfortable asking for help and struggled to assert their needs. When we ask for things too, it refuels us and plucks out any weeds of resentment, so we can give more.

If we embrace giving tree generosity, we may think of asking for things as selfish or imposing. But Kumashiro's research suggests that asking for what we need is in the service of not just ourselves but also our relationships. When we don't just give but also ask and receive, we protect ourselves from burning out, so that we can give more in the long term. We're less resentful when friends need something from us and better at showing up. The most generous people give themselves permission to ask for what they need because doing so refuels them, allowing them to be more generous in the long run.

In their year together, Park and Derrick developed a routine they enjoyed. Park worked nights in a parking garage and came home with breakfast. "You wake up in the morning and your best friend is there," Derrick said. They'd chill until Derrick left for work. Derrick would bring back dinner for the both of them, or they'd go to a nearby bar, where they'd have five-dollar wings and Henny-coolatas. Park gave Derrick a few hundred dollars when he could. He washed the dishes, made the shower sparkle, scooped poop for Sheen. "Maybe I'm giving more financially, but Park's giving me something I really needed. We were there for each other in the lowest times of our lives."

Use Boundaries to Strengthen Bonds

As I read about the concept of equilibrium, I was reminded of a short-lived friendship I had with a woman I'll call Margaret. We hung out a trickle of times, once at a park, then in a garden, and then for a walk, during which Margaret told me she was moving. I offered to help her pick up boxes since I had a car and she didn't. She took me up on my offer, and we drove to Lowe's together. The week after, during her actual move, she reached out again for help, also asking if I'd bring my big, burly relationship partner at the time to help too. He was reluctant. He didn't know Margaret and wasn't motivated to sacrifice his Saturday for her. But I convinced him to help because it was the right thing to do.

When we got to Margaret's apartment, she let me know her plans to use my car to move things to her new apartment. I told her that was fine, as long as it happened before 1:30, when I had to leave to make an appointment. It was 1:30 when Margaret finally got around to packing my car. I was frustrated but didn't want to leave her in the lurch. When we got to the new apartment with Margaret's stuff, it was 2:00 p.m. Margaret insisted we not only help take her stuff out of the car but carry it up the elevator to her new apartment. Other friends were helping too, but they were still at the old apartment helping with packing, so we were alone with Margaret. I felt too guilty to leave her with furniture, so we helped. By the time the car was unpacked, her mirror and clothes and tote bags strewn across her new apartment, it was ten minutes before my appointment began. I had planned to drop my partner home beforehand, but I told him I'd have to pay for his Lyft.

Before my bitterness at giving too much left me, Margaret reached out again, the next day, to see if I'd return with my car to help move what was left. This time, I told her I was too busy to help.

What became of Margaret and me? I lost all motivation to see her. She'd reach out and I'd reply, "Cool," or "Great," or "Thanks," or tell her I was busy. She kept reaching out, and I figured if she wouldn't take the hint, I needed to be honest rather than ghost. I told her I felt my boundaries had been crossed and this friendship wouldn't work for me. She never responded.

Throughout this whole ordeal, I felt deeply guilty and selfish. I wasn't upset that I didn't help Margaret that second day, I realized. I was upset that I didn't *want* to. And what did that say about me, if humans are supposed to enjoy being generous? But now I know why. I was in disequilibrium, according to Dr. Kumashiro's research, and when that happens, it's normal to need to pull back. Just because I wasn't selfless didn't mean I was selfish. It meant I was human.

The other thing I realized is that it wasn't fair for me to say I liked or disliked being generous based on my experience with Margaret. It was more accurate to say the degree to which I liked being generous fluctuated depending on whom I was generous with. For Margaret, I was unmotivated to help, not because I didn't like her but because I didn't really know her. If my closest friend was in a bind on their second day of moving, I'd shift around my interviews to show up. This all left me wondering, do the rules of generosity change with those you're closest to?

Generosity in Our Closest Friendships

I sent an Instagram post I found online to some friends. It read:

> "You should feel comfortable saying:
> 1. I am taking space and I will circle back later.
> 2. I'm not available. Please find someone else for support.
> 3. I'm drained. I will respond when I have energy again."

After sending this post to friends, I asked them: *What would you say if you were in distress and went to a close friend and they responded with one of these messages? No wrong answers.*

Here's my anecdata on how these statements made my friends feel:

> *I would wonder if they are mad at me, or if they are trying to push me away deliberately.*
> *I'd be hurt and probably wouldn't reach out to them again.*
> *It would send me deeper into whatever distress I'm in.*

My friends' responses to such boundaries convey something fundamental about friendship: we expect our friends to try their best to show up in our times of need. One study analyzed 491 responses to the question "What qualities do you look for in a good friend?"

from www.authentichappiness.com, and it found that supportiveness was one of the top three. Another study, one from 1984, analyzed people's views on the "rules" of friendship, four rules of which were highly endorsed across multiple cultures. One of these highly coveted rules was that a friend "should volunteer help in time of need." In that study, support given in times of need marked the difference between high- and low-quality friendships.

It is appropriate to share these kinds of boundaries with someone we don't know well or don't care to, but when we get close, the rules of generosity change. The psychology world used to assume these rules were static, no matter the relationship. Among strangers and friends, we are self-interested, willing to give to the extent we expect to receive. With strangers, we might cash in sooner, but with friends, we could wait to cash in later. That's what new age friendship implies; boundaries are immutable, universal no matter the type of relationship, as firm with a Starbucks barista as they should be with a best friend.

But Margaret S. Clark, a professor at Yale University, has done amazing work that shows that what's appropriate in a relationship depends on the nature of the relationship. As we get closer to one another, our relationships transform into what she calls "communal relationships," where even if it costs us, we give in times of need.*

Communal relationships, Clark argues, are ones where we "give benefits in response to needs to demonstrate general concern for the other person." The greater the communal strength of a relationship, the more we're willing to sacrifice when someone needs us. Communal relationships are the deepest and most significant rela-

---

* Dr. Clark has even gotten into an academic imbroglio with another researcher, C. Daniel Batson, who argued she's wrong about the rules of relationships changing depending on their depth. In true academic fashion, their brawl played out over a series of academic papers. Since then, there have been hundreds of studies verifying communal relationships.

tionships in our lives. Studies find that people are more willing to be vulnerable in these relationships—to express happiness or sadness. They are our closest relationships, according to other studies. One researcher defines communal relationships as the definition of love, as well as the "key to optimal relationship functioning and, indeed, the sine qua non of close relationships." These are the types of friendships we've been waiting for.

What maintains communal relationships is not boundaries, as we've come to define them. It's showing up. One study found that when a friend responds in times of need, people are more likely to support that friend deeply by doing things like telling them they're okay just as they are, listening to them, cheering them up, and telling them how close they feel to them. The more support we get from friends, another study found, the more support we give to them and the more secure and close we feel to them.

In other words, we find communal relationships when we offer them. You cannot develop deep friendship without being accountable to a friend in need, even when you're uncomfortably full from the grand slam at Denny's, or from watching *I Love Lucy* reruns, or from beating your top score in *Call of Duty*. When you choose to be a friend, you choose to show up. Research finds that support in times of need is a key factor that makes people more secure over time, and as other studies find, the more secure we are, the more supportive we are right back. When we feel prioritized in times of need—our needs attended to, our welfare considered—we reciprocate. So, for friendship to flourish, we need to know if we call a friend crying because we got fired from our job at the nuclear power plant, they won't text back, "I am currently unavailable."

Setting these kinds of individualistic boundaries destroys communal relationships because these statements say prioritize yourself, put yourself first, put the oxygen mask on yourself, even while your friend asphyxiates. They assume friendship is opt-in, something we can offer only when we're rested, exercised, worked out, bronzed, and full from a nutrient-dense meal. They suggest we shouldn't ever feel taxed, inconvenienced, or put out, and the instant we suspect we will be, it's our duty to apply the boundary as our first line of defense. Boundaries, in how we've come to understand them, are expressions of our deepest realms of individualism, justified under the guise of self-empowerment.

Is there no place for boundaries, then, in our most intimate friendships? No, that's not it. We still need boundaries, but of a different kind. Communal boundaries, swaddled in love rather than self-protection, are different. They're kinder, creative, more fluid, a negotiation that honors both parties. They're less binary—one person doesn't get their space while the other writhes in the gutter. In our friends' times of need, new age friendship boundaries default to the all-or-none of "Given my current state, I can't offer you anything," whereas communal boundaries require us to ask ourselves, "Given my current state, what can I offer?"

With communal boundaries, we show up for a friend in crisis because we practice mutuality. We zoom out to assess the friendship. We ask ourselves, if we consider both our needs, whose are more urgent? It's not a submission of self for the other, nor a domination of the other for the self. It is a coming together, a collaboration, a synergy. Communal boundaries are context-dependent; otherwise, they are walls. With communal boundaries, if I have a bad day at work and don't want to talk, I can say, "Let's talk some other time," when my friend calls me to debrief about the season finale of *Lost*, but not when they call because their kid is self-harming. Mutuality means that when someone important to us is in crisis, we prioritize them unless we are in crisis ourselves.

Communal boundaries, mutuality, are not meant to protect the self; they are meant to protect a relationship. As my neighbor Kirsten put it, "We often use boundaries in ways to disconnect, but boundaries should help our relationships flourish, so we can connect in a way to meet people's needs," or in the words of Prentis Hemphill, a healer, Somatics teacher, and writer, "Boundaries are the distance at which I can love you and me at the same time." Communal boundaries stop the car to refuel so it can keep driving, whereas individualistic boundaries stop the car to park it in the driveway.

Outside of crises, communal boundaries do not mean we always show up exactly how our friend wants, because attending to our needs too is in the service of the friendship. When our friend asks us to babysit but we had a date planned, or they ask us to walk their Pekinese when we live an hour away, we say no because if we decline now to attend to ourselves, we can give more in the long run. When Melody's best friend, Chelsea, moved to St. Louis to be near her, Chelsea wanted to hang out every day. Chelsea was single and unemployed, and Melody, juggling twelve-hour workdays and a boyfriend, just didn't have the same availability. Constantly worried she'd disappoint Chelsea, Melody wished she'd just brought up their clashing needs to negotiate a setup that worked for them both: "I could have said, 'I know it's hard to move to a new city, and I want to be there for you. My job is stressing me out, but you're important to me and I'd love to hang out. What if we have a weekly dinner?'"

On the flip side, mutuality also means we adjust to our friends not meeting 100 percent of our needs when doing so compromises our friend. Figuring out how much slack we give to friends isn't always easy. It's less of a science and more of an art and requires us to be honest to ourselves about how urgent our and our friend's needs are. For Chelsea, mutuality meant tolerating not seeing Melody as often as she'd like because Melody's priorities were also important to her. But if she was really struggling, she might have pushed back and asked Melody for two dinners a week.

Casey, who works at a nonprofit, didn't receive mutuality from her friend. Around the start of the COVID-19 pandemic, she suddenly starting fainting nearly every day, and the doctors couldn't figure out why. Her friend Elma asked her to join a dance competition. When Casey said no because of the pandemic, especially since she had a mysterious illness, Elma told Casey she was a bad friend and was abandoning her. The irony is that in demanding that her needs be met without considering that Casey's life was literally at stake, Elma was acting appallingly. When we embrace mutuality, we *want* our friends to take care of themselves, yet we want to take care of ourselves. Both are important. We can understand that our friends have boundaries to replenish themselves so they can keep showing up for us, or stay alive to show up for us in Casey's case. Their boundaries, then, are the ultimate act of generosity.

For mutuality to work, we must be clear with our close friends when we have an important need because in the words of author Neil Strauss, "Unspoken expectations are premeditated resentments." How can our friend know that now is a time to prioritize us if we don't say, "Hey, this is really important for me"? We need to get comfortable imposing when we need to impose. Because if the other person is comfortable asking and we are not, even our healthiest friendships will jut unevenly. Being understood isn't just about the other person putting in the time and effort to get us. It's also about us making ourselves understandable. Knowing this research, after I went through a breakup, I texted my friends, "Support for me right now looks like spending time with me and bringing over food."

Mutuality keeps us in equilibrium in the larger scheme of the friendship, but importantly, it allows disequilibrium and self-sacrifice to occur, not chronically but in moments of need. Sometimes we give more, like when Derrick let Park stay on his couch for a year. And then we take more, like when Derrick stayed on Park's couch after he moved to DC and visited New York, so, in the larger scheme of things, generosity equals out. It's not a tit-for-tat equality of keeping tabs, but instead we trust, if we are committed to showing up for each other, that things equal out.

Finding win-wins is also a form of mutuality, since it requires us to ask, "Is there a way to meet both our needs?" Melody realized she could have achieved a win-win with Chelsea if they co-worked a few days a week at the coffee shop near her apartment. Chelsea could have her company, and Melody could sift through her 187 work emails. My friend Allie Davis offered a touching win-win. She said that if a friend was in crisis and she was too, instead of telling the friend she's too overwhelmed to speak to them, she'd say, "Thanks for texting me. I'm really sorry you're going through that. I've been having a hard time too. Do you want to FaceTime to cry together?"

Mutuality win-wins mean even if I am embroiled in my own crisis when my friend needs me, I can still provide some empathy while also getting the space I need to recover. That might look like "That's so awful. I'm so sorry. I'm glad you reached out. I can chat later tomorrow." Consider how that rings differently than "I'm drained. I will respond when I have energy again." Both phrases achieve the same thing: a break to chat later, but one isn't just focused on ourselves. One affirms that our friend's needs are still a priority.

Individualistic boundaries	Communal boundaries
I prioritize my needs.	I consider both our needs and prioritize whoever's needs are more important.
I don't offer anything if I'm exhausted.	I evaluate what I can still offer despite being exhausted.
My boundaries are the same, no matter the person asking or the urgency of their needs.	My boundaries shift depending on my relationship with the asker and the urgency of their need.
Boundaries are used to protect me.	Boundaries are used to protect the friendship.

Individualistic boundaries	Communal boundaries
I consider my boundaries without regard for the other person's.	I welcome my friend's boundaries since I am invested in their well-being.
I never self-sacrifice.	I self-sacrifice when a close friend is in need.
When my needs conflict with a friend's, I prioritize myself.	When my needs conflict with a friend's, I assess if there's a way to meet both our needs.

Mutuality is how we balance selflessness and selfishness. It's where giving tree and new age generosity find compromise. But an important caveat to mutuality is that we cannot offer it to everyone. As much as we'd like to care for citizens of all seven continents and those of their corresponding archipelagos and islets, we cannot. The more contacts we have, one study found, the less time we spend with each one. That study also found that the larger our network, the weaker our relationships tend to be. If we try to invest in everyone, we may end up investing in no one.

To embrace mutuality, then, we first need to figure out who our friends are. Mutuality isn't something we can assume with someone we just met. It's a gradual process, and ultimately a by-product of a strong and stable friendship. If mutuality isn't, well, mutual, then we'll extend ourselves for friends who use individualistic boundaries on us.

But knowing who your friends are is tougher than you think, given that research finds that half our friends don't consider us friends. The authors of the study explain that most of us may deny that a friendship isn't reciprocal so as to not feel too bad about ourselves. This discrepancy may also be a by-product of the "false consensus effect"—our bias to assume others see things just as we do.

Shasta Nelson, a friendship expert, describes another type of conundrum in which one friend feels closer than the other. If you and a friend rank your friends from a 1 to a 10—10 being top friends and 1 being acquaintances—it's possible you rank them a 5, and they rank you a 10. You want to get lunch once a month, but they want to hang out every day, go to you with woes, ask you to come over with chicken noodle soup, and expect the same. If this occurs, we can talk to a friend about what they're willing to give, or we can assess the relationship ourselves by asking: Am I always the one reaching out? Asking for support? The only one being vulnerable? As Melody revealed, if the friendship is one-sided, we should bring up the issue, adjust expectations, or else seek mutuality elsewhere.

Knowing where we fall with people and adjusting expectations accordingly helps us not get hurt. If we're anxious, we might be tempted to push harder and ask for more when we sense a friend isn't as invested, but as we will learn in the affection chapter, love isn't forced. It is freely given. Just like people must sexually consent, new friends should emotionally consent to the level of intimacy we want. So, if someone isn't willing to consent, accept it and find another friend who will.

When people are generous to us, not because they love us but because we pressured them into being so, they will be more likely to resent rather than enjoy their giving. The motivation behind generosity predicts whether we enjoy it. One study involved people reporting on acts of giving and why they gave for two weeks. On days when they gave because they enjoyed it and it fulfilled them, they felt better and more energized and experienced upticks in self-esteem. On days when they gave because they felt obligated, worrying they'd be a bad person otherwise, they were worse off on these outcomes than people who didn't give at all. When I provided a level of generosity to Margaret that I wasn't ready for, it pushed me further away because I felt my generosity was the result of not love, but pressure.

We also feel obligated rather than energized by our generosity when we are asked to be generous to people we're not close to. In one study, people recalled a time they spent $20 on either a strong tie (e.g., a good friend, family member, or romantic partner) or a weak tie (e.g., an acquaintance, co-worker, or classmate). They felt better after recalling an instance of generosity with a strong tie. Another study found that people's mood improved after helping someone they desired a relationship with but not when helping someone they didn't.

Giving to someone we're close to also has a greater impact. A study found that people were happier to receive money from someone they were close to, rather than someone they weren't. More generally, the closer we get to someone, the more, as Dr. Clark puts it, we "automatically empathize with [them] and see their environment through their eyes," so giving to them feels like giving to ourselves. When we give to people we love, generosity isn't just a threat to self-care. It's also a form of it, allowing us to give more in the grand scheme.

Overall, these studies suggest that we should engage in mutuality with friends we're truly committed to, rather than with everybody. Be generous, but when generosity is taxing, let your generosity be proportional to the depth of the friendship and give yourself a get-out-of-guilt-free card for saying no when the friendship isn't as important. On the other hand, when it comes to our expectations, we should incrementally build them up rather than expecting an outpouring of generosity from the start. When the friendship is more established, it's more likely that our friends will give to us because they love us and want to. But when we put too much pressure on a budding friendship, we may drive people away because their giving comes from fear of disappointing us rather than love. Mutuality requires that both parties are willing.

Casey learned the hard way the importance of tapering generosity depending on the depth of the friendship. A natural empath and an absorbed listener, Casey was the confidante of choice for many, to the extent that her phone became a 24/7 therapy hotline. Once, when she was in high school, she was texting an upset person into the late hours of the night, even though her parents forbade phones in bed. When she texted that she should get to sleep, the text back read, "No. I need you right now. Show up for me." Her mom saw the glow from her cell phone through the crack of the door. As she came in to check on her, Casey chucked her phone under her bed so her mom wouldn't see. "When you have to lie to others about how much you're helping, then maybe you shouldn't be," she said.

Casey's generosity reached its limit one night when she received a call from an unknown caller, who said, "Matt's in the hospital. He broke his femur. What's wrong with you? You should be there already." As Casey drove to the hospital, she felt deeply ambivalent. Everyone should have someone to show up for them, that much she knew, but should that person be her? She had had maybe three conversations with Matt in her life. Then, when she arrived at the hospital, she got another call. It was someone else in crisis.

Casey is a naturally generous person who derives joy from helping. Her problem was not that she showed up in times of crisis. It's that she had no discernment. She'd do just as much for her friends as she would for a stressed acquaintance. Like the giving tree, she'd repeatedly give, at grave personal cost, to people who took from her but never gave to her. She wasn't sleeping or eating enough. Every time her phone pinged, she'd startle. When she waited an hour to respond, her phone would buzz with angry texts: "Why aren't you responding. I need help!" Her so-called friends would get offended if she made new ones. She wasn't only neglecting her needs. She was also letting people into her life who neglected them too.

"It was dependency, rather than friendship," Casey said. Dependency in relationships looks like one-sidedness, with the dependent person consistently initiating communication, mostly to talk about their crisis and rarely to just check in. The dependent person doesn't respect boundaries, feels entitled to consistent care, without considering the needs of the other party. They also make their healing the responsibility of the other party and neglect to assume responsibility for it too. My friend Zoe admitted to being dependent in the past: "I would use my friends to avoid my feelings. Instead of me wondering what I'm feeling about and sitting with it, I'd lob my feeling off to a friend with an urgent text."

Casey's friendships were like tearing out the chapter in a book where the tragic climax happens. Their stories did not have a beginning—as the relationship steadily builds over time, an outing to the movies, hot dogs on the pier, discernment happening as mutual investment grows. They didn't have the mundane moments—"I just wanted friendship where we could play board games together"—that signify that we're with friends in moments of tragedy but also in moments of mediocrity. She had to learn to avoid being so generous with people who wanted her in crisis but forgot her in peace.

Intentional Generosity

Generosity reveals our deeper existential concerns: What does it look like to make others and myself happy? What do boundaries look like as an act of love? What does it mean to be my authentic self while accommodating others? When we feel we should always give because it's the right thing to do, we will burn out. When we become too frugal with our generosity, we won't experience its joys or build our bonds. We need to stop seeing generosity as binary—*I should always give, or I have nothing to give.* We need to approach generosity with intentionality and mutuality. Generosity must occur on the backbone of self-awareness of what and who is important to us, as well as other-awareness, of what's important to our friends. It is an invitation to discern ourselves, our boundaries, and our people.

Casey found this out eventually, though she admits she's still a work in progress. She got her first taste of mutuality with her friend Tamara: "We weren't always in crisis. We went for ice cream, and watched television, and talked on the phone." Casey and Tamara were roommates, and when Casey took a little longer to wash the dishes during her finals week, that was okay with Tamara. Tamara made requests of Casey, rather than demands, to leave room for Casey to say, "Not now," if she had too much going on.

Then one day, Tamara's car broke down on the side of the road. Her fiancé called Casey to help because he was too far away to get her. Casey drove over an hour to pick up Tamara and was delighted at every mile. "If someone you don't have that relationship with asks for a lot," she said, "you have to grasp for that energy deep within you, take it from somewhere else. When it's someone you love, someone you're close to, you feel energized. You're like, 'Oh my gosh you're going through this, I am going to be there and I want to be there.'"

TAKEAWAYS

► To make and keep friends, be generous. Here are some suggestions:
  - Bake for friends.
  - Send friends cards.
  - Teach friends a skill.
  - Offer to connect friends with someone who might be helpful to them.
  - Offer to help friends reach a goal (e.g., to walk with them if they are trying to exercise more).
  - Spend more time with friends.

- Buy friends gifts when you see something they might like.
- Cook for friends.
- Offer to run errands for friends (walk their dog, pick up groceries).
- Venmo friends money for coffee or a meal to treat themselves.
- Drive friends to the airport.
- Let friends borrow clothes or books.
- Babysit friends' kids.
- Share helpful information with friends.
- Get friends gifts when you travel.

► Understand your generosity motives. Give because you love someone and want to show it. Don't give because someone doesn't love you and you want to change that.

► Look for win-wins in generosity. If a friend asks a lot of you, find ways you can benefit from the situation as well. Ask for what you need to make your generosity sustainable. This will prevent burnout so you can give more in the long run.

► Embrace mutuality with close friends by considering both people's needs and prioritizing the person most in need. To do so:
  - Tell friends when your needs are urgent.
  - Limit the number of friends you engage in mutuality with. Practice it only in friendships where there is reciprocity:
    - There may be low reciprocity if you answer yes to questions like: Am I always the one reaching

out? Asking for support? The only one being vulnerable?

- When giving is costly, the amount you give and expect to receive should be proportional to the depth of the friendship.

▶ There may be dependency, rather than friendship, if: one person consistently initiates communication to talk about a crisis, rarely checks in otherwise, doesn't respect boundaries, feels entitled to consistent care without consideration of the other party, and places responsibility for their healing solely on others.

CHAPTER 8

Giving Affection

How to Give and Receive Love

Rachel and Gabby have been friends for over two decades, and they still get high on each other's company. Their shared hobbies are dancing, ceramics, board games, and gushing about each other. In their friendship, there are no white lies. When Gabby asks, "Does this dress look good?" Rachel responds, "It's drooping a little in the middle. Maybe change?" Each revels in a friendship safe enough to tolerate total honesty. When they went to sleepaway camp together, people mixed up their names, even though they look nothing alike. One day at camp, Gabby introduced herself, speaking rapidly because she was nervous. No one understood what she said, until Rachel translated, revealing, "I speak Gabby."

When the two were living in separate cities, Gabby surprised Rachel with a visit on her birthday. Rachel was so excited, she collapsed. They are best friends, confidantes, and occasional emergency contacts. Gabby and Rachel are as close as two humans can be. The only way they could further their bond is if they proposed to each other in a formal ceremony in front of their loved ones, which is exactly what they did.

It all started one day when Gabby said to Rachel, "I have an idea! Why don't we trace each other's hands?" The two were lazed on a worn-out sofa donated by a local coffee shop while *Lost* hummed on the television. Rachel's eyebrows furrowed as she replied, "Why would we do that?"

"Because it could be fun," Gabby responded.

Rachel's birthday was coming up, and as Gabby's pencil tickled her index finger, she guessed Gabby's motives. "You're trying to figure out my ring size! If you're getting me a ring for my birthday, you better propose," Rachel joked.

The next week, for Rachel's birthday, ten of Rachel and Gabby's closest friends squeezed into the living room of their apartment. As people drank wine and emptied out the chips and dip, Gabby announced that she'd like everyone's attention. She got down on one knee and proposed. The ring was inscribed with their initials, and at its center was each of their birthstones, amethyst and peridot.

Gabby got another friend to officiate. "Rachel Jane Stein, will you be Gabby's best friend, forever, to have and to hold, as long as we both shall live?" "I will! I will!" Rachel said. Gabby reached under the coffee table to pull out a certificate, nestled inside a frame she had picked up at the thrift store. It read, "Certificate of Friendship." Gabby and Rachel signed it. "It's official," Rachel said as friends took pictures of the pair and Rachel waved her new ring. Rachel reflected on the experience by saying, "It was very Gabby. I laugh at how extra it was. She's so ridiculous. I love her."

On Gabby's birthday, the two went to 7-Eleven for Slurpees. After ordering, they returned to the car, blasting the heat while they slurped. When Gabby was halfway through her wild cherry, Rachel pulled a box out of her pocket. Gabby opened it to find a necklace. "I'd like to use this necklace to renew our vows," Rachel said, pulling out ten tabs of paper, each with commitments they would make to each other. Rachel, who has a side hustle cutting hair, gave Gabby one to sign: "I will never cut my own hair." Rachel signed a tab that read, "I will always cut Gabby's hair."

A year later, Gabby was studying abroad in Scotland. Rachel was traveling to Europe to visit family in Romania, and the two planned to meet in London. They went to a speakeasy, with Rachel's sister, Lily, and a man from their hostel, Roy. After the waiter took their order, Rachel got on one knee and proposed back to Gabby, "Will you be my friend forever?" Roy stepped outside to smoke because he couldn't handle all their affection. When the server returned, she asked Rachel, "Did that actually happen? Did you propose?" Lily said, "No, no, no, it's fake." After the server left, Gabby chided, "Why did you do that, Lily? We would have gotten free champagne! If they ever ask if it's your birthday or if it's a real proposal, you always say yes! Because then you get champagne! Life lesson."

Even though the proposals were a joke, they also kind of weren't. Rachel and Gabby are, in fact, committed to being each other's friends forever. When Gabby first proposed to Rachel at her birthday, Rachel insisted they write down what they'd actually commit to in the friendship. When Gabby looks back, she realizes she and Rachel love each other and are committed to fulfilling these vows. Now that they have friendship certificates and rings, there's not much else they can do to further their bond.

Onlookers to a friendship like Rachel and Gabby's wonder how they got so close. They seemed to have cracked the code on closeness. Meanwhile, so many of us are stuck in the friendly acquaintance stage, deprived of not just friends but true intimacy. We may have someone to go to the movies with, but no one to call from the hospital. We receive one hundred happy birthdays on Facebook, yet no one shows up at our party. It's not just people we're hungry for; it's *meaningful connection*. But how do we find it? As Rachel and Gabby will illustrate, affection can help us get there.

Why We Hide Affection from Friends

Affection is an expression that makes another person feel valued and loved, such as warm greetings, compliments, encouragement, praise, or appreciation. Rachel and Gabby share a level of affection typically quarantined to significant others. When Rachel's mom heard about the proposals, she said, "It's kind of weird, but it's also okay." Not only do they share rings and friendship ceremonies, but they also cuddle. For Rachel and Gabby, this is normal, but for most of us, in friendship, it isn't. But why?

It's not that we don't feel deep love for friends; it's just that we don't always feel comfortable expressing it. When I did a talk on how to make friends at work, I asked the audience to write down something positive they feel for a friend that they have yet to tell them. The responses poured in: "I want to tell my friend how much she has inspired me all these years of us being friends," "I want to tell my friends that they've made me a better person," "I hope my friend realizes what a beautiful soul she has," and "I hear your smile through the phone. It makes my day." I felt bittersweet for my audience: sweet because of their love, but bitter because it was yet unsaid.

Why do we go mum about our love toward friends? We just don't get the same permission to express it as we do for our spouses. Hallmark cards, love letters, and physical touch: in the US, so many earmarks of affection are confined to our spouses, although they need not be. For our significant others, we have anniversaries, Valentine's Day, and wedding vows to impart our love. For friends, well, there's International Friendship Day, but no one's heard of it (it's July 30). Its notoriety may rival Measure Your Feet Day (January 23) or National Garlic Day (April 19). It's only since 2010 that we've had Galentine's Day, which was popularized in an episode of *Parks and Recreation* when the main character, Leslie Knope, created the day to express her love for her female friends. The non-gender-specific Palentine's Day has cropped up since.

There are qualities inherent to friendship that prevent us from expressing affection to friends. By nature, friendship is less formal, more wild, and more versatile than romantic relationships, bearing no particular script, which means we just don't know if our friends are as invested as we are. As mentioned in the generosity chapter, approximately half the people we call friends don't call us friends. When we marry someone, we know they're committed. The ceremony, the vows, and the ring prove it. With family, mutual investment is assumed because "blood is thicker than water." But with friends, it's riskier to show affection because we aren't sure they feel the same way.

Also, technology has made figuring out your friends even more confusing. The term "friend" has been so eviscerated that even if we wanted to show love to friends, we would struggle to discern who they are. Do Facebook friends count? People who retweet us? That friend you haven't spoken to for five years but you mutually like each other's posts every other leap year?

Technology and social media have created a loose-tie culture: we have more so-called friends, and yet we feel close to fewer of them than ever. Instead of clarifying who those few are and investing in and celebrating them, we let an algorithm do it for us, leaving us to root for not necessarily our true friends, but whoever's good news crops up on our feed. Without social media, we might be forced to ask ourselves, *Who do I want to keep in my life in an intentional way?* Instead, we portion our affection to whoever is active on our most beloved platform. It's hard to express affection toward our friends when we're not even sure who they are.

Another reason showing love for friends isn't popular (relative to doing so for romantic partners) is because of the jumbling of any type of love with sexual love. We are petrified to express love for our friends because if we do, we risk accusations of being attracted to them. But this muddling reveals our collective confusion as to different forms of love. Angela Chen reveals in her book *Ace: What Asexuality Reveals About Desire, Society, and the Meaning of Sex,* that we feel platonic (appreciation and liking toward someone), romantic (heady passion and idealization of someone), or sexual (desire to have sex with someone) love separately.

We can feel passionate about someone (romantic love) without wanting to have sex with them (sexual love). This means we can feel romance in the confines of friendship. There's even a term for it—"romantic friendship." Throughout history, romance has been a part of friendship, arguably even more so than it was a part of marriage. The first definition of love alluded to friends: to "be pleased with, to regard with affection. We love a man who has done us a favor."

Before the eighteenth century, in Europe and the US, people—albeit predominately White people—did not necessarily love their spouse. Their marital partner was chosen for them by family for practical reasons. Family members chose someone from a family they would like to ally with or who could provide them with resources. As historian Stephanie Coontz put it, "For most of history it was inconceivable that people would choose their mates on the basis of something as fragile and irrational as love."

In Coontz's book *Marriage, a History: How Love Conquered Marriage,* she describes how even when marrying for love became popular in the Victorian era, people still turned to friendship for affection. Popular thinking at the time was that men and women were stark opposites and they needed to come together to complete each other. A man was rational and analytical. A woman was moral and pure. But the genders were so different that they had trouble connecting, and both men and women connected better with their same-gender friends. In Coontz's words, "Many people felt much closer to their own sex than to what was seen as the literally 'opposite'—and alien—sex." In 1863, Lucy Gilmer Breckinridge, a woman whose diary was later published, wrote that she worried she would "never learn to love any man . . . women are so lovely, so angelic. Oh what I would not give for a wife!"

At a time when love wasn't monopolized by spouses, remnants of romance were apparent among famous friends of the past. Alexander Pope, the English poet, wrote to Jonathan Swift, the satirist, "It is an honest truth, there's no one living or dead of whom I think oft'ner, or better than yourself." Herman Melville, who penned *Moby-Dick,* wrote to Nathaniel Hawthorne, author of *The Scarlet Letter,* "I shall leave the world, I feel, with more satisfaction for having come to know you. Knowing you persuades me more than the Bible of our immortality." And Frederick Douglass proclaimed that leaving friends was the hardest part of escaping the plantation: "The thought of leaving my friends was decidedly the most painful thought with which I had to contend. The love of them was my tender point and shook my decision more than all things else."

Romantic love in friendship isn't radical. It's traditional if you peek back far enough into our history. Even now, it is normal for close friends to feel the heady passion and idealization that we typically deem appropriate only for spouses. Nearly all of the best friends I've interviewed and read about have appeared to share some degree of romantic love, as I've defined it. They are excited about and territorial of each other, idealize each other, or want to spend all their time together.

When we pretend romantic love is abnormal in friendship, we leave people ashamed and confused by the deep love they feel for friends. Then, instead of expressing this love, they bury it. In the 1970s, in the feminist journal *Ain't I a Woman?,* a woman wrote that she shared close and affectionate love toward her friends until she read that these feelings warranted psychiatric counseling. She felt "hopelessly dirty and sick. I became suspicious of any uncontrolla-ble emotions and motives my strange new self might have." Because of how we conflate sexual and romantic love, Gabby also admits to being confused about her feelings toward Rachel: "I once asked my-self, 'Am I attracted to her?' And then I was like no, I'm not. How is that possible? It's hard to reconcile that. We cuddle together, but I'm not physically attracted to her. I just love her so much." *Romantic* attraction can crop up without *sexual* attraction. And just because we feel one doesn't mean we feel the other.

What happened? Why are we so much less comfortable now, sharing this depth of love with our friends? Our discomfort with affection in friendships coincides with the rise of homophobia, as it is expressed today. Before the 1900s, one's sexual behaviors didn't comprise an aspect of one's identity like they do today. Before 1868, there was no straight or gay, according to Hanne Blank, author of *Straight: The Surprisingly Short History of Heterosexuality*. Because sexual orientation wasn't an identity, people were harshly stigma-tized for having sex with someone of their gender but not for being or even *seeming* gay. They were free to carve their initials into trees and cuddle and sleep beside friends without stigma, because none of this was sexual. Friends also wrote passionate love letters to each other, like the one in which a nineteenth-century woman told a friend, "The expectation once more to see your face again, makes me feel hot and feverish." It wasn't until prominent psychiatrists, such as Sigmund Freud and Richard von Krafft-Ebing, characterized same-sex love as a sexual disorder,* creating the concept of sexual

---

* In the late nineteenth century, industrialization caused people to flock to cities. With less small-town gossip and more anonymity, people started to engage in all types of sexual acts they felt barred from when living in small towns, including sex with people of the same gender. People took up Krafft-Ebing and Freud's pseudosci-ence around sexuality because they were looking for a way to justify curbing the uptick in sex among people of the same gender that surged in these cities. See Blank's *Straight: The Surprisingly Short History of Heterosexuality* for more.

identity in the process, that homophobia as we know it rose and affection in friendship declined.

The rise of homophobia, or more specifically homohysteria, has ravaged straight men's friendships in particular. Homohysteria describes straight men's fears of being perceived as gay, and researchers argue that these fears impede emotional intimacy among men. Men who are especially homophobic, one study finds, are less likely to be vulnerable with their straight male friends, which then leads them to have less close and satisfying friendships. Before the nineteenth century, society was not homohysteric, so while sex among men was forbidden, men *were* vulnerable with each other; just like women at the time, they wrote each other love letters and cuddled. Now, some men feel compelled to clarify "no homo" when hugging or appreciating their friends, signaling that even bread crumbs of their affection are not homoerotic.

It's not that we don't love our friends like we do our spouses. In fact, one study finds that women experience more intimacy with their same-sex best friend than they do with their lover, and both genders report having more in common with best friends than with lovers. But when it comes to friends, we feel more pressure to conceal that love. Expressing it requires us to transcend homohysteria by challenging homophobia and acknowledging that sexual attraction isn't conveyed by the entire gamut of affectionate behaviors. Transcending it also looks like giving ourselves permission to express to our friends just how deeply we love them.

Affection Benefits Friendship

When we don't express affection, we are at risk of losing the friendship itself. Affection, it turns out, is a mighty force for nurturing connection and intimacy. In a study titled "The Development and

Maintenance of Friendship," Robert Hays, a professor at the University of Utah, tracked the behaviors of budding friendships. He followed potential friendship duos for twelve weeks and then followed up with them months later, to see if he could predict which pairs ended up as friends. What was different between the successful and unsuccessful friendship pairs? The successful pairs expressed high amounts of affection for each other.

Hays found that many of the things that bring us closer to our friends work particularly well at certain stages of friendship, maybe right at the beginning or only after we've gotten to know each other. Affection, however, created closeness at all stages. For people who are already friends, companionship, doing things like watching TV together, made them closer, whereas the power of this act at the beginning stages of friendship was less strong. Affection, however, brought people closer no matter how close they were already. It powers friendships when they're just an embryo, but also when they're a mature adult with a job, life insurance, streaks of gray, and a modest 401(k). Telling people you appreciate them, value them, or see so much good in them builds friendships, no matter how close you are. The more you show affection, the more likely you are to not just make friends, but also deepen the friendships you already have.

In another study, a researcher gave college students two packets of questionnaires and asked them to give one packet to someone they knew who expressed much affection toward others and the second to a person who expressed little affection. The highly affectionate people had strikingly different profiles than the non-affectionate. Not only were they less depressed, happier, and more self-assured, they also received more affection from others, had fuller social calendars, and were less isolated.

Expressing affection doesn't just benefit our friendships. It benefits us. Because we're social creatures, to prod us to connect, our bodies have a rule: whatever we do to connect with others also makes us healthy. Studies have shown that the affectionate are less depressed, have higher self-esteem, and have lower cholesterol, cortisol, and blood pressure. These studies reveal that while we think showing affection benefits others, it also kicks up positive energy inside us. When we judge, the negative energy corrodes us, but when we love, the warm feelings enrich us. How we view others determines what we experience inside ourselves. Knowing this research, I've started "love scrolling" my friends—the opposite of doom scrolling. I scroll through my newsfeed and tell friends how great they're doing and how proud and happy I am for them, and I notice the warmth I feel. It turns out that taking my affection to social media is a good strategy for making and keeping friends. One study found that posting on friends' walls, supporting them after bad news, and congratulating them via Facebook are all linked to more satisfying and closer friendships.

Why exactly does affection make friendship stronger? We find some clues in reciprocity of liking and inferred attraction theories. The crux of these theories is that people like people who like them. In a landmark study in 1958, strangers were brought together in a group to discuss how to improve class instruction. Before they arrived, they took personality tests, and at the start of the group, they received bogus information indicating that three group members were predicted to like them most, based on personality test results. At the end of the discussion, the researchers told group members that they might later be divided into teams and they should report who they wanted to pair with. By and large, people chose to pair with people they were made to believe liked them. These same results have arisen in studies where strangers interact and then report how much they like one another, or where people rate how much they like people already in their lives. People like the people they think like them.

This research challenges a misconception about making friends.

We think making friends is about being suave like James Bond, smart like Bill Gates, or funny like Chris Rock. We think it's about wowing people with our irresistible personalities, but it's not. In one study, people reported that being entertaining or persuasive was the least important quality in a friend, whereas the most important quality was that a friend made them feel good about themselves. People who excel at making friends have one thing in common, and it's less who they are and more how they treat people. They make people feel like they matter. Oprah Winfrey, one of the world's most likable celebrities, does this when she exclaims, "That's an aha moment" or "Tweetable!" whenever her guests say something profound. And nothing says "You matter" like buying someone a brand-new car! As she puts it, "We all want to be heard, to know that we matter and that what we had to say meant something."

Expressing Affection Is Less Awkward Than You Think

Despite the poignant impact of affection in friendship, one reason we avoid it is because we think our affection will come off as weird. I realized this when I taught a class called "Helping Skills," where college students learned basic tools for becoming therapists. Although students generally loved the class, there was one week that never failed to make everyone uncomfortable. In that week, we practiced a therapy skill called immediacy—directly expressing how we think or feel in a relationship.

"Today, you are going to express to one another the things you like about each other," I'd tell the class, my intro to that day's activity. There was always a sprawling silence, in which I was met with wide eyes, bums shifting in seats, and erasers being aggressively tinkered with. Students would offer a list of fears: "What if I freak someone out?" "What if I come off as clingy and desperate?" I would listen to them vent, and then wait out their silence, until a brave soul came forward to participate in the activity.

"Everything you say is so wise. It's like you're quiet but then when you talk, you drop so many truth bombs." "There's just something about you that's just so cool, and so confident, and I admire that." "Every day, I come in here, and you say hi to me and you make me feel so welcomed." The students would all share in a parade of appreciation. In my many years teaching the class, no one ever ended the week freaked out, despite initial fears.

Once the activity was over, the class dynamic was forever changed. It was transformative. People participated more, laughed more, said hi to one another in the hallways. It was like the class had been wearing a corset it finally abandoned. In the last class, we'd reflect on the course, and the students would say how "immediacy week" brought them closer than any other. One student shared, "This is how you strengthen a relationship, when you are intentional with telling someone what they mean to you."

We've explored why we often don't express affection in friendship. We also underestimate just how much we lose when we don't. My class illustrates a bias we have in how we view affection, one that's just like biases we've discussed around vulnerability and initiative—we think our affection will freak people out, but it actually makes them feel closer to us.

In one study, people wrote letters of gratitude and then indicated how happy or awkward the recipients would feel upon receiving the letter. The recipients reported how happy or awkward they actually felt. The participants, it turns out, overestimated how awkward the recipients felt and underestimated how good they felt when receiving the letter. A later study, in the same article, showed that the more we discount the power of our affection on its recipients, the less likely we are to express it. This bias is a real problem. As the study's authors state, "Misunderstanding how positively recipients will respond to an expression of gratitude may leave people choosing to express gratitude less often than they would actually want to, a potentially misplaced barrier to positive interactions."

Affection Makes Us Feel Safe

On one fall evening, when Gabby was in seventh grade, she wandered the suburban streets of Maryland. Her siblings had been fighting, screaming, and when she tried to step in, she was shoved to the side. They had started throwing objects, and that was when Gabby left to take shelter at Rachel's house. It was Shabbat, so she couldn't call or get a ride. She had to trek the few miles.

She knocked on Rachel's door and waited, nervous that she'd be told to go home. A part of her wanted to flee, but another part felt like she'd explode if she didn't seek comfort immediately. Rachel's mom opened the door.

"Is . . . Rachel . . . here?" Gabby asked, starting and stopping each word to gulp air, the way you do when you're trying not to cry.

"Oh, honey, what's wrong?" Rachel's mom asked. "You could always call us. We'll come get you. Even if it's Shabbat. Please call." Rachel came down the stairs and, seeing Gabby looking downward with tears all over her face, hugged her.

The two went to Rachel's room. Gabby collapsed on the bed, and Rachel held her as Gabby shared what had just happened. After that night, Rachel's family started to take Gabby in, and Gabby would spend many nights with Rachel's family, like she was their adopted daughter. Rachel leaned on Gabby too. When Rachel's favorite aunt got cancer, she shared her fears with Gabby.

A defining aspect of Rachel and Gabby's friendship, the major ingredient that made it so close, is safety. When one of them is in need, they know the other is there. Clearly, safety is cultivated through vulnerability and support, like what Rachel and Gabby offered each other when Gabby showed up at her house. But it's also cultivated through affection, which signals *I love and value you as you are and you're safe to be you with me.* Affection builds up someone's worth, makes them feel like they're enough, they're lovable. Gabby never received this at home. She remembers babysitting her niece and trying to make sure her niece never felt as unworthy as she did. She'd say, "We waited nine months for you. And the day you were born, we were so excited to get to know you, to get to know the things you like and the things you don't like. You as you are is enough."

But Gabby did receive this affection somewhere, and that was from Rachel. Their mutual friend proposals are the icing on the cake of their abundant expressions of affection toward each other. They also write each other long cards, essays that detail how important they are to each other. They praise each other in front of outside company. "She's just a lovable ball of energy and is very much herself. She's a wonderful, kind human," Rachel told another friend about Gabby. Neither of them ever has to fish for compliments, because praise is embedded in the language of their friendship. When Rachel told Gabby she would be interviewed for this book, Gabby said, "Make sure you tell her what an amazing friend you are, and how validating you are of everybody all the time."

Affection Makes Difficult Conversations Easier

Affection can strengthen friendships not just when we're happy with our friends but also when we're upset with them. When we show affection while bringing up a concern, people feel challenged in a way that gives them dignity and makes them feel loved and empowered, instead of worthless. This allows them to be more amenable to our concerns. In college, Gabby's boyfriend, Paul, was moving in with her and her roommates. But her other roommate, Tina, was sleeping in his room because her bed was covered in laundry. Gabby confronted Tina with a kiss on the forehead, a rub of her shoulder, and said, "I love you, but you can't keep running away from your shit. You have to deal with it. I see a pile of clothing in the bed, and I know that's why you're not sleeping there. I have to go to class. But when I get home, I'll do laundry with you. I'll help you. I'll bring back food and we'll do this together. But it has to happen." Tina reflected on this memory, saying, "Gabby will tell me in the most loving way to get my shit together. Other people tell me to do something, and I'm like, well fuck you. But with her, I actually listen because of how she says it."

Affection triggers something striking in the other person. As we touched on in the authenticity chapter, trying to protect ourselves is often at odds with protecting our relationships. When we try to protect ourselves—by shutting down, being passive, or trying to elevate ourselves above others—we often harm our relationships. And when we try to protect the relationship—by de-escalating conflict or being trusting—our self is more defenseless. To build better friendship, we need to figure out how to not just shift into pro-relationship (rather than self-protection) mode ourselves, but also to activate our friends' pro-relationship mode, so they'll invest in the friendship, despite the risk to their selves. Affection helps us do this.

According to "risk regulation theory" developed by Sandra Murray, a professor of psychology at the University of Buffalo, "confidence in a partner's positive regard and caring allows people to risk seeking dependence and connectedness." In other words, to invest in a relationship, we need proof we won't be rejected when doing so. Similarly, if we want people to invest in us, we need to make them feel safe to. And we grant this security when we show affection. We impart that we love, value, and accept someone, so they can feel safe to take the risks of intimacy with us.

Affection Makes Our Friends Secure

Up until now, we've learned how to become more secure in friend-ship. But to make and keep friends, risk regulation theory suggests that we don't just need to be more secure. We need to make others secure. We need to become attachment sanctuaries, terrains of safety, and we can do this through showing affection. Making oth-ers feel secure is not just a selfless act for our friends' benefit; it's in our best interest. Secure people, we've learned, are better friends—they are more vulnerable and authentic and take more initiative. When we make our friends know they are loved and accepted, they let their guard down and melt into a secure pro-relationship mode. They feel comfortable initiating with us, checking in with us, affirm-ing us, being vulnerable with us. They are invested in us. We bring out the best in them, and they bring out the best in us, in an upward spiral that brings out the best in friendship.

Risk regulation theory reveals just how harmful our culture of flakiness is. When we flake on someone last minute, we make them more insecure as we signal that we don't value them—the *opposite* of what makes people feel comfortable investing in us. Instead of putting them in pro-relationship mode, we swing them into self-protection mode, and they stop reaching out to us. Of course, when we flake, we don't always mean to convey that we don't like a person, but regardless of our intentions, the impact is all the same. I've been guilty of this myself. A friend of a friend invited me to her birthday, and it was later on in the evening and cold out. I had RSVPed yes, but as the hour drew nearer, I didn't want to venture out. This friend never invited me out again, and she even told our mutual friend how hurt she was that I flaked and that she worried I didn't like her.

What should we do instead? How can we use affection to make people feel secure enough to invest in us? If we meet a potential friend at a happy hour, instead of checking our texts during the conversation, we can greet them warmly and stay engaged. If we want our new friend to invite us for pizza, when they text to ask how we're doing, instead of saying "Everything's fine," we can say, "It's so good to hear from you! There's so much I've wanted to tell you about." If we want our friends to keep us abreast of their lives, when they tell us they received an award, instead of saying "That's cool," we say, "I'm so proud of you! There's no one I know who deserves this more!" Although when we crave connection we tend to focus on our needs, when we stop thinking about whether we belong and shift to making others feel like they belong, we'll inevitably belong too.

Gabby and Rachel's friendship aligns with the tenets of risk regulation theory. According to Gabby, "This friendship has helped me be more open to connecting with other people. It's helped me realize my self-worth. I know that I am worthy of love. Having that has made me braver. If I didn't have this friendship, I'd be much warier of going out and trying to connect with people, questioning whether I'm good enough. It's given me confidence." Because Rachel has made her feel secure, she feels comfortable investing not just in Rachel but in all her other friendships.

One of the important ways Rachel and Gabby show affection for each other is by showing enthusiasm for each other's good news. When Gabby told Rachel that she was considering having a baby on her own, Rachel was ecstatic: "If you decide you want to go through this, you should know your future baby already has an auntie who loves them a ton. They've got family. And you have someone who's going to Lamaze classes with you. I'm so excited for you, and I will be there!"

Research suggests that when Rachel responded with so much excitement at Gabby's news, she further strengthened their friendship. A study called "I Like That You Feel My Pain, But I Love That You Feel My Joy" found that we are more satisfied in our close relationships when other people are happy for our joy. In fact, this responsiveness more greatly predicted the quality of the relationship than how others responded to our suffering. Another study involved a person going into the lab and sharing one of the best events that had happened to them in the last few years with a "stranger" who was secretly working for the researcher. In one condition, the stranger responded enthusiastically ("Wow! That's great"), and in another, the stranger neutrally asked a list of questions about the event, like "What makes your event so positive for you?" Afterward, participants reported feeling more closeness and liking for the responsive partner. Lastly, as proof of risk regulation theory, a study found that in an interview, when the interviewer responded positively to something the interviewee expressed, the interviewee was more likely to return the money they were "accidentally overpaid" for their interview participation. When we show affection to people, they invest right back.

How to Show Affection

Risk regulation theory shows us that making friends is about making people feel safe, whether that means giving them more affection or learning how to better receive theirs. It also implicates us in the success of our friendships. Often, when our friendships are shallow, we blame our friends. "They're not my people," we might tell ourselves. That may be true. Sometimes people just don't get along, but risk regulation theory suggests that if we want better friendships, it's useful to turn the microscope back on ourselves, to assess "Do I make people feel safe? Do I show them I love and value them? Do I convey that they matter?"

One woman I interviewed, Anne, was aware she had walls but complained that others weren't trying hard enough to climb them.

But what Anne didn't realize was that others have walls too; in fact, it's healthy that they do. Expecting others to repeatedly make themselves vulnerable and reach out to us while we hide behind our walls—not showing any affection or openly receiving theirs—is expecting them to abandon their healthy mechanisms of self-protection, while failing to make them feel safe to do so. Instead of only asking why our friends don't try more, we also must evaluate whether we make them feel safe to.

Here is a list of ways to show affection to a friend:

- Tell them how much they mean to you.
- When they reach out, tell them how happy you are to hear from them.
- Be excited at their good news.
- Compliment them.
- Praise their hard work.
- Greet them warmly.
- Let them know when they share something that's meaningful to you.
- Tell them when you think of them in passing.
- Tell other people how great you think they are.
- Let them know when they impress you.
- Tell them they'll succeed in reaching their dreams.
- Tell them when you think they have a great idea.
- Smile at them genuinely.
- Remind them you are grateful to know them.

But affection doesn't always make people feel comfortable and safe. Many of us have experienced times when it's fallen flat. We may have told a friend we appreciate them, and they got awkward and changed the subject. If affection is so powerful for friendship, then why does this happen? The answer, it turns out, is that many of us don't know what affection *truly is*. As Kory's story will reveal, expressing affection can be harder than we think.

How to Give Love Friends Can Receive

When Kory became a graduate student at the University of Washington, he was assigned his very own office. Eventually, another graduate student, Scott, joined him. Scott adorned the wall with a picture of Stockholm, Sweden. Kory had been there the previous summer, so the two chatted about its wonders. Another day, Kory entered the office to find Scott sprawled on his desk, reading something and laughing so hard he was gasping for air. Kory watched, afraid Scott might roll off the desk, while thinking to himself, *Scott's a cool guy.*

Kory hoped Scott could be not just his colleague but also his friend, so one day, he invited Scott to dinner. The conversation flowed, and they got to know each other more, unencumbered by the formality that office walls requested of them. Kory is a highly affectionate person who grew up in a family where everyone hugged and kissed and said they loved each other. It was natural for him to pull in and hug Scott as they departed, to mark that he had come to feel at least a kernel of love for Scott. He felt Scott's body stiffen in his arms, and as their bodies peeled apart, things felt weird.

Kory thought about that awkward embrace more than he liked to. What did it mean that Scott recoiled at his hug? Was he uncomfortable with physical affection? Or uncomfortable with Kory? Did he not like Kory at all? Had Kory done something wrong, irreparably harmed the relationship with his enthusiasm? He waited for the opportunity to clear the air with Scott, and he found an in when the two attended a conference together in San Diego.

As they sat on a dock, gazing at the water, Kory chewed on his plan of action. Usually good at initiating tough conversations, Kory was nervous this time. Did he really want to hear if he had made the relationship unsalvageable? Where would that leave him—alone like driftwood pruned from its ship, floating lonely in the water? But then, if he did bring it up, he could mend things—apologize, pledge to never hug again, hug it out (JK, not that last part).

So, Kory brought it up. And Scott's response forever changed the course of his life. "There are other ways I am more comfortable giving and receiving affection. I'm not comfortable with hugs, but that doesn't mean I don't like you," Scott said. Kory came to understand affection like he never had before. He realized affection could be polarizing, that not everyone loved and appreciated it like he did. He also realized that someone could reject the *delivery* of your affection while welcoming the warm feelings that drove the act. Scott could reject his hug without rejecting him.

Now Kory Floyd is a foremost expert on affection and a professor and communication expert at the University of Arizona. His research has helped him make sense of what happened all those years ago with Scott. He's identified three components of affection: you feel love, appreciation, or fondness (so flattery and manipulation don't count!); you act to express those feelings; and the other person interprets and welcomes your behavior as reflecting those warm feelings. When he hugged Scott, he technically wasn't showing affection, because Scott hadn't perceived it that way. Kory explained that racial microaggressions exemplify failed affection: "You tell an African American they're really articulate, and they respond, 'Why wouldn't I be?' and you negatively stereotyped their race as less articulate rather than complimenting them."

To be effective at showing affection, Dr. Floyd argues, we need to calibrate the way we show affection with the way the other person receives it. "When you offer affection, it's coming from a certain perspective," he said. "There's an assumption—that your behavior will be received in an affirming way. But just because you like compliments doesn't mean another person will. You have to take their perspective."

Taking one another's perspective when expressing affection is something Gabby and Rachel had to learn. When they'd attend gatherings with friends, Rachel would introduce Gabby: "Hi. This is my friend Gabby. She's amazing in every way and you should get to know her." And then when mutual friends would ask Gabby questions, Rachel would answer, "Gabby would like a tea rather than coffee." Rachel did this because "I love Gabby so much and would just get so excited to talk about her." But Rachel's actions made Gabby uncomfortable and impeded her from connecting with their friends. Gabby brought it up to Rachel, and Rachel made a conscious effort to stop chiming in. Gabby would watch Rachel squirm, avert her eyes, and sit on her hands to stop inserting herself.

For another period of their friendship, Rachel would try to show love by offering Gabby unsolicited advice. Gabby would go to Rachel with her insecurities, and instead of Rachel just lending an ear, she'd tell Gabby how she could improve. "Please stop. I just need someone to listen, and I don't need you to fix it," Gabby told Rachel one evening. "Okay," Rachel said, "but check with me first to make sure I have space to give you an ear." Seeing Rachel adjust to her needs made their friendship much closer.

I have not been as good as Rachel at shifting my affection toward friends when they don't receive it as I intended. During one holiday season, some friends and I sat around an oval oak table and, after we did a gift exchange, we shared what we loved about one another. Most of us soaked it up, with one of our friends, fishing, said, "I like this game! What else do you all like about me?" But my friend Cassandra was unmoved. In fact, as I radiated all the things I loved and appreciated about her, she disagreed with each of them, as if we were debating the merits of *Groundhog Day.* I felt rejected and frustrated. I was trying to give her gifts, and she kept pelting them back, unopened. I noticed the next time I tried to compliment her, I disclaimed, "You're not allowed to reject any of this!"

I thought Cassandra was in the wrong for dismissing my compliments, but now I realize I was in the wrong for forcing them upon her. Dr. Floyd, Rachel, and Gabby helped me realize that, to my revelation, strong-arming someone into receiving love isn't loving at all; instead, being responsive to someone's boundaries is. Also, Dr. Floyd helped me realize I needed to take Cassandra's behavior less personally. People simply receive affection in different ways, and when they're not able to receive our affection, it doesn't mean they're rejecting us. It just means that our behavior isn't what affection looks like for them.

This understanding also helped me release resentment in friendships where I was taking deflection of my affection as rejection (and simultaneously developing the opening line to my next poem . . .), rather than as mismatched styles around affection. I once sent a friend a job listing I thought she might like, and she responded, "I already have a good job." I was trying to convey that I was looking out for her, but instead, I conveyed that her job wasn't good enough. I was upset that she received it that way, but I realized I could take more responsibility for my impact. Another time, an ex-partner and I met up with one of his closest friends. I really like this friend, so I was effusive when seeing him: "Hi! It's so good to see you! We've missed you." He didn't match my enthusiasm, and I remember wondering if he liked me. But now I think my excitement may have just overwhelmed him.

Dr. Floyd pointed out that people with anxious attachment often struggle with modulating their expression of love based on how someone receives it. If someone's sheepish about receiving their love, instead of backing off, they double down. "Anxious people never feel like there can be enough love. So they will smother the other person with affection to the point at which they can no longer keep up," he said. "The other person becomes overwhelmed. Their intention is to strengthen the relationship, but they paradoxically end up ruining it."

Dr. Floyd's wisdom on affection also reveals something larger about dynamics in friendships. Sometimes, we get so focused on what *should* happen in our friendships that we don't attend to what's *actually* happening. *This friend should like my compliments. They should like my hugs. They should want my praise,* we tell ourselves (or else, they should be there whenever I need them; they should be vulnerable; they shouldn't be vulnerable). This leaves us frustrated with them because we imposed a rule on them that they never agreed to.

We keep approaching the relationship in the same tired ways because of what we think should be true—we keep complimenting, keep praising, even as our friends wince, just like I did with Cassandra. If we can allow people to be the unique flowers that they are, if we can recognize that in relationships, there are few "shoulds," then we can be more amenable to adjusting our behaviors in ways that create greater harmony. Ironically, this may lead them to change into the more loving and attentive friend we want them to be, because by adjusting to their needs, we make them feel secure. It's classic risk regulation theory.

Sometimes, of course, it is impossible to adjust our affection without feeling too compromised, or what psychologists call "deselfed." In these cases, we can decide whether we want to keep the friendship or at what depth we can do so without feeling inauthentic. Gabby retains some friendships in which her friends have trouble receiving her affection. She has a friend, Tali, who is so uncomfortable with affection that whenever Gabby hugs her, she jokes, "Me putting my arms around you? This is a hug. We do this when we're happy or we want to show someone we care about them." And Tali jokes back, "GET YOUR HANDS OFF ME!" and hisses. But Gabby also acknowledges when others are uncomfortable with her affection: "It affects the level of closeness we can reach. If I'm toning it down, I'm not really bringing the full me. I'm bringing a consumable me." In fact, she thinks part of the reason her friendships with men aren't as deep is because it seems impossible for her to express affection without signaling sexual interest.

But when we are open to adjusting our affection, how do we do it? Dr. Floyd advises having conversations with friends about how they like to receive affection, which he does by asking, "What helps you feel my appreciation toward you?" This may seem unnatural, but I can attest that it feels good to be asked. When I was moving to Atlanta, Cassandra asked me, "What's your favorite way to keep in touch?" It felt so nice that she cared to ask.

Asking also allows us to express affirmation idiosyncratically, based on the particulars of our friendship, kind of like an affection "inside joke." Idiosyncratic affection will only amplify its loving impact, since, as research finds, exclusivity breeds friendships. In other words, when we have memories, language, or experiences that we share with only one person, it strengthens the relationship. Kat and Gwina were two friends I met at a happy hour who celebrated their friendaversary every year, on a day they dubbed "Katwina." Some friends go on yearly vacations together or have annual Friendsgivings. Whatever the occasion, we should develop rituals that allow us to show affection to friends.

How to Better Receive Love

But it's not just on our shoulders to curate our affection to our friends. To be a good friend, we need to expand the ways we receive love so that we don't reject our friends' warmth. This will benefit us too, since, as mentioned, anything we do that makes our friends feel less rejected allows them to invest more in the friendship. When it comes to giving and receiving affection, then, "It's more of a negotiation or a compromise," Dr. Floyd imparted. "In a good relationship, I will modify my behaviors to better match your comfort level. But at the same time, you will also try to become more receptive to my behaviors."

Avoidant people in particular struggle to negotiate affection. They tend to give it less and receive it poorly. A recovering-avoidant attorney, Dana, told me: "I've spent my life trying to show how smart I am to get people to like me, to have people say, 'Wow, she's intelligent, someone I'd like to have around me.' But in a subtle way, I was positioning myself to be above other people rather than alongside them. This constant need to be special and be seen as smart made it difficult for me to compliment others, because if they were special, then I might be less special myself. In a strange way, what I did to create connections with people actually disconnected me from them, because to be loved by other people requires accepting rather than surpassing them."

When it comes to receiving affection, avoidants don't trust others, so when others show affection, they assume it's because of ulterior motives. In one study, people wrote about benefits they received from friends. Two days later, in the lab, they were asked if they thought their friends benefited them because they felt they had to. But before answering this question, in an avoidance condition, half the participants wrote about someone they couldn't trust and felt uncomfortable being close to. Participants primed with avoidance were more likely to assume their friends benefited them out of obligation. Dana would add, "I used to get the sense that people were nice because they wanted something out of me. And then their niceness didn't count. It was uncomfortable, actually. It made me feel pressured rather than happy."

Avoidants are, of course, in self-protection mode when they

make unflattering assumptions about others' motives, and in doing so, as risk regulation theory tells us, they often harm their relationships. According to the authors of the study, "Perceiving benefits to be non-voluntary may protect them from temptations to increase dependency on a partner. Sadly, if such perceptions are conveyed to partners, partners may become frustrated, decrease true caring, and set a self-fulfilling prophecy into motion." This point is backed by one study that finds that people are less likely to show gratitude to someone they think won't receive it well.

Unless we have a reason to think otherwise, if someone expresses affection toward us, we should assume their intentions are pure. This not only feels better than assuming they have some other motive, but it also nurtures the friendship and our self-esteem, which is another important filter for how we receive love.

People with low self-esteem struggle to receive love because they don't notice when it's there. In a telling study called "Acceptance Is in the Eye of the Beholder," people had to film themselves discussing several conversation topics. They then had to watch a "response video" from a stranger who allegedly watched their video and then discussed those same topics. To raise the stakes, they were told they might meet the stranger face-to-face later. The "strangers" (who were actually actors) purposely affirmed the participants in the video by agreeing with the participant, "I'm with you on this one," smiling, and saying, outright, that they were interested: "So I hope to see you in the second part of this study." Even though all participants watched the *same* video of the stranger, when participants had lower self-esteem, they were less likely to pick up on these cues of affection and were less sure about whether the stranger liked them.* Even though we come to love ourselves through others

---

* When people with low self-esteem were told they wouldn't meet the stranger in person, they *were* able to pick up on acceptance cues. This suggests that it's not that people with low self-esteem are oblivious to signals of acceptance. Instead, they

loving us, what this study shows is that if we don't love ourselves, when others love us, we don't register it.

Low self-esteem can make another's love feel threatening. When people with low self-esteem receive compliments, the gap between how someone views them and how they view themselves triggers an identity crisis. According to one study, people with low self-esteem endorse statements like "I feel like I don't know exactly who I am after getting a compliment," and "When I am complimented, sometimes I feel like the other person clearly doesn't know me." When we compliment someone, we convey that they are great, and if they don't feel great, the compliment can make them feel, counterintuitively, misunderstood, unseen, or pressured to act good enough so they can merit the compliment. That same study showed that people with low self-esteem are more likely to devalue compliments. For them, it feels easier to reject a compliment than it is to reject their entire sense of who they are. When affection forces us to choose between being loved and being understood, we'd rather be understood.

The authors of the study stated, "If people do not trust in their partners' positive regard—which is chronically true for [people with low self-esteem]—they adopt self-protection goals, which drive behavior that can undermine opportunities to achieve satisfying relationships." Myles, a personal trainer, can attest to how struggling to receive love can harm our relationships. He told me, "I always feel like I'm the one doing more in a relationship, but really, people are loving me and I can't take it. I can't trust it." He grew up with parents who were always fighting, and with a father who had a temper. He remembers getting a bad grade. His father immediately attacked him: "Why are you such a failure? Why can't you do anything right?" When he cried, the abuse only got worse. He walked on eggshells

---

likely downplay acceptance cues so they won't feel worse if they're ultimately rejected. People with high self-esteem don't fear rejection as much, so they don't have to engage in this defense mechanism.

around his father, always fearing his rage, which could get triggered in a microsecond. Even in their happy moments, "it's terrifying to feel love because it's something dangerous that can be taken away from me."

To get better at taking in others' praise or compliments, it helps to pause and think about the other person's intentions in affirming us rather than just focusing on our interpretation of their comments. One study asked people to report on a compliment they received from a relationship partner. A third of participants then reflected on why their partner admired them and what it meant for them and the relationship, a third described the compliment, and a third described it in more detail. People with low self-esteem felt happier and more secure and valued the relationship more when they reflected on their partner's positive motives. These results reveal that thinking of the admiration underneath the compliment rather than how it might bite our insecurities will keep us from denying, refuting, or downplaying love. And it'll make us more secure. Therapy is also a good option to open us up to receiving love. Myles added that therapy helped him realize that love isn't always scary and to feel good enough about himself so that he can trust that when others said they loved him, they might actually mean it.

Loving You as You Are

In Rachel and Gabby's freshman-year ceramics class, Gabby made a harrowing sculpture of a home. Its walls were boarded, it had a hole in the roof, and it had copper-colored mold painted on it. It was a broken home, and it was meant to symbolize her and where she came from. But by her senior year, her family dynamic was healthier, and thanks in large part to Rachel, she felt healthier inside. She couldn't stand to look at the home every day, perched in her guest room, as she grew beyond its meaning. She asked Rachel if she'd help her smash it.

The two brought hammers to a ceramics shop and shattered every last piece of the home. The holey roof, the boarded walls, and the copper-colored mold were all hammered to smithereens. They made an event of it, taking pictures as they smashed. "That was the moment in our friendship where I felt proudest of Gabby," Rachel said.

As Gabby went home, proud to show her aunt the shards, her aunt told her she should never have done that—she should have never made a mess of her art. Even as Gabby told her it meant she was no longer broken, her aunt continued to scold her until Gabby felt ashamed. Her aunt's response, contrasted with Rachel's, showed her the power of affection and what it truly means. She said, "Rachel being so proud of me in that moment told me *I see all of you and I still love you. I love the good and I love the bad.* I think love is holding that space, creating that space for people to express their full selves, to have full freedom in the ways they want to live their lives, and to love them anyway. What she did to help me feel less broken was to love me as I am."

TAKEAWAYS

▸ Show more affection to your friends. They'll be happier to receive it than you think.
  ▪ Some ways to show affection are:
    • Tell them how much they mean to you.
    • When they reach out, tell them how happy you are to hear from them.
    • Be excited at their good news.
    • Compliment them.
    • Praise their hard work.
    • Greet them warmly.

- Let them know when they share something that's meaningful to you.
- Tell them when you think of them in passing.
- Tell other people how great you think they are.
- Let them know when they impress you.
- Tell them they'll succeed in reaching their dreams.
- Tell them when you think they have a great idea.
- Smile at them genuinely.
- Remind them you are grateful to know them.
- Develop rituals—like Palentine's Day or Friendsgiving—to show affection toward friends.

▶ To make new friends, use affection to make people feel safe to invest in you. If you meet a potential friend, greet them warmly. If you want a new friend to invite you for pizza, tell them how happy you are to hear from them when they reach out. And don't flake.

▶ Feeling romantic love for friends is normal. Allow yourself to express this love in ways your friend can receive it.

▶ If your friend gets uncomfortable with your affection, adapt by calibrating how you deliver your affection to how your friend receives it.
   - To do so, ask your friends, "What helps you feel my appreciation for you? How do you best like to receive it?"

▶ Be open to friends' affection by:
   - Assuming their intentions are pure.
   - Thinking about the positive and warm feelings they're expressing when they show affection toward you rather than your own hesitation in reaction to it.

Conclusion

I hope you're finishing this book with new insights on how to make and keep friends. I hope it challenged you and gave you direction. I hope you'll be a little less afraid, a little more loving, a little more willing to be intentional, to take responsibility for making our world less lonely and more kind. I hope you'll see giving love as just as much a gift as receiving it. I hope you'll be more willing to be vulnerable and tell the people in your life just how much they've uplifted you. Ultimately, I hope you find and keep friends who love you as you are and show up when you need them, and I hope you'll be that friend too. But there's one more piece of advice I need to impart to help you actualize all of this.

Billy Baker is a journalist and father who works for the *Boston Globe*. He wrote a memoir, *We Need to Hang Out,* about his quest to make friends. The book idea originated from a *Boston Globe* article, one of the most popular in the news outlet's history. The article detailed men's struggles in making friends, and Billy's in particular. So many could relate to Billy's friendlessness that the article went viral. When I interviewed Billy, I asked him what he learned in his journey to make friends. "I've always been a mostly good human being, in a box-checky way," he said. "I woke up every day and I was going to be a good husband and a good father and I was gonna go to the gym and I was gonna eat my broccoli and I was gonna be a good employee. What I have done is added 'be a good friend' to the list."

It's easy to scrap friends from the list. There's so much we juggle, from spouses, to children, to health, to work that never ceases. Friendship takes energy that we don't feel like we have. It's effort to think about what your friend wants for their birthday, or bring up a problem, or answer a friend's panicked call at 1:00 a.m., or pick them up from the airport, or reach out, or pause to reflect and express how much they mean to you. And it's not always clear that it's worth it.

But it is.

I've pelted you with studies to demonstrate just how worth it it is. As a reminder: at the start of this book, I shared how having social connection is one of the strongest determinants of our happiness. Out of 106 factors that influence depression, having a confidante is the most powerful. Loneliness is more fatal than a poor diet or lack of exercise, as corrosive as smoking fifteen cigarettes a day. Friendship literally saves our lives. This isn't intuitive, though, because connection's influence is intangible. It doesn't have the same perceivable impact on our bodies as ingesting asparagus or feeling beads of sweat trickle down our arm. It's an invisible healer, so it's easy to diminish the importance of adding it to the list.

Until it isn't so invisible. I wrote this book during the COVID-19 pandemic, when my regular weekend plans morphed into plans to stay home indefinitely. The toxicity of loneliness was a slow poison: a tamping of joy, a malaise, a not-quite-myself-ness. But when my sporadic walk dates with friends came around, I'd inflate with life. Warmth, joy, purpose, my very spirit, it all poured back into me. The impact of a simple interaction was dramatic. Friendship felt like CPR. What was once buried beneath work and chores became the foundation of my vitality to do the rest of these things. What was once muddled in its impact became undeniable. What was once often simple fun became my pulse.

All the studies I read lived inside me. Yes, friendship is curative, said my heart after being vulnerable to a friend in my darkest hours. Yes, it is grounding, said my mood after a hike with a friend. Yes, it is necessary, said somewhere deep and true inside me.

So, after you start to practice all you've learned in this book to make and keep friends, there's one last thing I ask: Don't take friendship for granted. Don't be passive, letting friendship fizzle because you forgot to reach out. Don't dip out when friends need you. Don't wait for calamity to rock you into realizing friendship is priceless. Engrave friendship on your list. Make being a good friend a part of who you are, because a deep and true core that needs to belong lies within us all.

Acknowledgments

I would have never written this book if it wasn't for the wellness group that changed my life forever. Lauri Ng, Heather and Fiona McQueen, Mikelann Scerbo, Bri Canty—I am better because I've known you. Thank you for agreeing to my really intense group rules of looking up research articles to support the "wellness" of your idea. I took it all the way!

Thanks to Darren Agboh for bringing me tea and kombucha, telling me you'll buy a hundred copies of my book (you don't have to, because the moral support was worth a hundred copies), and accepting me in my wild-haired, multiday-pajamaed, mad scientist state when writing this. Thank you to Tuxedo the dog for being my sweet, cuddly reprieve when I needed one.

Thanks to my agent, Todd Shuster, and former agent, Justin Brouckaert, for challenging me to make *Platonic* into a book that I am so proud to say reflects who I am. Your counsel was wise, and it made this book better. Thanks to Erin Files for making *Platonic* an international affair. Thank you to my team at Putnam and my editor there, Michelle Howry, and her editorial assistant, Ashley Di Dio. Thank you to all the folks at Putnam who worked their behind-the-scenes magic to manifest *Platonic*, including Andrea Monagle,

Acknowledgments

Janice Barral, Erin Byrne, Nancy Resnick, Ashley Hewlett, Elora Weil, Emily Mlynek, and Samantha Bryant. Your feedback turned *Platonic* into what it was meant to be. Thank you to Ellen Hendriksen for referring me to Aevitas and helping my dreams come true. Teara Jamison fact-checked this book and dazzled me along the way with her commitment to make *Platonic* the best version of itself.

Thank you to my writing critique group—Rhaina Cohen, Brandon Tensley, Jenny Schmidt, and Emily Tamkin. Absolutely every one of you is brilliant, and I struck gold when I found you as partners in writing and in friendship. Thanks to Adam Smiley Poswolsky for co-hosting our all-star author support group. Thank you to Joy Harden Bradford, who helped crack me out of the ivory tower by welcoming me on *Therapy for Black Girls.*

Thank you to my mom, Gina Franco, for teaching me what it means to want everyone in your life to succeed. Thank you to my dad, Stefano Franco, for raising us kids to be intellectually curious beyond measure. Thank you to my brother, Stephen Franco, for growing with me. Thank you to my sister, Tania Vazquez, for making sure we all have some common sense, and to Billy Vazquez, for helping her raise the greatest people ever, my nieces, Angelica Vazquez and Natasha Vazquez. I love you both *so* much.

Thank you to Kana Felix for being the type of person who heals everyone around you, me included. Thanks to Racheli Katz for keeping me grounded when I faced reviewer number two and life. Thank you to Ginnie Seger for sending me that video by Cheryl Strayed at my lowest and for being a model of great friendship. Thanks to Rabia Friedman for showing me what it looks like when two friends simply click. Thank you to Krizia Gupiteo for being the most considerate, dedicated friend. Thank you to Harbani Ahuja for being a generous and loving soul. Thanks to Vanessa Williams for being my forever favorite adventure buddy. Thank you to Mikelann Scerbo (again) for just being the kindest person on the planet. Thanks to Leah Fuller,

Acknowledgments

who has shown me what it takes to make a friendship last a lifetime. Thank you to Lauri Ng (again) for getting me. Thanks to Michael Abdullah for picking me up in the rain literally and figuratively. Thank you to Keshia Ashe for being everyone's biggest cheerleader. Thank you to my neighbors. We helped each other survive the pandemic, and the way we support each other brings me so much joy.

Thank you to *everybody* whose story contributed to this book. I kept many of you anonymous, but I hope you'll smile with recognition when you see yourself in these pages.

Thank you to *all* the academics who contributed their time to *Platonic*. Your research astounds me, and I am so excited for everyone it will help. Thank you to my PhD advisor, Karen O'Brien, for helping fuel my passion for research. You nurtured my love of science when it was a vulnerable seed, and you tended it and it grew. Thank you to Mia Smith-Bynum, my mentor, for always treating me like family and being a fabulous Black woman role model. Speaking of Black women role models, thank you to my mentor Beverly Tatum for telling me that I should go for *Platonic*. If we had never had that lunch where you gave me the permission I needed, I'm not sure I'd have written this book. Thank you to my PhD program at the University of Maryland and internship at the University of Maryland Counseling Center for helping me understand that at our core, we are all love.

Notes

Introduction: The Secret to Making Friends as an Adult

xx   **other babies cry:** Grace B. Martin and Russell D. Clark, "Distress Crying in Neonates: Species and Peer Specificity," *Developmental Psychology* 18, no. 1 (1982): 3–9, https://doi.org/10.1037/0012-1649.18.1.3.

Chapter 1: How Friendship Transforms Our Lives

6   **eudaimonia, or flourishing:** Dirk Baltzly and Nick Eliopoulos, "The Classical Ideals of Friendship," in *Friendship: A History,* ed. Barbara Caine (New York: Equinox, 2009).

6   **in the seventeenth century:** Mia, "History of Friendship: From Ancient Times to the XXI Century," *Youth Time Magazine,* May 2, 2016, https://youth -time.eu/history-of-friendship-from-ancient-times-to-the-xxi-century.

6   **superior to romance:** Juliet Lapidos, "What's Plato Got to Do with It?," *Slate,* September 26, 2010, https://slate.com/human-interest/2010/09/the-origins -of-the-term-platonic-friendship.html.

7   **the strongest preventor:** Karmel W. Choi et al., "An Exposure-Wide and Mendelian Randomization Approach to Identifying Modifiable Factors for the Prevention of Depression," *American Journal of Psychiatry* 177, no. 10 (October 2020): 944–54, https://doi.org/10.1176/appi.ajp.2020.19111158.

7   **The impact of loneliness:** Julianne Holt-Lunstad, Timothy B. Smith, and J. Bradley Layton, "Social Relationships and Mortality Risk: A Meta-Analytic Review," *PLoS Medicine* 7, no. 7 (2010): e1000316, https://doi.org/10.1371/journal .pmed.1000316; Julianne Holt-Lunstad, "The Potential Public Health Relevance of Social Isolation and Loneliness: Prevalence, Epidemiology, and Risk Factors," *Public Policy & Aging Report* 27, no. 4 (2017): 127–30, https://doi.org/10.1093/ppar /prx030.

7   **level of social connection:** Ed Diener and Martin E. P. Seligman, "Very Happy People," *Psychological Science* 13, no. 1 (2002): 81–84, https://doi.org/10.1111/1467 -9280.00415.

7 **rated an alleged terrorist:** Daniel M. T. Fessler and Colin Holbrook, "Friends Shrink Foes: The Presence of Comrades Decreases the Envisioned Physical Formidability of an Opponent," *Psychological Science* 24, no. 5 (2013): 797–802, https://doi.org/10.1177/0956797612461508.

7 **judged a hill:** Simone Schnall, Kent D. Harber, Jeanine K. Stefanucci, and Dennis R. Proffitt, "Social Support and the Perception of Geographical Slant," *Journal of Experimental Social Psychology* 44, no. 5 (2008): 1246–55, https://doi.org/10.1016/j.jesp.2008.04.011.

7 **exercise decreases our risk of death:** Željko Pedišić et al., "Is Running Associated with a Lower Risk of All-Cause, Cardiovascular and Cancer Mortality, and Is the More the Better? A Systematic Review and Meta-Analysis," *British Journal of Sports Medicine* 54, no. 15 (2019): 898–905, https://doi.org/10.1136/bjsports-2018-100493.

7 **diet by up to 24 percent:** Xianglan Zhang et al., "Cruciferous Vegetable Consumption Is Associated with a Reduced Risk of Total and Cardiovascular Disease Mortality," *American Journal of Clinical Nutrition* 94, no. 1 (2011): 240–46, https://doi.org/10.3945/ajcn.110.009340.

7 **large social network:** Julianne Holt-Lunstad, Theodore F. Robles, and David A. Sbarra, "Advancing Social Connection as a Public Health Priority in the United States," *American Psychologist* 72, no. 6 (2017): 517–30, https://doi.org/10.1037/amp0000103.

8 **romantic partner or children:** Nathan W. Hudson, Richard E. Lucas, and M. Brent Donnellan, "Are We Happier with Others? An Investigation of the Links between Spending Time with Others and Subjective Well-Being," *Journal of Personality and Social Psychology* 119, no. 3 (2020): 672–94, https://doi.org/10.1037/pspp0000290.

10 **benefitting the outgroup:** Thomas F. Pettigrew, "Generalized Intergroup Contact Effects on Prejudice," *Personality and Social Psychology Bulletin* 23, no. 2 (1997): 173–85, https://doi.org/10.1177/0146167297232006.

10 **hostility toward outgroups:** Stephen C. Wright, Arthur Aron, Tracy McLaughlin-Volpe, and Stacy A. Ropp, "The Extended Contact Effect: Knowledge of Cross-Group Friendships and Prejudice," *Journal of Personality and Social Psychology* 73, no. 1 (1997): 73–90, https://doi.org/10.1037/0022-3514.73.1.73.

10 **A 2013 meta-analysis:** Cornelia Wrzus, Martha Hänel, Jenny Wagner, and Franz J. Neyer, "Social Network Changes and Life Events across the Life Span: A Meta-Analysis," *Psychological Bulletin* 139, no. 1 (2013): 53–80, https://doi.org/10.1037/a0028601.

11 **increase our trust in others:** Mariska van der Horst and Hilde Coffé, "How Friendship Network Characteristics Influence Subjective Well-Being," *Social Indicators Research* 107, no. 3 (2012): 509–29, https://doi.org/10.1007/s11205-011-9861-2.

11 **Germany, Czech Republic, and Cameroon:** Jan Hofer et al., "The Higher Your Implicit Affiliation-Intimacy Motive, the More Loneliness Can Turn You into a Social Cynic: A Cross-Cultural Study," *Journal of Personality* 85, no. 2 (2017): 179–91, https://doi.org/10.1111/jopy.12232.

11 **social cynicism:** Kwok Leung et al., "Social Axioms: The Search for Universal Dimensions of General Beliefs about How the World Functions," *Journal of*

Cross-Cultural Psychology 33, no. 3 (2002): 286–302, https://doi.org/10.1177/0022022102033003005.

12 ***strength and endurance:*** Laura E. VanderDrift, Juan E. Wilson, and Christopher R. Agnew, "On the Benefits of Valuing Being Friends for Nonmarital Romantic Partners," *Journal of Social and Personal Relationships* 30, no. 1 (2013): 115–31, https://doi.org/10.1177/0265407512453009.

15 **Judge David Davis:** Charles B. Strozier with Wayne Soini, *Your Friend Forever, A. Lincoln: The Enduring Friendship of Abraham Lincoln and Joshua Speed* (New York: Columbia University Press, 2018).

15 **Webster shared his hope:** Strozier with Soini, *Your Friend Forever, A. Lincoln.*

16 **health and well-being:** William J. Chopik, "Associations among Relational Values, Support, Health, and Well-Being across the Adult Lifespan," *Personal Relationships* 24, no. 2 (2017): 408–22, https://doi.org/10.1111/pere.12187.

17 **"unhuman":** David Elkind, "'Good Me' or 'Bad Me'—The Sullivan Approach to Personality," *New York Times,* September 24, 1972, https://www.nytimes.com/1972/09/24/archives/-good-me-or-bad-me-the-sullivan-approach-to-personality-starting.html.

17 **according to Sullivan:** Elkind, "'Good Me' or 'Bad Me'—The Sullivan Approach to Personality,"

19 **shame is highest:** Ulrich Orth, Richard W. Robins, and Christopher J. Soto, "Tracking the Trajectory of Shame, Guilt, and Pride across the Life Span," *Journal of Personality and Social Psychology* 99, no. 6 (2010): 1061–71, https://doi.org/10.1037/a0021342.

20 **We turn to friends:** Nandita Vijayakumar and Jennifer H. Pfeifer, "Self-Disclosure during Adolescence: Exploring the Means, Targets, and Types of Personal Exchanges," *Current Opinion in Psychology* 31 (2020): 135–40, https://doi.org/10.1016/j.copsyc.2019.08.005.

20 **kindness toward friends:** Laura M. Padilla-Walker et al., "Adolescents' Prosocial Behavior toward Family, Friends, and Strangers: A Person-Centered Approach," *Journal of Research on Adolescence* 25, no. 1 (2015): 135–50, https://doi.org/10.1111/jora.12102.

20 **correlated with greater empathy:** Savannah Boele et al., "Linking Parent–Child and Peer Relationship Quality to Empathy in Adolescence: A Multilevel Meta-Analysis," *Journal of Youth and Adolescence* 48, no. 6 (2019): 1033–55, https://doi.org/10.1007/s10964-019-00993-5.

20 **kids with better friends:** Neeltje P. van den Bedem et al., "Interrelation between Empathy and Friendship Development during (Pre)Adolescence and the Moderating Effect of Developmental Language Disorder: A Longitudinal Study," *Social Development* 28, no. 3 (2019): 599–619, https://doi.org/10.1111/sode.12353.

21 **seeing friends excluded:** Meghan L. Meyer et al., "Empathy for the Social Suffering of Friends and Strangers Recruits Distinct Patterns of Brain Activation," *Social Cognitive and Affective Neuroscience* 8, no. 4 (2013): 446–54, https://doi.org/10.1093/scan/nss019.

21 **friends during formative years:** Catherine L. Bagwell, Andrew F. Newcomb, and William M. Bukowski, "Preadolescent Friendship and Peer Rejection as Predictors of Adult Adjustment," *Child Development* 69, no. 1 (1998): 140–53, https://doi.org/10.2307/1132076.

24 **Bobo doll experiment:** Albert Bandura, Dorothea Ross, and Sheila A. Ross, "Transmission of Aggression through Imitation of Aggressive Models," *Journal of Abnormal and Social Psychology* 63, no. 3 (1961): 575–82, https://doi.org/10.1037/h0045925.

24 **self-expansion theory:** Brent A. Mattingly and Gary W. Lewandowski Jr., "Broadening Horizons: Self-Expansion in Relational and Non-Relational Contexts," *Social and Personality Psychology Compass* 8, no. 1 (2014): 30–40, https://doi.org/10.1111/spc3.12080.

25 **people who were given money:** Arthur Aron, Elaine N. Aron, Michael Tudor, and Greg Nelson, "Close Relationships as Including Other in the Self," *Journal of Personality and Social Psychology* 60, no. 2 (1991): 241–53, https://doi.org/10.1037/0022-3514.60.2.241.

25 **more likely to mistake traits:** Debra J. Mashek, Arthur Aron, and Maria Boncimino, "Confusions of Self with Close Others," *Personality and Social Psychology Bulletin* 29, no. 3 (2003): 382–92, https://doi.org/10.1177/0146167202250220.

25 **people took longer to recognize:** Sarah Ketay et al., "Seeing You in Me: Preliminary Evidence for Perceptual Overlap between Self and Close Others," *Journal of Social and Personal Relationships* 36, no. 8 (2019): 2474–86, https://doi.org/10.1177/0265407518788702.

26 **"If I am close to you":** Arthur Aron et al., "Including Others in the Self," *European Review of Social Psychology* 15, no. 1 (2004): 101–32, https://doi.org/10.1080/10463280440000008.

26 **self is simply a reflection:** Arthur Aron, Christina C. Norman, and Elaine N. Aron, "The Self-Expansion Model and Motivation," *Representative Research in Social Psychology* 22 (1998): 1–13.

27 **in that nasal spray:** Paul J. Zak, Angela A. Stanton, and Sheila Ahmadi, "Oxytocin Increases Generosity in Humans," *PLoS ONE* 2, no. 11 (2007): e1128, https://doi.org/10.1371/journal.pone.0001128; Michael Kosfeld et al., "Oxytocin Increases Trust in Humans," *Nature* 435, no. 7042 (2005): 673–76, https://doi.org/10.1038/nature03701.

27 **triggers empathy:** Sarina M. Rodrigues et al., "Oxytocin Receptor Genetic Variation Relates to Empathy and Stress Reactivity in Humans," *Proceedings of the National Academy of Sciences of the United States of America* 106, no. 50 (2009): 21437–41, https://doi.org/10.1073/pnas.0909579106.

27 **attention to others:** Inna Schneiderman, Orna Zagoory-Sharon, James F. Leckman, and Ruth Feldman, "Oxytocin during the Initial Stages of Romantic Attachment: Relations to Couples' Interactive Reciprocity," *Psychoneuroendocrinology* 37, no. 8 (2012): 1277–85, https://doi.org/10.1016/j.psyneuen.2011.12.021.

27 **male chimpanzees:** C. Crockford et al., "Urinary Oxytocin and Social Bonding in Related and Unrelated Wild Chimpanzees," *Proceedings of the Royal Society B: Biological Sciences* 280, no. 1755 (2013): 20122765, https://doi.org/10.1098/rspb.2012.2765.

27 **social hormone, vasopressin:** Tamara A. R. Weinstein et al., "Early Involvement in Friendships Predicts Later Plasma Concentrations of Oxytocin and Vasopressin in Juvenile Rhesus Macaques (*Macaca Mulatta*)," *Frontiers in Behavioral Neuroscience* 8 (2014): 1–13, https://doi.org/10.3389/fnbeh.2014.00295.

27 **higher levels of oxytocin:** Ruth Feldman et al., "Parental Oxytocin and Early Caregiving Jointly Shape Children's Oxytocin Response and Social Reciprocity," *Neuropsychopharmacology* 38, no. 7 (2013): 1154–62, https://doi.org/10.1038/npp .2013.22.

28 **"elixir of youth":** Susan E. Erdman, "Microbes and Healthful Longevity," *Aging* 8, no. 5 (2016): 839–40, https://doi.org/10.18632/aging.100969.

28 **calms stress responses:** J. Gutkowska and M. Jankowski, "Oxytocin Revisited: Its Role in Cardiovascular Regulation," *Journal of Neuroendocrinology* 24, no. 4 (2012): 599–608, https://doi.org/10.1111/j.1365-2826.2011.02235.x.

28 **decrease cortisol levels:** Kerstin Uvnäs-Moberg, "Oxytocin May Mediate the Benefits of Positive Social Interaction and Emotions," *Psychoneuroendocrinology* 23, no. 8 (1998): 819–35, https://doi.org/10.1016/s0306-4530(98)00056-0.

Chapter 2: How Our Past Relationships Affect Our Present

33 **initiating new friendships:** Omri Gillath, Gery C. Karantzas, and Emre Selcuk, "A Net of Friends: Investigating Friendship by Integrating Attachment Theory and Social Network Analysis," *Personality and Social Psychology Bulletin* 43, no. 11 (2017): 1546–65, https://doi.org/10.1177/0146167217719731.

33 **closer and more enduring:** Juwon Lee and Omri Gillath, "Perceived Closeness to Multiple Social Connections and Attachment Style: A Longitudinal Examination," *Social Psychological and Personality Science* 7, no. 7 (2016): 680–89, https://doi.org/10.1177/1948550616644963.

33 **super friends have better mental health:** Trisha Raque-Bogdan et al., "Attachment and Mental and Physical Health: Self-Compassion and Mattering as Mediators," *Journal of Counseling Psychology* 58, no. 2 (2011): 272–78, https://doi .org/10.1037/a0023041.

33 **open to new ideas:** Matthew J. Jarvinen and Thomas B. Paulus, "Attachment and Cognitive Openness: Emotional Underpinnings of Intellectual Humility," *Journal of Positive Psychology* 12, no. 1 (2016): 74–86, https://doi.org/10.1080 /17439760.2016.1167944.

33 **harbor less prejudice:** Mario Mikulincer and Phillip R. Shaver, "Attachment Theory and Intergroup Bias: Evidence That Priming the Secure Base Schema Attenuates Negative Reactions to Out-Groups," *Journal of Personality and Social Psychology* 81, no. 1 (2001): 97–115, https://doi.org/10.1037/0022-3514.81.1.97.

33 **more satisfied at work:** Cindy Hazan and Phillip R. Shaver, "Love and Work: Attachment-Theoretical Perspective," *Journal of Personality and Social Psychology* 59, no. 2 (1990): 270–80, https://doi.org/10.1037/0022-3514.59.2.270.

33 **feel less regret:** Alexander M. Schoemann, Omri Gillath, and Amanda K. Sesko, "Regrets, I've Had a Few: Effects of Dispositional and Manipulated Attachment on Regret," *Journal of Social and Personal Relationships* 29, no. 6 (2012): 795–819, https://doi.org/10.1177/0265407512443612.

33 **In typically stressful events:** Lisa M. Diamond, Angela M. Hicks, and Kimberly Otter-Henderson, "Physiological Evidence for Repressive Coping Among Avoidantly Attached Adults," *Journal of Social and Personal Relationships* 23, no. 2 (2006): 205–29, https://doi.org/10.1177/0265407506062470.

33 **heart attacks, headaches, stomach troubles:** Jennifer Puig, Michelle M. Englund, Jeffry A. Simpson, and W. Andrew Collins, "Predicting Adult Physical

Illness from Infant Attachment: A Prospective Longitudinal Study," *Health Psychology* 32, no. 4 (2013): 409–17, https://doi.org/10.1037/a0028889; Lisa M. Diamond, Angela M. Hicks, and Kimberly Otter-Henderson, "Physiological Evidence for Repressive Coping among Avoidantly Attached Adults," *Journal of Social and Personal Relationships* 23, no. 2 (2006): 205–29, https://doi.org/10.1177/0265407506062470.

33   **milk fiasco:** Jude Cassidy, Steven J. Kirsh, Krista L. Scolton, and Ross D. Parke, "Attachment and Representations of Peer Relationships," *Developmental Psychology* 32, no. 5 (1996): 892–904, https://doi.org/10.1037/0012-1649.32.5.892; Kathleen M. Dwyer et al., "Attachment, Social Information Processing, and Friendship Quality of Early Adolescent Girls and Boys," *Journal of Social and Personal Relationships* 27, no. 1 (2010): 91–116, https://doi.org/10.1177/0265407509346420.

34   **our genes play a role:** Omri Gillath, Phillip R. Shaver, Jong-Min Baek, and David S. Chun, "Genetic Correlates of Adult Attachment Style," *Personality and Social Psychology Bulletin* 34, no. 10 (2008): 1396–1405, https://doi.org/10.1177/0146167208321484.

35   **72 percent of people:** Everett Waters et al., "Attachment Security in Infancy and Early Adulthood: A Twenty-Year Longitudinal Study," *Child Development* 71, no. 3 (2000): 684–89, https://doi.org/10.1111/1467-8624.00176.

35   **as low as 26 percent:** Julie Wargo Aikins, Carollee Howes, and Claire Hamilton, "Attachment Stability and the Emergence of Unresolved Representations during Adolescence," *Attachment & Human Development* 11, no. 5 (2009): 491–512, https://doi.org/10.1080/14616730903017019.

40   **coined the term "pronoia":** Fred H. Goldner, "Pronoia," *Social Problems* 30, no. 1 (1982): 82–91, https://doi.org/10.2307/800186.

40   **finance game:** Ernst Fehr and Bettina Rockenbach, "Detrimental Effects of Sanctions on Human Altruism," *Nature* 422, no. 6928 (2003): 137–40, https://doi.org/10.1038/nature01474.

40   **"If you trust people":** Tom Clarke, "Students Prove Trust Begets Trust," *Nature* (2003), https://www.nature.com/news/2003/030310/full/news030310-8.html.

41   **strong predictor of resilience:** Pernille Darling Rasmussen et al., "Attachment as a Core Feature of Resilience: A Systematic Review and Meta-Analysis," *Psychological Reports* 122, no. 4 (2018): 1259–96, https://doi.org/10.1177/0033294118785577.

41   **stress regulation:** Jeffry A. Simpson and W. Steven Rholes, "Adult Attachment, Stress, and Romantic Relationships," *Current Opinion in Psychology* 13 (2017): 19–24, https://doi.org/10.1016/j.copsyc.2016.04.006.

41   **heart rate variability:** Simpson and Rholes, "Adult Attachment, Stress, and Romantic Relationships."

41   **more likely to initiate:** Omri Gillath, Gery C. Karantzas, and Emre Selcuk, "A Net of Friends: Investigating Friendship by Integrating Attachment Theory and Social Network Analysis," *Personality and Social Psychology Bulletin* 43, no. 11 (2017): 1546–65, https://doi.org/10.1177/0146167217719731.

41   **address conflict:** Julie Petersen and Benjamin Le, "Psychological Distress, Attachment, and Conflict Resolution in Romantic Relationships," *Modern Psychological Studies* 23, no. 1 (2017): 1–26.

41   **share intimate things:** Chandra M. Grabill and Kathryn A. Kerns, "Attachment Style and Intimacy in Friendship," *Personal Relationships* 7, no. 4 (2000): 363–78, https://doi.org/10.1111/j.1475-6811.2000.tb00022.x.

42   **better at maintaining friendships:** Gillath, Karantzas, and Selcuk, "A Net of Friends."

42   **less likely to get into conflict:** Petersen and Le, "Psychological Distress, Attachment, and Conflict Resolution in Romantic Relationships."

42   **Secure people are more giving:** Mario Mikulincer, Phillip R. Shaver, Omri Gillath, and Rachel A. Nitzberg, "Attachment, Caregiving, and Altruism: Boosting Attachment Security Increases Compassion and Helping," *Journal of Personality and Social Psychology* 89, no. 5 (2005): 817–39, https://doi.org/10.1037 /0022-3514.89.5.817; Kathleen A. Lawler-Row, Jarred W. Younger, Rachel L. Piferi, and Warren H. Jones, "The Role of Adult Attachment Style in Forgiveness Following an Interpersonal Offense," *Journal of Counseling & Development* 84, no. 4 (2006): 493–502, https://doi.org/10.1002/j.1556-6678.2006.tb00434.x; Omri Gillath, Amanda K. Sesko, Phillip R. Shaver, and David S. Chun, "Attachment, Authenticity, and Honesty: Dispositional and Experimentally Induced Security Can Reduce Self- and Other-Deception," *Journal of Personality and Social Psychology* 98, no. 5 (2010): 841–55, https://doi.org/10.1037/a0019206.

42   **giving and receiving support:** Nancy L. Collins and Brooke C. Feeney, "A Safe Haven: An Attachment Theory Perspective on Support Seeking and Caregiving in Intimate Relationships," *Journal of Personality and Social Psychology* 78, no. 6 (2000): 1053–73, https://doi.org/10.1037/0022-3514.78.6.1053; Roseanne DeFronzo, Catherine Panzarella, and Andrew C. Butler, "Attachment, Support Seeking, and Adaptive Inferential Feedback: Implications for Psychological Health," *Cognitive and Behavioral Practice* 8, no. 1 (2001): 48–52, https://doi.org /10.1016/s1077-7229(01)80043-2; Mario Mikulincer and Orna Nachshon, "Attachment Styles and Patterns of Self-Disclosure," *Journal of Personality and Social Psychology* 61, no. 2 (1991): 321–31, https://doi.org/10.1037/0022-3514.61.2.321.

43   **increases their security over time:** Fang Zhang and Gisela Labouvie-Vief, "Stability and Fluctuation in Adult Attachment Style over a 6-Year Period," *Attachment & Human Development* 6, no. 4 (2004): 419–37, https://doi.org/10.1080 /1461673042000303127.

43   **more accepting of others:** Grabill and Kerns, "Attachment Style and Intimacy in Friendship."

44   **skin conductance:** Susan Cain, *Quiet: The Power of Introverts in a World That Can't Stop Talking* (New York: Penguin Books, 2013).

45   **work affects their happiness:** Hazan and Shaver, "Love and Work."

45   **An avoidant patient:** Mary E. Connors, "The Renunciation of Love: Dismissive Attachment and Its Treatment," *Psychoanalytic Psychology* 14, no. 4 (1997): 475–93, https://doi.org/10.1037/h0079736.

45   **avoidant individuals reduce their dependence:** Gillath, Karantzas, and Selcuk, "A Net of Friends."

46   **more likely to end friendships:** Gillath, Karantzas, and Selcuk, "A Net of Friends."

46   **eject using indirect routes:** Tara J. Collins and Omri Gillath, "Attachment, Breakup Strategies, and Associated Outcomes: The Effects of Security

Enhancement on the Selection of Breakup Strategies," *Journal of Research in Personality* 46, no. 2 (2012): 210–22, https://doi.org/10.1016/j.jrp.2012.01.008.

46   **their nervous systems frenzied:** Lisa M. Diamond, Angela M. Hicks, and Kimberly Otter-Henderson, "Physiological Evidence for Repressive Coping among Avoidantly Attached Adults," *Journal of Social and Personal Relationships* 23, no. 2 (2006): 205–29, https://doi.org/10.1177/0265407506062470; Mario Mikulincer and Phillip R. Shaver, "The Attachment Behavioral System in Adulthood: Activation, Psychodynamics, and Interpersonal Processes," in *Advances in Experimental Social Psychology* (Cambridge, MA: Elsevier, 2003), 53–152, https://doi.org/10.1016/s0065-2601(03)01002-5.

47   **avoidants are shame-prone:** Sarah A. H. Atkins, "The Relationship between Shame and Attachment Styles" (PhD diss., University of North Texas, 2016).

47   **poorer immune functioning:** Lachlan A. McWilliams and S. Jeffrey Bailey, "Associations between Adult Attachment Ratings and Health Conditions: Evidence from the National Comorbidity Survey Replication," *Health Psychology* 29, no. 4 (2010): 446–53, https://doi.org/10.1037/a0020061; Angelo Picardi et al., "Attachment Security and Immunity in Healthy Women," *Psychosomatic Medicine* 69, no. 1 (2007): 40–46, https://doi.org/10.1037/a0020061.

48   **more likely to bully:** Michael Troy and L. Alan Sroufe, "Victimization among Preschoolers: Role of Attachment Relationship History," *Journal of the American Academy of Child & Adolescent Psychiatry* 26, no. 2 (1987): 166–72, https://doi.org/10.1097/00004583-198703000-00007.

49   **"avoidant attachment history":** Robert Karen, *Becoming Attached: Unfolding the Mystery of the Infant-Mother Bond and Its Impact on Later Life* (New York: Grand Central Publishing, 1994).

49   **less warm, supportive, and close friendships:** Wyndol Furman, "Working Models of Friendships," *Journal of Social and Personal Relationships* 18, no. 5 (2001): 583–602, https://doi.org/10.1177/0265407501185002; Gillath, Karantzas, and Selcuk, "A Net of Friends"; Emily L. Loeb, Jessica A. Stern, Meghan A. Costello and Joseph P. Allen, "With(out) a Little Help from My Friends: Insecure Attachment in Adolescence, Support-Seeking, and Adult Negativity and Hostility," *Attachment & Human Development* 23, no. 5 (2020): 624–42, https://doi.org/10.1080/14616734.2020.1821722.

49   **less invested, committed, and ultimately satisfied:** Chong Man Chow and Cin Cin Tan, "Attachment and Commitment in Dyadic Friendships: Mediating Roles of Satisfaction, Quality of Alternatives, and Investment Size," *Journal of Relationships Research* 4, no. e4 (2013): 1–11, https://doi.org/10.1017/jrr.2013.4.

49   **avoidants are less likely to initiate:** Gillath, Karantzas, and Selcuk, "A Net of Friends."

49   **experience less enjoyment and intimacy:** Marie-Cecile O. Tidwell, Harry T. Reis, and Phillip R. Shaver, "Attachment, Attractiveness, and Social Interaction: A Diary Study," *Journal of Personality and Social Psychology* 71, no. 4 (1996): 729–45, https://doi.org/10.1037/0022-3514.71.4.729.

51   **adjust their initial optimism:** Mario Mikulincer and Daphna Arad, "Attachment Working Models and Cognitive Openness in Close Relationships: A Test of Chronic and Temporary Accessibility Effects," *Journal of Personality and Social Psychology* 77, no. 4 (1999): 710–25, https://doi.org/10.1037/0022-3514.77.4.710.

51 **secure people modulate:** Mikulincer and Nachson, "Attachment Styles and Patterns of Self-Disclosure."

51 **building resentment for their unmet needs:** Tara Kidd and David Sheffield, "Attachment Style and Symptom Reporting: Examining the Mediating Effects of Anger and Social Support," *British Journal of Health Psychology* 10, no. 4 (2005): 531–41, https://doi.org/10.1111/j.2044-8287.2005.tb00485.x.

51 **leak their feelings passive-aggressively:** Marrie H. J. Bekker, Nathan Bachrach, and Marcel A. Croon, "The Relationships of Antisocial Behavior with Attachment Styles, Autonomy-Connectedness, and Alexithymia," *Journal of Clinical Psychology* 63, no. 6 (2007): 507–27, https://doi.org/10.1002/jclp.20363.

52 **anxious people tend to wallow:** Katherine Pascuzzo, Chantal Cyr, and Ellen Moss, "Longitudinal Association between Adolescent Attachment, Adult Romantic Attachment, and Emotion Regulation Strategies," *Attachment & Human Development* 15, no. 1 (2012): 83–103, https://doi.org/10.1080/14616734.2013.745713.

52 **when rejection was simulated:** C. Nathan DeWall et al., "Do Neural Responses to Rejection Depend on Attachment Style? An fMRI Study," *Social Cognitive and Affective Neuroscience* 7, no. 2 (2011): 184–92, https://doi.org/10.1093/scan/nsq107.

53 **anxious people viewed a threatening face:** Luke Norman et al., "Attachment-Security Priming Attenuates Amygdala Activation to Social and Linguistic Threat," *Social Cognitive and Affective Neuroscience* 10, no. 6 (2014): 832–39, https://doi.org/10.1093/scan/nsu127.

53 **feel low self-worth:** Rohmann, Elke, Eva Neumann, Michael Jürgen Herner, and Hans-Werner Bierhoff, "Grandiose and Vulnerable Narcissism," *European Psychologist* 17, no. 4 (January 2012): 279–90, https://doi.org/10.1027/1016-9040/a000100.

53 **ones being slighted:** Elke Rohmann, Eva Neumann, Michael Jürgen Herner, and Hans-Werner Bierhoff, "Grandiose and Vulnerable Narcissism," *European Psychologist* 17, no. 4 (2012): 279–90, https://doi.org/10.1027/1016-9040/a000100; Anna Z. Czarna, Marcin Zajenkowski, Oliwia Maciantowicz, and Kinga Szymaniak, "The Relationship of Narcissism with Tendency to React with Anger and Hostility: The Roles of Neuroticism and Emotion Regulation Ability," *Current Psychology* 40 (2019): 5499–514, https://doi.org/10.1007/s12144-019-00504-6.

54 **"exaggerated sense of entitlement":** Mario Mikulincer and Phillip R. Shaver, "An Attachment Perspective on Psychopathology," *World Psychiatry* 11, no. 1 (2012): 11–15, https://doi.org/10.1016/j.wpsyc.2012.01.003.

54 **anxious people were quicker at recognizing:** Mark W. Baldwin and Aaron C. Kay, "Adult Attachment and the Inhibition of Rejection," *Journal of Social and Clinical Psychology* 22, no. 3 (2003): 275–93, https://doi.org/10.1521/jscp.22.3.275.22890.

54 **more emotionally intense and volatile:** Ashley N. Cooper, Casey J. Totenhagen, Brandon T. McDaniel, and Melissa A. Curran, "Volatility in Daily Relationship Quality: The Roles of Attachment and Gender," *Journal of Social and Personal Relationships* 35, no. 3 (2017): 348–71, https://doi.org/10.1177/0265407517690038; Mario Mikulincer and Michal Selinger, "The Interplay

between Attachment and Affiliation Systems in Adolescents' Same-Sex Friendships: The Role of Attachment Style," *Journal of Social and Personal Relationships* 18, no. 1 (2001): 81–106, https://doi.org/10.1177/0265407501181004.

54   **perceive transgressions as more serious:** Kirsten M. Blount-Matthews, "Attachment and Forgiveness in Human Development: A Multi-Method Approach" (PhD diss., University of California, Berkeley, 2004), ProQuest (3167189); Marcia Webb et al., "Dispositional Forgiveness and Adult Attachment Styles," *Journal of Social Psychology* 146, no. 4 (2006): 509–12, https://doi.org/10.3200/socp .146.4.509-512.

55   **"The disorder leads to conditions":** L. Alan Sroufe, "Considering Normal and Abnormal Together: The Essence of Developmental Psychopathology," *Development and Psychopathology* 2, no. 4 (1990): 335–47, https://doi.org/10.1017/s09545 79400005769.

Chapter 3: Taking Initiative

64   **The word "lonely":** Fay Bound Alberti, *A Biography of Loneliness: The History of an Emotion* (Oxford: Oxford University Press, 2019).

64   **increased residential mobility:** Omri Gillath and Lucas A. Keefer, "Generalizing Disposability: Residential Mobility and the Willingness to Dissolve Social Ties," *Personal Relationships* 23, no. 2 (2016): 186–98, https://doi.org/10.1111 /pere.12119.

64   **"by definition not mutually helpful":** Robert Karen, *Becoming Attached: Unfolding the Mystery of the Infant-Mother Bond and Its Impact on Later Life* (New York: Grand Central Publishing, 1994).

65   **heavy social media users:** Jean M. Twenge, Brian H. Spitzberg, and W. Keith Campbell, "Less In-Person Social Interaction with Peers among U.S. Adolescents in the 21st Century and Links to Loneliness," *Journal of Social and Personal Relationships* 36, no 6. (2019): 1892–1913, https://doi.org/10.1177/0265407519836170.

65   **61 percent of Americans:** "Loneliness and the Workplace: 2020 U.S. Report," Cigna, January 2020, https://www.cigna.com/static/www-cigna-com/docs /about-us/newsroom/studies-and-reports/combatting-loneliness/cigna-2020 -loneliness-report.pdf.

66   **four fewer friends:** Cornelia Wrzus, Martha Hänel, Jenny Wagner, and Franz J. Neyer, "Social Network Changes and Life Events across the Life Span: A Meta-Analysis," *Psychological Bulletin* 139, no. 1 (2013): 53–80, https://doi.org/10.1037 /a0028601.

66   **four times as many people:** Daniel A. Cox, "The State of American Friendship: Change, Challenges, and Loss," Survey Center on American Life, June 8, 2021, https://www.americansurveycenter.org/research/the-state-of-american -friendship-change-challenges-and-loss.

66   **Circumstances are more dire:** Daniel A. Cox, "Men's Social Circles Are Shrinking," Survey Center on American Life, June 29, 2021, https://www.amer icansurveycenter.org/why-mens-social-circles-are-shrinking.

67   **were less lonely:** Nancy E. Newall et al., "Causal Beliefs, Social Participation, and Loneliness among Older Adults: A Longitudinal Study," *Journal of Social and Personal Relationships* 26, no. 2–3 (2009): 273–90, https://doi.org/10.1177 /0265407509106718.

70 **essential for connection:** Alex Williams, "Why Is It Hard to Make Friends over 30?," *New York Times,* July 13, 2012, www.nytimes.com/2012/07/15/fashion /the-challenge-of-making-friends-as-an-adult.html.

72 **betters our romantic relationships:** Christine M. Proulx, Heather M. Helms, Robert M. Milardo, and C. Chris Payne, "Relational Support from Friends and Wives' Family Relationships: The Role of Husbands' Interference," *Journal of Social and Personal Relationships* 26, no. 2–3 (2009): 195–210, https://doi.org /10.1177/0265407509106709.

72 **pattern of stress hormones:** Elizabeth Keneski, Lisa A. Neff, and Timothy J. Loving, "The Importance of a Few Good Friends: Perceived Network Support Moderates the Association between Daily Marital Conflict and Diurnal Cortisol," *Social Psychological and Personality Science* 9, no. 8 (2017): 962–71, https:// doi.org/10.1177/1948550617731499.

72 **linked to better self-esteem:** Kirsten Voss, Dorothy Markiewicz, and Anna Beth Doyle, "Friendship, Marriage and Self-Esteem," *Journal of Social and Personal Relationships* 16, no. 1 (1999): 103–22, https://doi.org/10.1177/026540759 9161006.

73 **tend to have stronger friendships:** Heather R. Walen and Margie E. Lachman, "Social Support and Strain from Partner, Family, and Friends: Costs and Benefits for Men and Women in Adulthood," *Journal of Social and Personal Relationships* 17, no. 1 (2000): 5–30, https://doi.org/10.1177/0265407500171001.

73 **insecure people were primed with security:** Omri Gillath, Gery C. Karantzas, and Emre Selcuk, "A Net of Friends: Investigating Friendship by Integrating Attachment Theory and Social Network Analysis," *Personality and Social Psychology Bulletin* 43, no. 11 (2017): 1546–65, https://doi.org/10.1177/0146167217719731.

73 **assume others like us:** Sandra L. Murray, John G. Holmes, and Dale W. Griffin, "Self-Esteem and the Quest for Felt Security: How Perceived Regard Regulates Attachment Processes," *Journal of Personality and Social Psychology* 78, no. 3 (2000): 478–98, https://doi.org/10.1037/0022-3514.78.3.478.

74 **the rejection sensitive are more likely:** Shuling Gao, Mark Assink, Andrea Cipriani, and Kangguang Lin, "Associations between Rejection Sensitivity and Mental Health Outcomes: A Meta-Analytic Review," *Clinical Psychology Review* 57 (2017): 59–74, https://doi.org/10.1016/j.cpr.2017.08.007; Geraldine Downey and Scott I. Feldman, "Implications of Rejection Sensitivity for Intimate Relationships," *Journal of Personality and Social Psychology* 70, no. 6 (1996): 1327–43, https://doi.org/10.1037/0022-3514.70.6.1327.

74 **report that their romantic partner:** Downey and Feldman, "Implications of Rejection Sensitivity for Intimate Relationships."

74 **becoming distant or cold:** Kevin B. Meehan et al., "Rejection Sensitivity and Interpersonal Behavior in Daily Life," *Personality and Individual Differences* 126 (2018): 109–15, https://doi.org/10.1016/j.paid.2018.01.029.

74 **makes their relationship partners more dissatisfied:** Downey and Feldman, "Implications of Rejection Sensitivity for Intimate Relationships."

75 **"if people expect acceptance":** Danu Anthony Stinson et al., "Deconstructing the 'Reign of Error': Interpersonal Warmth Explains the Self-Fulfilling Prophecy of Anticipated Acceptance," *Personality and Social Psychology Bulletin* 35, no. 9 (2009): 1165–78, https://doi.org/10.1177/0146167209338629.

75   **shared more about themselves:** Rebecca C. Curtis and Kim Miller, "Believing Another Likes or Dislikes You: Behaviors Making the Beliefs Come True," *Journal of Personality and Social Psychology* 51, no. 2 (1986): 284–90, https://doi.org/10.1037/0022-3514.51.2.284.

76   **"liking gap":** Erica J. Boothby, Gus Cooney, Gillian M. Sandstrom, and Margaret S. Clark, "The Liking Gap in Conversations: Do People Like Us More Than We Think?," *Psychological Science* 29, no. 11 (2018): 1742–56, https://doi.org/10.1177/0956797618783714.

79   **rated the class's social climate:** Sanna Eronen and Jari-Erik Nurmi, "Social Reaction Styles, Interpersonal Behaviours and Person Perception: A Multi-Informant Approach," *Journal of Social and Personal Relationships* 16, no. 3 (1999): 315–33, https://doi.org/10.1177/0265407599163003.

85   **each other's friendship potential:** Michael Sunnafrank and Artemio Ramirez Jr., "At First Sight: Persistent Relational Effects of Get-Acquainted Conversations," *Journal of Social and Personal Relationships* 21, no. 3 (2004): 361–79, https://doi.org/10.1177/0265407504042837.

86   **90 percent of cadets listed someone:** Mady W. Segal. "Alphabet and Attraction: An Unobtrusive Measure of the Effect of Propinquity in a Field Setting," *Journal of Personality and Social Psychology* 30, no. 5 (1974): 654–57, https://doi.org/10.1037/h0037446.

86   **costs diminish the likelihood:** Robert B. Hays, "The Day-to-Day Functioning of Close versus Casual Friendships," *Journal of Social and Personal Relationships* 6, no. 1 (1989): 21–37, https://doi.org/10.1177/026540758900600102.

87   **They reported liking the profile:** John M. Darley and Ellen Berscheid, "Increased Liking as a Result of the Anticipation of Personal Contact," *Human Relations* 20, no. 1 (1967): 29–40, https://doi.org/10.1177/001872676702000103.

87   **students reported liking the most the stranger:** Richard L. Moreland and Scott R. Beach, "Exposure Effects in the Classroom: The Development of Affinity among Students," *Journal of Experimental Social Psychology* 28, no. 3 (1992): 255–76, https://doi.org/10.1016/0022-1031(92)90055-o.

88   **live in the dorm's center:** Leon Festinger, Stanley Schachter, and Kurt Back, *Social Pressures in Informal Groups: A Study of Human Factors in Housing* (New York: Harper and Brothers, 1950).

88   **sharing a statement or insight:** David Hoffeld, "Three Scientifically Proven Steps for Talking with Strangers," *Fast Company,* June 14, 2016, http://www.fastcompany.com/3060762/three-scientifically-proven-steps-for-talking-with-strange.

89   **talk to a stranger:** Nicholas Epley and Juliana Schroeder, "Mistakenly Seeking Solitude," *Journal of Experimental Psychology: General* 143, no. 5 (2014): 1980–99, https://doi.org/10.1037/a0037323.

Chapter 4: Expressing Vulnerability

96   **feeling less close to others:** Sanjay Srivastava et al., "The Social Costs of Emotional Suppression: A Prospective Study of the Transition to College," *Journal of Personality and Social Psychology* 96, no. 4 (2009): 883–97, https://doi.org/10.1037/a0014755.

96 **help a woman giving a speech:** Steven M. Graham, Julie Y. Huang, Margaret S. Clark, and Vicki S. Helgeson, "The Positives of Negative Emotions: Willingness to Express Negative Emotions Promotes Relationships," *Personality and Social Psychology Bulletin* 34, no. 3 (2008): 394–406, https://doi.org/10.1177/01461 67207311281.

99 **"An incredible bond":** Lily Velez, "Why Letting Ourselves Be Weak Is Actually the Key to Becoming Strong," *tiny buddha,* accessed December 1, 2021, https:// tinybuddha.com/blog/weak-actually-key-becoming-strong.

100 **the science of suppression:** Mario Mikulincer, Tamar Dolev, and Phillip R. Shaver, "Attachment-Related Strategies during Thought Suppression: Ironic Rebounds and Vulnerable Self-Representations," *Journal of Personality and Social Psychology* 87, no. 6 (2004): 940–56, https://doi.org/10.1037/0022-3514.87.6.940.

103 **The secure were less vulnerable:** Mario Mikulincer, Netta Horesh, Ilana Eilati, and Moshe Kotler, "The Association between Adult Attachment Style and Mental Health in Extreme Life-Endangering Conditions," *Personality and Individual Differences* 27, no. 5 (1999): 831–42, https://doi.org/10.1016/S0191-8869 (99)00032-X.

104 **keeping secrets leads us to ruminate:** Michael L. Slepian, Jinseok S. Chun, and Malia F. Mason, "The Experience of Secrecy," *Journal of Personality and Social Psychology* 113, no. 1 (2017): 1–33, https://doi.org/10.1037/pspa0000085; Michael L. Slepian, James N. Kirby, and Elise K. Kalokerinos, "Shame, Guilt, and Secrets on the Mind," *Emotion* 20, no. 2 (2020): 323–28, https://doi.org/10.1037 /emo0000542.

104 **Self-concealment:** Kathleen Y. Kawamura and Randy O. Frost, "Self-Concealment as a Mediator in the Relationship between Perfectionism and Psychological Distress," *Cognitive Therapy and Research* 28, no. 2 (2004): 183–91, https://doi.org/10.1023/b:cotr.0000021539.48926.c1.

104 **more isolated and fatigued:** Michael L. Slepian, Nir Halevy, and Adam D. Galinsky, "The Solitude of Secrecy: Thinking about Secrets Evokes Goal Conflict and Feelings of Fatigue," *Personality and Social Psychology Bulletin* 45, no. 7 (2018): 1129–51, https://doi.org/10.1177/0146167218810770.

104 **experienced the death of a spouse:** James W. Pennebaker and Joan R. Susman, "Disclosure of Traumas and Psychosomatic Processes," *Social Science & Medicine* 26, no. 3 (1988): 327–32, https://doi.org/10.1016/0277-9536(88)90397-8.

105 *no one* **to confide in:** Miller McPherson, Lynn Smith-Lovin, and Matthew E. Brashears, "Social Isolation in America: Changes in Core Discussion Networks over Two Decades," *American Sociological Review* 71, no. 3 (2006): 353–75, https://doi.org/10.1177/000312240607100301.

105 **"We don't usually see big social changes":** "Social Isolation: Americans Have Fewer Close Confidantes," *All Things Considered,* June 24, 2006, https:// www.npr.org/templates/story/story.php?storyId=5509381.

107 **"undercurrent of our natural state":** David Whyte, *Consolations: The Solace, Nourishment and Underlying Meaning of Everyday Words* (Langley, WA: Many Rivers Press, 2019).

107 **The singers assumed:** Anna Bruk, Sabine G. Scholl, and Herbert Bless, "Beautiful Mess Effect: Self–Other Differences in Evaluation of Showing

Vulnerability," *Journal of Personality and Social Psychology* 115, no. 2 (2018): 192–205, https://doi.org/10.1037/pspa0000120.

108 **This discrepancy occurred:** Dena M. Gromet and Emily Pronin, "What Were You Worried About? Actors' Concerns About Revealing Fears and Insecurities Relative to Observers' Reactions," *Self and Identity* 8, no. 4 (2009): 342–64, https://doi.org/10.1080/15298860802299392.

108 **results from ninety-four different analyses:** Nancy L. Collins and Lynn Carol Miller, "Self-Disclosure and Liking: A Meta-Analytic Review," *Psychological Bulletin* 116, no. 3 (1994): 457–75, https://doi.org/10.1037/0033-2909.116.3.457.

108 **students who were vulnerable:** Arthur Aron et al., "The Experimental Generation of Interpersonal Closeness: A Procedure and Some Preliminary Findings," *Personality and Social Psychology Bulletin* 23, no. 4 (1997): 363–77, https://doi.org/10.1177/0146167297234003.

109 **Giving our friends the opportunity:** Roy F. Baumeister, Kathleen D. Vohs, Jennifer L. Aaker, and Emily N. Garbinsky, "Some Key Differences between a Happy Life and a Meaningful Life," *Journal of Positive Psychology* 8, no. 6 (2013): 505–16, https://doi.org/10.1080/17439760.2013.830764; Stephanie L. Brown, Randolph M. Nesse, Amiram D. Vinokur, and Dylan M. Smith, "Providing Social Support May Be More Beneficial Than Receiving It: Results from a Prospective Study of Mortality," *Psychological Science* 14, no. 4 (2003): 320–27, https://doi.org/10.1111/1467-9280.14461; Sylvia A. Morelli, Ihno A. Lee, Molly E. Arnn, and Jamil Zaki, "Emotional and Instrumental Support Provision Interact to Predict Well-Being," *Emotion* 15, no. 4 (2015): 484–93, https://doi.org/10.1037/emo0000084.

109 **we share our secrets:** Michael L. Slepian and Katharine H. Greenaway, "The Benefits and Burdens of Keeping Others' Secrets," *Journal of Experimental Social Psychology* 78 (2018): 220–32, https://doi.org/10.1016/j.jesp.2018.02.005.

109 **express negative emotions:** Graham, Huang, Clark, and Helgeson, "The Positives of Negative Emotions: Willingness to Express Negative Emotions Promotes Relationships."

111 **she divulged to her classmates:** Rachel Bloom, *I Want to Be Where the Normal People Are* (New York: Grand Central Publishing, 2020).

111 **They liked the medium discloser:** Paul C. Cozby, "Self-Disclosure, Reciprocity and Liking," *Sociometry* 35, no. 1 (1972): 151–60, https://doi.org/10.2307/2786555.

112 **disclosed to someone avoidant:** Mario Mikulincer and Orna Nachshon, "Attachment Styles and Patterns of Self-Disclosure," *Journal of Personality and Social Psychology* 61, no. 2 (1991): 321–31, https://doi.org/10.1037/0022-3514.61.2.321.

113 **positive view of their vulnerability:** Anna Bruk, "Self-Other Differences in the Evaluation of Showing Vulnerability" (PhD diss., University of Mannheim, 2019).

116 **one meta-analysis:** Charles F. Bond Jr. and Bella M. DePaulo, "Accuracy of Deception Judgments," *Personality and Social Psychology Review* 10, no. 3 (2006): 214–34, https://doi.org/10.1207/s15327957pspr1003_2.

120 **An older meta-analysis:** Kathryn Dindia and Mike Allen, "Sex Differences in Self-Disclosure: A Meta-Analysis," *Psychological Bulletin* 112, no. 1 (1992): 106–24, https://doi.org/10.1037/0033-2909.112.1.106.

120 **twice as likely to receive emotional support:** Daniel A. Cox, "The State of American Friendship: Change, Challenges, and Loss," *American Perspectives Survey,* June 8, 2021, https://www.americansurveycenter.org/research/the -state-of-american-friendship-change-challenges-and-loss.

121 **women are more likely to suppress their anger:** Melissa Dittmann, "Anger across the Gender Divide," *Monitor on Psychology* 34, no. 3 (2003): 52, https:// www.apa.org/monitor/mar03/angeracross.

121 **When men act angrily:** Victoria L. Brescoll and Eric Luis Uhlmann, "Can an Angry Woman Get Ahead?: Status Conferral, Gender, and Expression of Emotion in the Workplace," *Psychological Science* 19, no. 3 (2008): 268–75, https://doi .org/10.1111/j.1467-9280.2008.02079.x.

122 **One 2013 study:** A. Celeste Gaia, "The Role of Gender Stereotypes in the Social Acceptability of the Expression of Intimacy," *Social Science Journal* 50, no. 4 (2013): 591–602, https://doi.org/10.1016/j.soscij.2013.08.006.

124 **people who dominate others:** Kristin D. Neff and Susan Harter, "Relationship Styles of Self-Focused Autonomy, Other-Focused Connectedness, and Mutuality across Multiple Relationship Contexts," *Journal of Social and Personal Relationships* 20, no. 1 (2003): 81–99, https://doi.org/10.1177/02654075030201004.

125 **"I began to realize":** Benjy Hansen-Bundy, "My Time Inside a Group Where Men Confront Their Feelings," *GQ,* October 29, 2019, https://www.gq.com/story /inside-a-group-where-men-confront-their-feelings.

126 **Those least able to cope:** Michael L. Slepian and Edythe Moulton-Tetlock, "Confiding Secrets and Well-Being," *Social Psychological and Personality Science* 10, no. 4 (2018): 472–84, https://doi.org/10.1177/1948550618765069.

126 **attempted to hide their feelings:** James C. Coyne and David A. F. Smith, "Couples Coping with a Myocardial Infarction: Contextual Perspective on Patient Self-Efficacy," *Journal of Family Psychology* 8, no. 1 (1994): 43–54, https:// doi.org/10.1037/0893-3200.8.1.43.

126 **"core feature of resilience":** Pernille Darling Rasmussen et al., "Attachment as a Core Feature of Resilience: A Systematic Review and Meta-Analysis," *Psychological Reports* 122, no. 4 (2018): 1259–96, https://doi.org/10.1177/003329411 8785577.

126 **better at seeking support:** Omri Gillath et al., "Automatic Activation of Attachment-Related Goals," *Personality and Social Psychology Bulletin* 32, no. 10 (2006): 1375–88, https://doi.org/10.1177/0146167206290339.

128 **The survivors harvested the resources:** Nick P. Winder and Isabelle C. Winder, "Complexity, Compassion and Self-Organisation: Human Evolution and the Vulnerable Ape Hypothesis," *Internet Archaeology* 40 (2015), https://doi .org/10.11141/ia.40.3.

Chapter 5: Pursuing Authenticity

137 **"Owning one's personal experiences":** Susan Harter, "Authenticity," in *Oxford Handbook of Positive Psychology,* ed. C. R. Snyder and Shane J. Lopez (Oxford: Oxford University Press, 2002), 382–93.

138 **people report being most authentic:** Ralph H. Turner and Victoria Billings, "The Social Contexts of Self-Feeling," in *The Self-Society Dynamic: Cognition, Emotion, and Action,* ed. Judith A. Howard and Peter L. Callero (Cambridge,

England: Cambridge University Press, 1991), 103–22, https://doi.org/10.1017/CBO9780511527722.007.

138 **others are judging them:** Alison P. Lenton, Martin Bruder, Letitia Slabu, and Constantine Sedikides, "How Does 'Being Real' Feel? The Experience of State Authenticity," *Journal of Personality* 81, no. 3 (2013): 276–89, https://doi.org/10.1111/j.1467-6494.2012.00805.x.

138 **anxious, stressed, or depressed:** Lenton, Bruder, Slabu, and Sedikides, "How Does 'Being Real' Feel? The Experience of State Authenticity."

138 **competence, belonging, and self-esteem:** Lenton, Bruder, Slabu, and Sedikides, "How Does 'Being Real' Feel? The Experience of State Authenticity."

139 **discovering one's true nature:** Shane W. Bench, Rebecca J. Schlegel, William E. Davis, and Matthew Vess, "Thinking about Change in the Self and Others: The Role of Self-Discovery Metaphors and the True Self," *Social Cognition* 33, no. 3 (2015): 169–85, https://doi.org/10.1521/soco.2015.33.3.2.

141 **your response depends on the computer task:** Mario Mikulincer, Phillip R. Shaver, Omri Gillath, and Rachel A. Nitzberg, "Attachment, Caregiving, and Altruism: Boosting Attachment Security Increases Compassion and Helping," *Journal of Personality and Social Psychology* 89, no. 5 (2005): 817–39, https://doi.org/10.1037/0022-3514.89.5.817.

143 **links authenticity to less moral disengagement:** Michael Knoll, Robert G. Lord, Lars-Eric Petersen, and Oliver Weigelt, "Examining the Moral Grey Zone: The Role of Moral Disengagement, Authenticity, and Situational Strength in Predicting Unethical Managerial Behavior," *Journal of Applied Social Psychology* 46, no. 1 (2015): 65–78, https://doi.org/10.1111/jasp.12353.

143 **the participants were more present:** Charles T. Taylor and Lynn E. Alden, "To See Ourselves as Others See Us: An Experimental Integration of the Intra and Interpersonal Consequences of Self-Protection in Social Anxiety Disorder," *Journal of Abnormal Psychology* 120, no. 1 (2011): 129–41, https://doi.org/10.1037/a0022127.

144 **greater satisfaction in friendship:** Kätlin Peets and Ernest V. E. Hodges, "Authenticity in Friendships and Well-Being in Adolescence," *Social Development* 27, no. 1 (2017): 140–53, https://doi.org/10.1111/sode.12254.

144 **Inauthenticity is linked to depression:** Amanda J. Wenzel and Rachel G. Lucas-Thompson, "Authenticity in College-Aged Males and Females, How Close Others Are Perceived, and Mental Health Outcomes," *Sex Roles* 67, no. 5–6 (2012): 334–50, https://doi.org/10.1007/s11199-012-0182-y.

144 **effects of inauthenticity:** Francesca Gino, Maryam Kouchaki, and Adam D. Galinsky, "The Moral Virtue of Authenticity: How Inauthenticity Produces Feelings of Immorality and Impurity," *Psychological Science* 26, no. 7 (2015): 983–96, https://doi.org/10.1177/0956797615575277.

145 **We're less accommodating:** Kathleen D. Vohs, Roy F. Baumeister, and Natalie J. Ciarocco, "Self-Regulation and Self-Presentation: Regulatory Resource Depletion Impairs Impression Management and Effortful Self-Presentation Depletes Regulatory Resources," *Journal of Personality and Social Psychology* 88, no. 4 (2005): 632–57, https://doi.org/10.1037/0022-3514.88.4.632.

147 **linked to greater mutuality:** Reese Y. W. Tou, Zachary G. Baker, Benjamin W. Hadden, and Yi-Cheng Lin, "The Real Me: Authenticity, Interpersonal Goals,

and Conflict Tactics," *Personality and Individual Differences* 86 (2015): 189–94, https://doi.org/10.1016/j.paid.2015.05.033.

147 **most authentic moments:** Lenton, Bruder, Slabu, and Sedikides, "How Does 'Being Real' Feel? The Experience of State Authenticity."

150 **Authentic people were more mindful:** Chad E. Lakey, Michael H. Kernis, Whitney L. Heppner, and Charles E. Lance, "Individual Differences in Authenticity and Mindfulness as Predictors of Verbal Defensiveness," *Journal of Research in Personality* 42, no. 1 (2008): 230–38, https://doi.org/10.1016/j.jrp.2007.05.002.

156 **correlated with optimism:** Frederick W. Stander, Leon T. de Beer, and Marius W. Stander, "Authentic Leadership as a Source of Optimism, Trust in the Organisation and Work Engagement in the Public Health Care Sector," *SA Journal of Human Resource Management* 13, no. 1 (2015), https://doi.org/10.4102/sajhrm.v13i1.675.

157 **Black children were viewed:** Amy G. Halberstadt et al., "Preservice Teachers' Racialized Emotion Recognition, Anger Bias, and Hostility Attributions," *Contemporary Educational Psychology* 54 (July 2018): 125–38, https://doi.org/10.1016/j.cedpsych.2018.06.004.

157 **less fully human:** Nour Kteily, Emile Bruneau, Adam Waytz, and Sarah Cotterill, "The Ascent of Man: Theoretical and Empirical Evidence for Blatant Dehumanization," *Journal of Personality and Social Psychology* 109, no. 5 (2015): 901–31, https://doi.org/10.1037/pspp0000048.

157 **women who assert their ideas:** Melissa J. Williams and Larissa Z. Tiedens, "The Subtle Suspension of Backlash: A Meta-Analysis of Penalties for Women's Implicit and Explicit Dominance Behavior," *Psychological Bulletin* 142, no. 2 (2016): 165–97, https://doi.org/10.1037/bul0000039.

158 **"I never wanna be seen":** Nicole R. Holliday and Lauren Squires, "Sociolinguistic Labor, Linguistic Climate, and Race(ism) on Campus: Black College Students' Experiences with Language at Predominantly White Institutions," *Journal of Sociolinguistics* 25, no. 3 (2020): 418–37, https://doi.org/10.1111/josl.12438.

158 **"Renee is more conservative":** Courtney L. McCluney, Kathrina Robotham, Serenity Lee, Richard Smith, and Myles Durkee, "The Costs of Code-Switching," *Harvard Business Review,* November 15, 2019, http://www.hbr.org/2019/11/the-costs-of-codeswitching.

158 **Women who dressed provocatively:** Valerie Johnson and Regan A. R. Gurung, "Defusing the Objectification of Women by Other Women: The Role of Competence," *Sex Roles* 65, no. 3–4 (2011): 177–88, https://doi.org/10.1007/s11199-011-0006-5.

159 **formal clothing:** Regan A. R. Gurung, Rosalyn Stoa, Nicholas Livingston, and Hannah Mather, "Can Success Deflect Racism? Clothing and Perceptions of African American Men," *Journal of Social Psychology* 226, no. 1 (2020): 119–28, https://doi.org/10.1080/00224545.2020.1787938.

159 **retain accents:** Carina Bauman, "Social Evaluation of Asian Accented English," *University of Pennsylvania Working Papers in Linguistics* 19, no. 2 (2013), https://repository.upenn.edu/pwpl/vol19/iss2/3.

164 **A similar pattern:** Emile G. Bruneau and Rebecca Saxe, "The Power of Being Heard: The Benefits of 'Perspective-Giving' in the Context of Intergroup

Conflict," *Journal of Experimental Social Psychology* 48, no. 4 (2012): 855–66, https://doi.org/10.1016/j.jesp.2012.02.017.

Chapter 6: Harmonizing with Anger

174 **correlated with hostility, depression, and anxiety:** Bukre Kahramanol and Ihsan Dag, "Alexithymia, Anger and Anger Expression Styles as Predictors of Psychological Symptoms," *Düşünen Adam: Journal of Psychiatry and Neurological Sciences* 31, no. 1 (2018): 30–39, https://doi.org/10.5350/dajpn2018310103.

174 **drive anger and impede intimacy:** Mark H. Butler, Kierea C. Meloy-Miller, Ryan B. Seedall, and J. Logan Dicus, "Anger Can Help: A Transactional Model and Three Pathways of the Experience and Expression of Anger," *Family Process* 57, no. 3 (2018): 817–35, https://doi.org/10.1111/famp.12311.

175 **"insufficiently processed emotions":** Butler, Meloy-Miller, Seedall, and Dicus, "Anger Can Help."

176 **Dynamic safety:** Virginia Goldner, "Review Essay: Attachment and Eros: Opposed or Synergistic?," *Psychoanalytic Dialogues* 14, no. 3 (2004): 381–96, https://doi.org/10.1080/10481881409348793.

176 **confronting the perpetrator:** Rachel M. McLaren and Keli Ryan Steuber, "Emotions, Communicative Responses, and Relational Consequences of Boundary Turbulence," *Journal of Social and Personal Relationships* 30, no. 5 (2012): 606–26, https://doi.org/10.1177/0265407512463997.

176 **more socially competent:** Duane Buhrmester, Wyndol Furman, Mitchell T. Wittenberg, and Harry T. Reis, "Five Domains of Interpersonal Competence in Peer Relationships," *Journal of Personality and Social Psychology* 55, no. 6 (1988): 991–1008, https://doi.org/10.1037/0022-3514.55.6.991.

176 **addressing an issue:** Stephen M. Drigotas, Gregory A. Whitney, and Caryl E. Rusbult, "On the Peculiarities of Loyalty: A Diary Study of Responses to Dissatisfaction in Everyday Life," *Personality and Social Psychology Bulletin* 21, no. 6 (1995): 596–609, https://doi.org/10.1177/0146167295216006.

176 **minimizing the problem:** Nickola C. Overall, Garth J. O. Fletcher, Jeffry A. Simpson, and Chris G. Sibley, "Regulating Partners in Intimate Relationships: The Costs and Benefits of Different Communication Strategies," *Journal of Personality and Social Psychology* 96, no. 3 (2009): 620–39, https://doi.org/10.1037/a0012961.

176 **"everyday episodes of anger":** Tori DeAngelis, "When Anger's a Plus," *APA Monitor* 34, no. 3 (2003): 44, https://www.apa.org/monitor/mar03/whenanger.

176 **expressing anger:** DeAngelis, "When Anger's a Plus."

177 **voice their concerns constructively:** Catherine A. Sanderson, Katie B. Rahm, and Sarah A. Beigbeder, "The Link between the Pursuit of Intimacy Goals and Satisfaction in Close Same-Sex Friendships: An Examination of the Underlying Processes," *Journal of Social and Personal Relationships* 22, no. 1 (2005): 75–98, https://doi.org/10.1177/0265407505049322.

177 **more likely to avoid problems:** Daniel J. Canary, Laura Stafford, Kimberley S. Hause, and Lisa A. Wallace, "An Inductive Analysis of Relational Maintenance Strategies: Comparisons among Lovers, Relatives, Friends, and Others," *Communication Research Reports* 10, no. 1 (1993): 3–14, https://doi.org/10.1080/08824099309359913; Cheryl Harasymchuk and Beverley Fehr, "Responses to

Dissatisfaction in Friendships and Romantic Relationships: An Interpersonal Script Analysis," *Journal of Social and Personal Relationships* 36, no. 6 (2018): 1651–70, https://doi.org/10.1177/0265407518769451.

182　**aggression or withdrawal:** Laura K. Guerrero, Lisa Farinelli, and Bree Mc-Ewan, "Attachment and Relational Satisfaction: The Mediating Effect of Emotional Communication," *Communication Monographs* 76, no. 4 (2009): 487–514, https://doi.org/10.1080/03637750903300254; Christopher L. Heavey, Andrew Christensen, and Neil M. Malamuth, "The Longitudinal Impact of Demand and Withdrawal during Marital Conflict," *Journal of Consulting and Clinical Psychology* 63, no. 5 (1995): 797–801, https://doi.org/10.1037/0022-006x.63.5.797.

193　**responsiveness improves relationships:** For a review of responsiveness studies, see Harry T. Reis and Margaret S. Clark, "Responsiveness," in *The Oxford Handbook of Close Relationships,* ed. Jeffry Simpson and Lorne Campbell (Oxford: Oxford University Press, 2015), 400–423, https://doi.org/10.1093/oxfordhb/9780195398694.013.0018.

198　**"anger orgasm":** Thomas J. Scheff, "Catharsis and Other Heresies: A Theory of Emotion," *Journal of Social, Evolutionary, and Cultural Psychology* 1, no. 3 (2007): 98–113, http://dx.doi.org/10.1037/h0099826.

Chapter 7: Offering Generosity

203　**generous people have closer relationships:** "Study: It Pays to Be Generous," The Ascent, updated November 7, 2019, accessed March 24, 2021, https://www.fool.com/the-ascent/research/study-it-pays-be-generous.

203　**generous kids are more liked:** Kathryn R. Wentzel and Cynthia A. Erdley, "Strategies for Making Friends: Relations to Social Behavior and Peer Acceptance in Early Adolescence," *Developmental Psychology* 29, no. 5 (1993): 819–26, https://doi.org/10.1037/0012-1649.29.5.819.

203　**best-friendless fifth graders:** Julie C. Bowker et al., "Distinguishing Children Who Form New Best-Friendships from Those Who Do Not," *Journal of Social and Personal Relationships* 27, no. 6 (2010): 707–25, https://doi.org/10.1177/0265407510373259.

204　**2,803 high schoolers:** Joseph Ciarrochi, Baljinder K. Sahdra, Patricia H. Hawley, and Emma K. Devine, "The Upsides and Downsides of the Dark Side: A Longitudinal Study into the Role of Prosocial and Antisocial Strategies in Close Friendship Formation," *Frontiers in Psychology* 10 (2019): 114, https://doi.org/10.3389/fpsyg.2019.00114.

204　**Participants who received help:** Monica Y. Bartlett et al., "Gratitude: Prompting Behaviours That Build Relationships," *Cognition & Emotion* 26, no. 1 (2012): 2–13, https://doi.org/10.1080/02699931.2011.561297.

204　**aggressive people and prosocial people:** Ciarrochi, Sahdra, Hawley, and Devine, "The Upsides and Downsides of the Dark Side."

205　**"Charity is equal in importance":** Jon D. Levenson, Dudley C. Rose, Jocelyn Cesari, Chris Berlin, and Harpreet Singh, "Why Give? Religious Roots of Charity," Harvard Divinity School News Archive, November 26, 2018, https://hds.harvard.edu/news/2013/12/13/why-give-religious-roots-charity.

208　**170 statutes to promote self-esteem:** Will Storr, *Selfie: How We Became So Self-Obsessed and What It's Doing to Us* (New York: Overlook Press, 2018).

208 **Promoting high self-esteem:** Jean M. Twenge et al., "Egos Inflating over Time: A Cross-Temporal Meta-Analysis of the Narcissistic Personality Inventory," *Journal of Personality* 76, no. 4 (2008): 875–902, https://doi.org/10.1111/j .1467-6494.2008.00507.x.

208 **"the costs of high self-esteem":** Roy F. Baumeister, Jennifer D. Campbell, Joachim I. Krueger, and Kathleen D. Vohs, "Does High Self-Esteem Cause Better Performance, Interpersonal Success, Happiness, or Healthier Lifestyles?," *Psychological Science in the Public Interest* 4, no. 1 (2003): 1–44, https://doi.org/10 .1111/1529-1006.01431.

210 **"Being treated by family members":** Benedict Carey, "A Trauma Expert Puts the Meghan and Harry Interview in Context," *New York Times,* March 9, 2021, https://www.nytimes.com/2021/03/09/health/meghan-harry-mental-health -trauma.html.

211 **they want people to care about them:** Rodney L. Bassett and Jennifer Aubé, "'Please Care about Me!' or 'I Am Pleased to Care about You!' Considering Adaptive and Maladaptive Versions of Unmitigated Communion," *Journal of Psychology and Theology* 41, no. 2 (2013): 107–19, https://doi.org/10.1177/009164711 304100201.

211 **one study on volunteering:** Omri Gillath et al., "Attachment, Caregiving, and Volunteering: Placing Volunteerism in an Attachment-Theoretical Framework," *Personal Relationships* 12, no. 4 (2005): 425–46, https://doi.org/10.1111/j .1475-6811.2005.00124.x.

211 **This type of anxious giving:** Scott Barry Kaufman and Emanuel Jauk, "Healthy Selfishness and Pathological Altruism: Measuring Two Paradoxical Forms of Selfishness," *Frontiers in Psychology* 11 (2020): 1006, https://doi.org/10 .3389/fpsyg.2020.01006.

215 **Evan Leedy, a college student:** Bill Laitner, "For Walking Man James Robertson, 3 Whirlwind Days," *Detroit Free Press,* February 3, 2015, https://www.freep .com/story/news/local/michigan/oakland/2015/02/03/robertson-meets -fundraiser/22785185.

215 **Estella Pyfrom:** Kyle Almond, "And the Top 10 CNN Heroes of 2013 Are . . . ," CNN, October 10, 2013, https://www.cnn.com/2013/10/10/world/cnnheroes -top-10.

215 **"boundless generosity":** Governor General of Canada, "Governor General's Caring Canadian Award," updated March 26, 2018, accessed March 23, 2021, https://archive.gg.ca/honours/awards/cca/index_e.asp.

216 **motivated to get an award:** Lawrence J. Walker and Jeremy A. Frimer, "Moral Personality of Brave and Caring Exemplars," *Journal of Personality and Social Psychology* 93, no. 5 (2007): 845–60, https://doi.org/10.1037/0022-3514.93.5.845.

216 **Spending on others:** Elizabeth W. Dunn, Ashley V. Whillans, Michael I. Norton, and Lara B. Aknin, "Prosocial Spending and Buying Time: Money as a Tool for Increasing Subjective Well-Being," *Advances in Experimental Social Psychology* 61 (2020): 67–126, https://doi.org/10.1016/bs.aesp.2019.09.001.

217 **people who self-sacrificed:** Francesca Righetti, John K. Sakaluk, Ruddy Faure, and Emily A. Impett, "The Link between Sacrifice and Relational and Personal Well-Being: A Meta-Analysis," *Psychological Bulletin* 146, no. 10 (2020): 900–921, https://doi.org/10.1037/bul0000297.

Notes

217   **These selfless individuals:** Sharon Danoff-Burg, Tracey A. Revenson, Kimber-lee J. Trudeau, and Stephen A. Paget, "Unmitigated Communion, Social Con-straints, and Psychological Distress among Women with Rheumatoid Arthritis," *Journal of Personality* 72, no. 1 (2004): 29–46, https://doi.org/10.1111 /j.0022-3506.2004.00255.x; Vicki S. Helgeson and Heidi L. Fritz, "A Theory of Unmitigated Communion," *Personality and Social Psychology Review* 2, no. 3 (1998): 173–83, https://doi.org/10.1207/s15327957pspr0203_2; Vicki S. Helgeson and Dianne K. Palladino, "Agentic and Communal Traits and Health: Adoles-cents with and without Diabetes," *Personality and Social Psychology Bulletin* 38, no. 4 (2011): 415–28, https://doi.org/10.1177/0146167211427149.

217   **people who were motivated to give:** Bonnie M. Le et al., "Communal Motiva-tion and Well-Being in Interpersonal Relationships: An Integrative Review and Meta-Analysis," *Psychological Bulletin* 144, no. 1 (2018): 1–25, https://doi.org/10 .1037/bul0000133.

218   **people maintained equilibrium:** Madoka Kumashiro, Caryl E. Rusbult, and Eli J. Finkel, "Navigating Personal and Relational Concerns: The Quest for Equi-librium," *Journal of Personality and Social Psychology* 95, no. 1 (2008): 94–110, https://doi.org/10.1037/0022-3514.95.1.94.

218   **When we ask for things:** Heidi L. Fritz and Vicki S. Helgeson, "Distinctions of Unmitigated Communion from Communion: Self-Neglect and Overinvolve-ment with Others," *Journal of Personality and Social Psychology* 75, no. 1 (1998): 121–40, https://doi.org/10.1037/0022-3514.75.1.121.

221   **One study analyzed 491 responses:** Christopher P. Roberts-Griffin, "What Is a Good Friend: A Qualitative Analysis of Desired Friendship Qualities," *Penn McNair Research Journal* 3, no. 1 (2011), https://repository.upenn.edu/mcnair _scholars/vol3/iss1/5.

222   **support given in times of need:** Michael Argyle and Monika Henderson, "The Rules of Friendship," *Journal of Social and Personal Relationships* 1, no. 2 (1984): 211–37, https://doi.org/10.1177/0265407584012005.

222   **we are self-interested:** Margaret Clark and Oriana Aragón, "Communal (and Other) Relationships: History, Theory Development, Recent Findings, and Fu-ture Directions," in *The Oxford Handbook of Close Relationships*, ed. Jeffry Simp-son and Lorne Campbell (Oxford: Oxford University Press, 2013), 255–80, http:// doi.org/10.1093/oxfordhb/9780195398694.001.0001.

222   **Communal relationships:** Margaret S. Clark and Judson Mills, "The Differ-ence between Communal and Exchange Relationships: What It Is and Is Not," *Personality and Social Psychology Bulletin* 19, no. 6 (1993): 684–91, https://doi .org/10.1177/0146167293196003.

223   **to express happiness or sadness:** Katherine R. Von Culin, Jennifer L. Hirsch, and Margaret S. Clark, "Willingness to Express Emotion Depends upon Per-ceiving Partner Care," *Cognition and Emotion* 32, no. 3 (2018): 641–50, https:// doi.org/10.1080/02699931.2017.1331906.

223   **our closest relationships:** Clark and Mills, "The Difference between Com-munal and Exchange Relationships"; Judson Mills, Margaret S. Clark, Thomas E. Ford, and Melanie Johnson, "Measurement of Communal Strength," *Personal Relationships* 11, no. 2 (2004): 213–30, https://doi.org/10.1111/j.1475-6811.2004 .00079.x.

Notes

223 **the definition of love:** Margaret S. Clark, Jennifer L. Hirsch, and Joan K. Monin, "Love Conceptualized as Mutual Communal Responsiveness," in *The New Psychology of Love*, ed. Robert J. Sternberg and Karin Sternberg (Cambridge, England: Cambridge University Press, 2019), 84–116.

223 **"key to optimal relationship functioning":** Margaret S. Clark and Edward P. Lemay, "Close Relationships," in *Handbook of Social Psychology*, ed. Susan T. Fiske, Daniel T. Gilbert, and Gardner Lindzey (Hoboken, NJ: John Wiley & Sons, 2010), 898–940.

223 **when a friend responds in times of need:** Edward P. Lemay and Margaret S. Clark, "How the Head Liberates the Heart: Projection of Communal Responsiveness Guides Relationship Promotion," *Journal of Personality and Social Psychology* 94, no. 4 (2008): 647–71, https://doi.org/10.1037/0022-3514.94.4.647.

223 **The more support we get from friends:** Edward L. Deci et al., "On the Benefits of Giving as Well as Receiving Autonomy Support: Mutuality in Close Friendships," *Personality and Social Psychology Bulletin* 32, no. 3 (2006): 313–27, https://doi.org/10.1177/0146167205282148.

223 **more secure over time:** Catherine Cozzarelli, Joseph A. Karafa, Nancy L. Collins, and Michael J. Tagler, "Stability and Change in Adult Attachment Styles: Associations with Personal Vulnerabilities, Life Events, and Global Construals of Self and Others," *Journal of Social and Clinical Psychology* 22, no. 3 (2003): 315–46, https://doi.org/10.1521/jscp.22.3.315.22888.

223 **the more secure we are:** Jennifer A. Bartz and John E. Lydon, "Relationship-Specific Attachment, Risk Regulation, and Communal Norm Adherence in Close Relationships," *Journal of Experimental Social Psychology* 44, no. 3 (2008): 655–63, https://doi.org/10.1016/j.jesp.2007.04.003; Fritz and Helgeson, "Distinctions of Unmitigated Communion from Communion"; Mario Mikulincer and Phillip R. Shaver, "Attachment Security, Compassion, and Altruism," *Current Directions in Psychological Science* 14, no. 1 (2005): 34–38, https://doi.org/10.1111/j.0963-7214.2005.00330.x.

228 **the larger our network:** Giovanna Miritello et al., "Time as a Limited Resource: Communication Strategy in Mobile Phone Networks," *Social Networks* 35, no. 1 (2013): 89–95, https://doi.org/10.1016/j.socnet.2013.01.003.

228 **half our friends:** Abdullah Almaatouq, Laura Radaelli, Alex Pentland, and Erez Shmueli, "Are You Your Friends' Friend? Poor Perception of Friendship Ties Limits the Ability to Promote Behavioral Change," *PLoS ONE* 11, no. 3 (2016): e0151588, https://doi.org/10.1371/journal.pone.0151588.

229 **they gave because they felt obligated:** Netta Weinstein and Richard M. Ryan, "When Helping Helps: Autonomous Motivation for Prosocial Behavior and Its Influence on Well-Being for the Helper and Recipient," *Journal of Personality and Social Psychology* 98, no. 2 (2010): 222–44, https://doi.org/10.1037/a0016984.

230 **recalling an instance of generosity:** Lara B. Aknin, Gillian M. Sandstrom, Elizabeth W. Dunn, and Michael I. Norton, "It's the Recipient That Counts: Spending Money on Strong Social Ties Leads to Greater Happiness Than Spending on Weak Social Ties," *PLoS ONE* 6, no. 2 (2011): e17018, https://doi.org/10.1371/journal.pone.0017018.

230 **people's mood improved:** Gail M. Williamson and Margaret S. Clark, "Impact of Desired Relationship Type on Affective Reactions to Choosing and Being

Required to Help," *Personality and Social Psychology Bulletin* 18, no. 1 (1992): 10–18, https://doi.org/10.1177/0146167292181002.

230 **people were happier to receive:** Wuke Zhang et al., "Recipients' Happiness in Prosocial Spending: The Role of Social Ties," *Journal of Consumer Affairs* 55, no. 4 (2020): 1333–51, https://doi.org/10.1111/joca.12312.

230 **"automatically empathize with [them]":** Margaret S. Clark, Lucylle A. Armentano, Erica J. Boothby, and Jennifer L. Hirsch, "Communal Relational Context (or Lack Thereof) Shapes Emotional Lives," *Current Opinion in Psychology* 17 (2017): 176–83, https://doi.org/10.1016/j.copsyc.2017.07.023.

Chapter 8: Giving Affection

240 **half the people we call friends:** Abdullah Almaatouq, Laura Radaelli, Alex Pentland, and Erez Shmueli, "Are You Your Friends' Friend? Poor Perception of Friendship Ties Limits the Ability to Promote Behavioral Change," *PLoS ONE* 11, no. 3 (2016): e0151588, https://doi.org/10.1371/journal.pone.0151588.

241 **first definition of love:** Stephanie Coontz, *Marriage, a History: How Love Conquered Marriage* (New York: Penguin Books, 2006).

241 **"For most of history":** Coontz, *Marriage, a History.*

241 **same-gender friends:** Coontz, *Marriage, a History.*

243 **a nineteenth-century woman told:** Coontz, *Marriage, a History.*

244 **affection in friendship declined:** Brandon Ambrosino, "The Invention of 'Heterosexuality,'" BBC, March 15, 2017, https://www.bbc.com/future/article/20170315-the-invention-of-heterosexuality; Lillian Faderman, *Surpassing the Love of Men: Romantic Friendship and Love between Women from the Renaissance to the Present* (New York: Harper Paperbacks, 1998).

244 **fears impede emotional intimacy:** Mark McCormack and Eric Anderson, "The Influence of Declining Homophobia on Men's Gender in the United States: An Argument for the Study of Homohysteria," *Sex Roles* 71, no. 3–4 (2014): 109–20, https://doi.org/10.1007/s11199-014-0358-8.

244 **Men who are especially homophobic:** Mark T. Morman, Paul Schrodt, and Michael J. Tornes, "Self-Disclosure Mediates the Effects of Gender Orientation and Homophobia on the Relationship Quality of Male Same-Sex Friendships," *Journal of Social and Personal Relationships* 30, no. 5 (2012): 582–605, https://doi.org/10.1177/0265407512463991.

244 **women experience more intimacy:** Anna Machin, "Treasure Your Friends," *Aeon,* June 4, 2021, https://aeon.co/essays/treasure-your-friends-the-top-of-your-love-hierarchy.

245 **high amounts of affection:** Robert B. Hays, "The Development and Maintenance of Friendship," *Journal of Social and Personal Relationships* 1, no. 1 (1984): 75–98, https://doi.org/10.1177/0265407584011005.

245 **received more affection:** Kory Floyd, "Human Affection Exchange: V. Attributes of the Highly Affectionate," *Communication Quarterly* 50, no. 2 (2002): 135–52, https://doi.org/10.1080/01463370209385653.

246 **the affectionate are less depressed:** Kory Floyd, Colin Hesse, and Mark T. Haynes, "Human Affection Exchange: XV. Metabolic and Cardiovascular Correlates of Trait Expressed Affection," *Communication Quarterly* 55, no. 1 (2007): 79–94, https://doi.org/10.1080/01463370600998715; Kory Floyd et al.,

"Human Affection Exchange: VIII. Further Evidence of the Benefits of Expressed Affection," *Communication Quarterly* 53, no. 3 (2005): 285–303, https://doi.org/10.1080/01463370500101071; Kory Floyd, Alan C. Mikkelson, Colin Hesse, and Perry M. Pauley, "Affectionate Writing Reduces Total Cholesterol: Two Randomized, Controlled Trials," *Human Communication Research* 33, no. 2 (2007): 119–42, https://doi.org/10.1111/j.1468-2958.2007.00293.x; Kory Floyd et al., "Human Affection Exchange: XIII. Affectionate Communication Accelerates Neuroendocrine Stress Recovery," *Health Communication* 22, no. 2 (2007): 123–32, https://doi.org/10.1080/10410230701454015.

246 **posting on friends' walls:** Bree McEwan, "Sharing, Caring, and Surveilling: An Actor–Partner Interdependence Model Examination of Facebook Relational Maintenance Strategies," *Cyberpsychology, Behavior, and Social Networking* 16, no. 12 (2013): 863–69, https://doi.org/10.1089/cyber.2012.0717.

246 **people chose to pair:** Carl W. Backman and Paul F. Secord, "The Effect of Perceived Liking on Interpersonal Attraction," *Human Relations* 12, no. 4 (1959): 379–84, https://doi.org/10.1177/001872675901200407.

246 **they think like them:** Susan Sprecher et al., "You Validate Me, You Like Me, You're Fun, You Expand Me: 'I'm Yours!,'" *Current Research in Social Psychology* 21, no. 5 (2013): 22–34, http://www.uiowa.edu/~grpproc/crisp/crisp.html; Adam J. Hampton, Amanda N. Fisher Boyd, and Susan Sprecher, "You're Like Me and I Like You: Mediators of the Similarity–Liking Link Assessed before and after a Getting-Acquainted Social Interaction," *Journal of Social and Personal Relationships* 36, no. 7 (2018): 2221–44, https://doi.org/10.1177/0265407518790411.

247 **being entertaining or persuasive:** Brant R. Burleson, Adrianne W. Kunkel, Wendy Samter, and Kathy J. Working, "Men's and Women's Evaluations of Communication Skills in Personal Relationships: When Sex Differences Make a Difference and When They Don't," *Journal of Social and Personal Relationships* 13, no 2. (1996): 201–24, https://doi.org/10.1177/0265407596132003.

248 **discount the power of our affection:** Amit Kumar and Nicholas Epley, "Undervaluing Gratitude: Expressers Misunderstand the Consequences of Showing Appreciation," *Psychological Science* 29, no. 9 (2018): 1423–35, https://doi.org/10.1177/0956797618772506.

251 **need proof we won't be rejected:** Sandra L. Murray, John G. Holmes, and Nancy L. Collins, "Optimizing Assurance: The Risk Regulation System in Relationships," *Psychological Bulletin* 132, no. 5 (2006): 641–66, https://doi.org/10.1037/0033-2909.132.5.641.

254 **more greatly predicted the quality:** Michael R. Andreychik, "I Like That You Feel My Pain, but I Love That You Feel My Joy: Empathy for a Partner's Negative versus Positive Emotions Independently Affect Relationship Quality," *Journal of Social and Personal Relationships* 36, no. 3 (2017): 834–54, https://doi.org/10.1177/0265407517746518.

254 **liking for the responsive partner:** Harry T. Reis et al., "Are You Happy for Me? How Sharing Positive Events with Others Provides Personal and Interpersonal Benefits," *Journal of Personality and Social Psychology* 99, no. 2 (2010): 311–29, https://doi.org/10.1037/a0018344.

254   **as proof of risk regulation theory:** Reis et al., "Are You Happy for Me?"

261   **Idiosyncratic affection:** Robert B. Hays, "The Day-to-Day Functioning of Close versus Casual Friendships," *Journal of Social and Personal Relationships* 6, no. 1 (1989): 21–37, https://doi.org/10.1177/026540758900600102.

262   **primed with avoidance:** Lindsey A. Beck and Margaret S. Clark, "Looking a Gift Horse in the Mouth as a Defense against Increasing Intimacy," *Journal of Experimental Social Psychology* 46, no. 4 (2010): 676–79, https://doi.org/10.1016/j.jesp.2010.02.006.

263   **"perceptions are conveyed to partners":** Beck and Clark, "Looking a Gift Horse in the Mouth as a Defense against Increasing Intimacy."

263   **less likely to show gratitude:** Kumar and Epley, "Undervaluing Gratitude."

263   **participants had lower self-esteem:** Jessica J. Cameron, Danu Anthony Stinson, Roslyn Gaetz, and Stacey Balchen, "Acceptance Is in the Eye of the Beholder: Self-Esteem and Motivated Perceptions of Acceptance from the Opposite Sex," *Journal of Personality and Social Psychology* 99, no. 3 (2010): 513–29, https://doi.org/10.1037/a0018558.

264   **devalue compliments:** David R. Kille, Richard P. Eibach, Joanne V. Wood, and John G. Holmes, "Who Can't Take a Compliment? The Role of Construal Level and Self-Esteem in Accepting Positive Feedback from Close Others," *Journal of Experimental Social Psychology* 68 (2017): 40–49, https://doi.org/10.1016/j.jesp.2016.05.003.

265   **partner's positive motives:** Denise C. Marigold, John G. Holmes, and Michael Ross, "More Than Words: Reframing Compliments from Romantic Partners Fosters Security in Low Self-Esteem Individuals," *Journal of Personality and Social Psychology* 92, no. 2 (2007): 232–48, https://doi.org/10.1037/0022-3514.92.2.232.

Index

Index

Index

bias. *See also* behavior of others; friendship across differences
  affection viewed with, 248–249
  false consensus effect, 228
  liking gap, 76
  negativity bias, 196
  social cynicism, 11
  understanding our own behavior, 36, 107 (*see also* attachment theory)
Bingham, James Hervey, 15
A Biography of Loneliness (Alberti), 209
Blank, Hanne, 243
Bloom, Rachel, 111
Bobo doll experiment, 24
Boothby, Erica J., 76
Boston Globe, 269–270
boundaries, 219–230
  communal boundaries and mutuality, 224–230
  communal relationships, defined, 222–223
  communal vs. individualistic, 223–224, 227–228
  depth of friendship and, 230–232
  expectations of support from others, 221–222
  false consensus effect and, 228
  feeling pressured by others, 219–221, 229–230
Bowlby, John, 64, 138, 175
Bowling Alone (Putnam), 11, 64–65
brain anatomy, 53
brain and behavior. *See* attachment theory; behavior of others; emotion
Breckinridge, Lucy Gilmer, 242
Brooks, David, xxi
Brown, Brené, 97–98, 106, 185–186
Bruk, Anna, 105–106, 107–108, 110, 112, 113, 123
Bruneau, Emile, 164
Buddhism, *mudita* (sympathetic joy), 9
burdened virtues, 158
burn out, avoiding, 218. *See also* boundaries

California, Task Force to Promote Self-Esteem, 207–208
Carnegie, Dale, 144

catharsis, 198
Cerny, Marenka, 151, 152
Chen, Angela, 241
children. *See also* attachment theory
  choice of friends by, 25–26
  chumship and, 28
  empathy of, 20
  teenagers/adolescents, shame felt by, 19–21
A Christmas Carol, 139–140
chumships, 20, 28
Clark, Margaret S., 222, 230
clothing, 158–159
co-dependency, 50–51
code switching, 158
cognitive load condition, 101–102
common humanity, 113
communal relationships
  communal boundaries and mutuality, 224–230
  communal vs. individualistic boundaries, 223–224, 227–228
  defined, 222–223
communication
  about anger, 182–190
  acceptance cues, 263–264n
  attachment style and, 42
  for constructive conflict, 185
  for expressing affection, 244–247, 250–251, 256–261
  listening and, 134–137, 168–169, 258
  nonverbal cues, 96
  sharing concerns, 185–186
  spontaneous, 88
  of vulnerability, 95–97
community and friendship networks
  community, defined, 147–148
  curative effect of, xiii–xv
  group vs. individual therapy, xv–xviii
  network size and time for friends, 228
  sacrificing friends for work, 65
  shrinking trend of, 10–11, 66, 105
confidantes
  depression prevented by, 7
  need for, 5–6, 16–19, 105 (*see also* vulnerability)
  scaffold vulnerability and, 116

Index

Index

Index

Index

Index

Index

Index